# CONTRIBUTIONS
# OF SURVEY METHODS
# TO ECONOMICS

SURVEY RESEARCH CENTER
A DIVISION OF THE INSTITUTE FOR SOCIAL RESEARCH
UNIVERSITY OF MICHIGAN

# CONTRIBUTIONS
# OF SURVEY METHODS
# TO ECONOMICS

GEORGE KATONA
LAWRENCE R. KLEIN
JOHN B. LANSING
JAMES N. MORGAN

*Edited with an Introduction by*
LAWRENCE R. KLEIN

1 9 5 4
COLUMBIA UNIVERSITY PRESS   NEW YORK

LIBRARY OF CONGRESS CATALOG CARD NUMBER: 54–6915

MANUFACTURED IN THE UNITED STATES OF AMERICA

# THE SURVEY RESEARCH CENTER

The Institute for Social Research is part of the University of Michigan and devoted to interdisciplinary research in the social sciences. It is engaged both in basic research and in conducting studies of general public interest for agencies of the government and private business firms. Work is not undertaken unless it promises a publication which may contribute to the accumulation of scientific knowledge.

The Institute has two divisions. One division, the Survey Research Center, is principally concerned with the collection and analysis of empirical data on economic behavior, human relations in large organizations, and political behavior.

The second division, the Research Center for Group Dynamics, studies the behavior of people in groups—in industry, education, government, and community life as well as in the laboratory—in an effort to discover what determines group effectiveness and human satisfactions.

The Survey Research Center relies on the sample interview as a basic tool in empirical and social research, both using and developing this new technique. The present publication is an outgrowth of the extensive survey research carried out during the past several years by the Economic Behavior Program of the Survey Research Center. The Economic Behavior Program has conducted annually since 1946 the Surveys of Consumer Finances for the Board of Governors of the Federal Reserve System. Data collected in these surveys provide the principal material on which the studies in this book are based. Other surveys of the Economic Behavior Program have included studies of decision making by individuals in purchasing government bonds, life insurance, common stock, and residential housing. Some surveys of business decisions have also been made.

This book is not devoted to the description or tabulation of survey findings. It represents an attempt to analyze survey results for the benefit and promotion of economic theory. A listing of selected survey findings reported by the Economic Behavior Program is given in the bibliography at the end of this volume.

# ACKNOWLEDGMENTS

The four authors of this volume, staff members of the Survey Research Center of the University of Michigan, have drawn upon assistance of other organizations and colleagues, whose support has been essential to the carrying out of the research described here.

The Surveys of Consumer Finances, which provide the main statistical raw material used, are conducted by the Survey Research Center for, and in cooperation with, the Board of Governors of the Federal Reserve System. A. L. Mills, Jr., Ralph A. Young, and Homer Jones deserve special acknowledgment for their continued assistance and encouragement of the annual Surveys of Consumer Finances. The Board of Governors has generously approved the use of these data for purposes of basic economic research by the Survey Research Center. The analyses reported in the subsequent pages transcend the original employment of the Survey data for the study of immediate problems of the economy.

A special aspect of the survey data used in some of the studies to be presented consists of reinterview material from a sample of urban respondents who were visited in connection with two successive annual surveys. The Rockefeller Foundation provided necessary financial assistance for analyzing the reinterview data, parts of which are described in other publications. The statistical material made available by the reinterview technique has been widely used at the Survey Research Center for various problems of economic analysis. The Rockefeller Foundation has also supplied assistance to the Economic Behavior Program of the Survey Research Center for theoretical studies and for writing this book.

For two years, 1949–50 and 1950–51, L. R. Klein and J. N. Morgan held postdoctoral fellowships supported by the Carnegie Corporation of New York for the purpose of stimulating interdisciplinary studies at the Survey Research Center. These fellowships were issued jointly through the Department of Economics and the Survey Research Center of the University of Michigan. Klein's work during these two years was also supported by the National Bureau of Economic Research, Inc. The stimulation of advice and criticism offered by staff members of the National Bureau of Economic Research was indispensable to the successful completion of Klein's research.

The indebtedness of the authors to their colleagues at the Survey Research Center is very great. Their associates have provided opportunities for research as well as new ideas, criticism, and technical competence in carrying out the sampling, interviewing, coding, and analysis aspects of extensive surveys. Gratitude must be expressed to Rensis Likert, Angus Campbell, Charles Cannell, Roe Goodman, Leslie Kish, and many others.

# CONTENTS

# CONTRIBUTIONS
# OF SURVEY METHODS
# TO ECONOMICS

# INTRODUCTION

## by *Lawrence R. Klein*

The Surveys of Consumer Finances conducted annually by the Survey Research Center for the Board of Governors of the Federal Reserve System have become indispensable components of our fund of basic statistical information. In this volume we undertake probing into these data for purposes of economic research rather than the assessment of the immediate economic climate, which latter objective has largely occupied the activities of those collecting and using these materials. The survey method embodies an essentially new tool for economic research, and it is hoped that the studies reported here will acquaint economists and statisticians with its potential uses. While attacking substantive problems of wide interest in the area of consumer behavior, the authors of this volume explore techniques whereby survey material can be used to advantage in economic research. The emphasis is on economic research and economic problems, but the continuous reliance on sociological and psychological theory shows clearly the need for special treatment in which many branches of social science are carefully blended to produce results otherwise unobtainable. It is the essence of survey research that several branches of social science can be combined in any particular application. This imparts a fresh aspect to the study of economic problems in consumer behavior.

Economic research, as the term is used here, implies the testing of hypotheses about economic behavior suggested by theory, a knowledge of our institutions, independent empirical studies, and other sources. Hypothesis testing is, however, only a first step. In the next stage, an attempt is made to derive quantitative estimates of the characteristics of acceptable hypotheses. In general, research is understood, in the present context, as a search for empirically validated generalizations about economic behavior. It is not a wild search, but one systematized through the drawing upon several fields of social theory and other advance sources of knowledge. These sought-after generalizations take the form of relationships showing how one set of variables influences another. The ultimate goal is to trace the pattern of relationships deeply enough, so that the basic determining set of variables depends on past events or on causal forces outside the realm of the behavior being studied. These aspects are essential for the final stage of research—prediction, using the term in a broad sense.

Potentially, survey methods may be applied throughout the economy wherever human beings are the actors. Questioning of humans on the results and underlying bases of their actions is the main function of survey methods. The Surveys of Consumer Finances have been, however, substantially confined to the household sector of the economy; therefore the present volume emphasizes research in consumer economics. Surveys of business firms, conducted in order to throw light on the economics of business behavior, will form the subject of future investigations.

In giving reports on the behavior and attitudes of individual consumers, the survey method realizes its strongest substantive contribution. Statistical materials are sparse and incomplete on the economic activity of consumers. Households do not generally maintain and publish accounting records of their behavior as do business firms; hence, through direct contact in personal interview surveys, data are gathered which fill important gaps in our basic knowledge of the economy. The specific research problem consists of using this informative collection of new data for quantitative studies of consumer behavior. Problems that economists have often talked about in theoretical works but never approached empirically for want of data are now investigated in consumer surveys.

A conceptual basis for the study of the consumer sector is necessary as a point of departure in any serious research undertaking. In the first chapter of this volume, J. B. Lansing takes up the conceptual problems of defining the consuming unit and outlining an accounting framework in which to measure the results of consumer economic behavior. These concepts are fundamental in the design and interpretation of the Surveys of Consumer Finances or like investigations. They shed light on the identification of the actors we want to study and on the relevance of different variables in consumer decisions.

A description of concepts, while of the utmost importance, is not enough. Into this framework must be built a theory of consumer behavior, an analysis of the types of decision consumers make and the way in which the variables considered in survey questionnaires shape the relationship. George Katona in his chapter gives an analysis of consumer behavior in terms of both economic and psychological variables. His theoretical scheme is quite general, leaving much freedom for the consideration of a wide range of specific questions. In this sense, his theory provides a fruitful research model. Not only is Katona's theoretical treatment unique in the application of psychological methods; it also uses a special type of survey to make some empirical calculations throwing light on the theory. This survey sample is a reinterview sample consisting of consumer units who were interviewed on two successive occasions one year apart.

A variety of statistical methods could be used to analyze survey data. At the first stage, univariate frequency distributions and bivariate cross-tabulations can be studied for the existence of basic relationships. Data of these types are more informative if they are analyzed in successive time periods. The statistical methods used in Katona's chapter are of this type. The next stage of statistical analysis may consist of more complex calculations to establish multivariate relations connecting many variables simultaneously. One multivariate approach is through the analysis of variance. This method serves best to indicate the existence or nonexistence of significant relations among the variables considered. It has the advantage of making relatively weak assumptions about the form of the relationship and can be used to study interactions among variables. Studying the behavior of various mean values makes it possible to judge the direction of significant effects in the analysis of variance, but the method does not permit us to measure the size of the parameters in the significant relationships.

J. N. Morgan applies the techniques of variance analysis to the study of savings behavior. He combines such explanatory variables as income, liquid assets, home ownership status, city size, age, and number of persons in the spending unit. This study is noteworthy for its attempt to design computations that meet, as closely as possible, the more stringent assumptions of variance analysis. Detailed variance analyses with samples of economic data are rare. An interesting aspect of Morgan's research is the way in which the exhaustive statistical calculations can be built into the theoretical scheme of Katona. Both authors rely heavily on psychological and sociological variables in explaining economic behavior.

Variance analysis is useful in showing which relations are significant and in breaking the ground for statistical estimation of the magnitude of parameters of these relations. L. R. Klein uses multiple regression techniques for estimating the parameters of multivariate savings relations jointly involving economic, demographic, and psychological variables. Some of the same relations studied by Katona and Morgan are again studied by regression methods. The degree and magnitude as well as the direction of relations are estimated by Klein. A feature of his approach is that consumer units are not grouped. Each case is regarded as a separate observation; therefore he is able to apply large-sample statistical methods.

As Lansing has argued in his chapter, several alternative savings concepts are plausible, and each is useful for different objectives. While Morgan concentrates most of his analysis on a savings concept including consumer durables as a component, Klein's analysis differs in that expenditures on durables are separately studied in relation to explanatory variables. The savings concept used by Klein is identical with that discussed by Lansing as the concept used in the Surveys of Consumer Finances; both exclude money spent on durable goods.

While the objective of the studies included in this volume is to investigate basic questions of economic research from survey data, our ultimate aim is to diagnose and predict economic activity. The patterns of behavior discerned from our studies of survey data are really desired for use in business cycle analysis. Klein, in a final chapter, discusses the use of survey methods in business cycle research.

There is a degree of independence among the seven chapters of this book, but they are closely bound by a common purpose and a common source of information. The different chapters take up diverse steps in using survey data for fundamental research purposes. Because of our lack of familiarity with this new tool, we must experiment with different techniques of analysis. Yet these different approaches complement one another and, in the end, enable us to reach much firmer conclusions. A single survey would not be adequate to give us confidence in our approach, but we find in repeated samples the same types of relationship resulting from application of the same techniques of analysis.

An emphasis has been placed on methodology, and, truly, a major purpose of the contributions is to explore the use of new methodological techniques. Simultaneously, however, economic problems of substance are attacked and brought closer to solution. The quantification of consumer behavior patterns is an outstanding problem of substance. Data on the various factors influencing the levels of consumer savings and expenditures on durable goods contribute much to our knowledge of fluctuations in general economic activity. Significant conclusions reached in the chapters to follow are:

1. Expenditures on durables and many components of savings are not determined by habitual decisions. They fluctuate and thereby influence general economic activity, but their predictability is enhanced by a study of their relation to income, past income

change, past liquid assets, and consumer attitudes or expectations.

2. Some components of saving, which can be specifically measured and identified in survey data, are determined by contract or by routine and do not play the same instigating role in economic fluctuations.

3. The saving process of an individual is not simple or explainable in terms of one or two variables. A complex of interrelated variables working in a nonlinear fashion affect behavior. The statistical calculations in this volume actually try to measure the characteristics of these nonlinear multivariate savings patterns.

4. The much discussed relationship between wealth and saving or spending is investigated here, and it is found that liquid assets have a significant influence on consumer behavior, but this relation is not of the simple form assumed in most discussions of the theory of employment.

5. Consumer income expectations and general economic outlook are found to be related to actual behavior. Individual subjective variables can be measured in personal interviews with consumers and fitted into behavior patterns.

These substantive conclusions are stated in rather general terms here, but are meant to serve merely as an introduction to the specific details presented at some length in the several chapters.

# I: CONCEPTS USED IN SURVEYS

## by John B. Lansing

INTRODUCTION

The collection of data by means of sample surveys is not a purely mechanical operation. Since the resources which can be devoted to sample surveys are limited, initial choices must be made as to what data to collect. When a body of data has been collected, sometimes it is possible to make the expenditure of resources necessary to organize it in more than one way, but often one method of organization must be chosen to the exclusion of others. Broad choices must be made between one set of concepts and another—be they traditional concepts such as income or saving or concepts less frequently used in economic analysis such as attitudes and expectations. Narrower choices must be made in the setting up of particular categories and definitions. Once it has been decided that saving, for example, is to be studied, it must also be decided what definition of saving is to be used and how each individual component of saving is to be handled in each interview.

It is ordinarily obvious what topics a survey covers, and users of the data may have no special interest in reasons why chosen topics were selected. It is far from obvious how the narrow choices are made and how the definitions are worked out in the unusual cases, but users of the data are likely to find the mass of detail overwhelming. Most readers of this volume will find it enough to understand the development of the major concepts used in the Surveys of Consumer Finances, and it is to this topic that this chapter is devoted.

The discussion starts with two basic elements—the unit of analysis (the spending unit) and the time span of analysis (the accounting period). A description of the frequency of specific economic activities among households lays the foundation for discussions of alternative systems of concepts, the choice made among these possibilities in the Survey, and similarities and differences between the concepts used in the Survey and those used elsewhere. A note at the conclusion of the chapter discusses briefly the reinterviews conducted in 1949 which form the basis for part of the analysis described in later chapters.

To evaluate data from surveys, information is also needed about the reliability of the data and, hence, about sampling and interviewing techniques. These topics are not treated systematically in this volume, since there exists a growing literature on surveys in general and a special, more restricted literature on the Surveys of Consumer Finances. The interested reader may consult on surveys in general the volume entitled *Research Methods in the Behavioral Sciences*,[1] and techniques used in the Surveys of Consumer Finances have been described in the article, "Methods of the Survey of Consumer Finances," *Federal Reserve Bulletin,* July 1950.[2]

### THE UNIT OF ANALYSIS

*The spending unit.* Economists customarily divide the economic system into the three components of consumer sector, business sector, and government. The consumer sector is regarded as composed of households. By households are meant the units which make decisions on such matters as the furnishing of productive services, the allocation of income among different uses, and the form in which assets will be held. The focus is on the unit's decision-making functions.

[1] Edited by Leon Festinger and Daniel Katz (Dryden Press, 1953). See especially Ch. 1, "The Sample Survey," by Angus Campbell and George Katona; Ch. 5, "Selection of Sample," by Leslie Kish; and Ch. 8, "Collection of Data by Interviewing," by Charles F. Cannell and Robert L. Kahn.

[2] Vol. XXXVI, No. 2, pp. 795–809. See also Part 5 of George Katona, *Psychological Analysis of Economic Behavior* (New York: McGraw-Hill, 1951), and, on sampling methods, Roe Goodman and Eleanor E. Maccoby, "Sampling Methods and Sampling Errors in Surveys of Consumer Finances," *International Journal of Opinion and Attitude Research,* II, 3 (1947), 349–60.

Such a definition of a household is helpful as a standard in empirical study of consumer units, but it leaves unsaid much that must be settled before an operational definition of a household can be established. The first preliminary investigation of the distribution of holdings of Government bonds and other liquid assets ran headlong into this problem. When an interviewer went to a single-family house and talked to the husband about the affairs of himself, his wife, and his infant, he felt he was talking to the head of a consumer unit. When there was an adult, unmarried child in the family, however, interviewers found that although sometimes the husband and father was informed about the son's or daughter's liquid asset holdings, sometimes he knew nothing about them. In the latter situation the interviewer had to make a second interview to complete his information about the family. From a conceptual point of view it became apparent that a son or daughter who kept his finances entirely separate was not a member of the same "household" as the parents, or at least he was only a partial member. He was, to use a concept adopted at that time, a separate "spending unit."

Since the "spending unit" is operationally defined, a precise statement of the operations by which it is defined is a prerequisite to conclusions on how closely a spending unit conforms to the theoretical construct of a household. In sampling spending units in the Surveys of Consumer Finances, dwelling units are selected at random by methods which need not concern us here. Interviewers then go to each dwelling unit in the sample and ascertain how many spending units it contains.

The definition of a dwelling unit is: A group of rooms (or only one room) forming separate living quarters and containing cooking facilities. For this purpose, cooking facilities are something more permanent and substantial than a hot plate. Typical dwelling units are the following: (1) a one family house or one-half of a two family house; (2) an apartment; (3) a trailer which has cooking facilities; (4) living quarters in back of stores or over garages, shacks in back yards, etc.; (5) a rooming house (but not the individual rooms in a rooming house); (6) an apartment in an apartment hotel.

Occasionally, difficulties arise in applying this definition because it is not clear whether certain living quarters are merely rooms and, as such, parts of one large dwelling unit, or light housekeeping apartments and, as such, individual dwelling units. This type of difficulty, however, rarely affects the definition of a spending unit since the inhabitants of living quarters of this general description are almost always unrelated to the owner. In a few cases, however, there is some ambiguity as to how far a family has gone in dividing a building between them into several units. For example, one respondent in a survey owns a two story house. He converted the second floor into an apartment some time ago and rented it to outsiders. Recently, however, his mother and brother have been living with him in the second story apartment and he has been supporting them. Here it seemed clear that the family was one unit and the building was counted as one dwelling unit and the family treated as one spending unit.

The decision to treat as separate spending units all persons living in separate dwelling units implies a sociological generalization: People who have separate living quarters have separate economic resources and make separate economic decisions. Experience with this definition is that it is close to the facts except in a few situations where the boundaries of the family effectively extend beyond the dwelling unit, as will be discussed below.

Once he has located the dwelling unit to his satisfaction, the interviewer inquires about the family units which live within. The definition of a family unit is as follows: All persons living in the same dwelling and related by blood, marriage, or adoption. There is seldom any difficulty in ascertaining what persons are related to each other by blood, marriage, or adoption, but it is not always clear who is "living" in the dwelling unit. Should college students who are away from home attending school at the time of the interview be counted as part of their parents' family and spending unit, or should they be counted as independent units? Students who are entirely self-supporting, or are partially self-supporting and earning more than $10 a week, are counted as separate spending units.[3] Students entirely or predominantly supported by their parents are counted as part of their parents' spending unit. From the point of view of the theorist, the question of what unit is the decision-making unit seems to depend on the decisions being investigated. Students dependent on their parents for support make decisions about purchasing food or phonograph records, but they do not have any important income and are not likely to make decisions about purchasing houses or common stock. The rule that they do not count as separate units in the Surveys reflects the fact that the Surveys are more concerned with income, houses, and common stock than with food and phonograph records.[4]

A group in a way similar to students are members of the family absent on active duty in the armed forces. For example, an interviewer may come upon a woman supported by her husband who is now in the army and living on a military reservation. He is in practice not counted as a member of the wife's spending unit. That part of the husband's income which he keeps entirely for his own use is excluded from the income of the unit. That part of his income which goes into assets jointly held with his wife (e.g., Series E bonds) plus that part which he transfers to her for her support is considered income of the unit interviewed.

Having decided who the members of the family unit are, the interviewer considers all persons living in the dwelling unit who are not

---

[3] In the 1953 Survey the amount was changed from $10 to $15.

[4] In the 1954 Survey the rules for the treatment of students were modified. Students living away from their parents are now regarded as part of the institutional population if they live in dormitories, fraternities, or large boarding houses. Members of this population are excluded from the universe sampled. As far as the parental spending unit is concerned, these students are now regarded as outside dependents rather than members. Married students or other students living in the ordinary dwelling units are now treated as independent spending units regardless of the source of their support.

members of the principal family unit as comprising one or more "unrelated secondary spending units." For the most part, these spending units consist of roomers and servants; sometimes, however, two families or two unrelated unmarried persons share an apartment.

Within the family unit itself the interviewer asks three questions concerning each individual aged eighteen years or over other than the head. These questions are: (1) Does he receive $10 or more per week from any source?[5] (2) Does he keep his finances separate? (3) Does he contribute less than one-half of his income to the spending unit containing the head of the family? If the answers to all of these questions are "Yes," the individual is classified as a separate spending unit. If the answer to any one of them is "No," he is part of the same spending unit as the head of the family. The head, incidentally, is the male member of the married couple if one is present; otherwise it is whoever is regarded as head by the members of the family.

A typical related secondary spending unit is an unmarried son or daughter living with his parents, earning a wage or salary, and contributing only a small fraction of it to the upkeep of the establishment. The economic reasoning which lies behind the decision to treat such individuals as separate units is that they do in fact make separate decisions. By definition, they have an income and keep more than one-half of it to themselves, to spend for one good or another or to save in one form or another, as they see fit. In the spending of that part of their income which they may contribute to the common pool it may be argued that they should be treated as members of the larger unit, the family. But since money is the yardstick of importance, both to the market and to the economist, the fact that they contribute less than one-half of their money speaks in favor of the spending unit, in which they are treated separately, as the *principal* decision making unit.

The frequency of different types of spending units is indicated in Table 1.

[5] In the 1953 Survey the amount was changed from $10 to $15.

TABLE 1

DISTRIBUTION OF SPENDING UNITS BY TYPE OF UNIT—1952

| | | *Percent* |
|---|---|---|
| Primary spending unit | | 85.6 |
| Related secondary spending unit | | 11.0 |
| Child over 18 | 7.3 | |
| Father or mother | 0.9 | |
| Other relative | 2.8 | |
| Unrelated secondary spending unit | | 3.4 |
| Roomer | 2.7 | |
| Servant | 0.3 | |
| Other | 0.4 | |
| Total | | 100.0 |

There are additional problems which arise in using the spending unit as a basic unit of analysis. Some of these problems would arise also with any other similar unit. One characteristic of the population of consumers is that it is made up of people whose situation changes with the passage of time. The economist in general is equally interested in the situation at a particular moment in time (the period when the unit is being interviewed) and in the past and the future. The character of the spending unit is quite likely to change during any extended period. Related secondaries usually come into being as a transitional stage in the individual's life cycle and are therefore particularly volatile. Children grow up, go to work, start keeping separate finances, get married, and set up separate households of their own. The exact sequence of events varies from individual to individual and the denotation of related secondaries from one point of view is a method for deciding at what point the stage of financial independence is to be regarded as achieved. Yet, there is not always a complete instantaneous transition from financial dependence to financial independence. In addition, births, deaths, divorces, and other events change the composition of the household.

Again, what formerly were two spending units may be combined into one, on the occasion, say, of the retirement of an individual or of his becoming unemployed. For individuals who move in and out of the labor market as a result of seasonal unemployment or seasonal retirement from the labor force there may be some ambiguity as to what is meant by "now" making $15 a week or more.[3] Unemployed adult children living with their parents are counted as part of the parental spending unit unless there is evidence that they keep their finances separate. Rare problems of this type are on the periphery of the concept. The people involved are in a state of transition, and as soon as they settle into one arrangement or another it becomes possible to define a meaningful economic unit.

In the Surveys of Consumer Finances, attention is focused on the situation at the time of interview and in the calendar year prior to the interview, for reasons discussed in the next section of this chapter. The procedure used in the Surveys is to consider as members of the spending unit those people who are members of it at the time of interview. In the case of a marriage, for example, the income of the unit is the income over the year of all people who are at present members of the spending unit. If a person is interviewed who was divorced during the year, his income includes one-half of the income of the couple during the period prior to the divorce. When a death has occurred within a spending unit, the income of the person who died is counted as part of the income of the unit for the year. In those cases, however, where the death of an individual extinguishes the spending unit, the income of the deceased prior to the time of his death is lost.

Another problem is the variation in financial arrangements from one type of family to another. We do not have much evidence on the extent and nature of this variety. Some families, no doubt, pool their incomes for some purposes, and some for others. In some families, the decisions as to how the pooled income is to be spent are made in one manner, and in some families, no doubt, these decisions are made differently. For example, when there are two related spending units living together, is there one car, or two? If one, who pays for the family car and who uses it? Who makes the purchases of durable goods?

The most common transaction involving spending units who live in separate dwelling units is the purchase of a house. We know that there are instances in which members of the family living at some distance from a particular spending unit will help finance this transaction. The relevant unit then becomes much larger. Exact information on the frequency of this type of arrangement is not available at the time of writing, but it appears that at least 80 percent of the purchases of houses for owner occupancy involve only the people who are to live in the house.

Another complication, which arises most frequently with related secondary spending units, is that a unit may receive an income and keep it separate, thus qualifying as a separate spending unit, and yet may be dependent for a large part of its support on other spending units. Such a unit makes its own decisions about its own resources and, hence, must be handled separately; but it makes these decisions in the light of the knowledge that it can count on someone to provide part of the goods and services it consumes. In studies of the welfare position of households this type of problem is particularly vexatious.

One difficulty arising out of this dependency of one unit on another is that regular cash contributions may be counted both as the income of the donor and of the recipient. The affairs of the spending unit receiving the contributions may be entirely unintelligible unless these contributions are counted as income. For this reason they are counted in that way in the Surveys of Consumer Finances. To avoid double counting, ideally these contributions should be deducted from the income of the donor. Since the amounts involved are not large or frequent, motives of economy of questions have led to omission of that information.

In a few instances, money is paid by one member of a family to another in exchange for services rendered. In one family, for example, the mother, who owns a farm, pays wages to her son as a farm laborer. Transactions of this sort may involve a different price for the services than would be paid in the open market. In practice the price is accepted at its face value, and the funds are taken as income to the one member and a business expense to the other (the two keeping in this case their finances separate and representing two spending units).

There are also a few instances of unrelated persons who live together and pool their income as completely as members of any family. The 1951 Survey turned up, for example, two elderly women who lived together and pooled their pensions of $55 a month apiece for all expenditures of any sort. This type of arrangement, however, is rare.

Economists make a sharp distinction between households and business enterprises. This distinction is difficult to maintain empirically for two groups—owners of unincorporated businesses and farm operators. Some owners of an unincorporated business keep their business and their household affairs entirely separate. Others, however, may even use the same bank account for business and personal use. A few may live on the business premises, for example, in the back of a store or over a garage, and may be unable to separate the rent which is used for business purposes and that which is used for their dwelling. A few owners of grocery stores and restaurants may take inventories for personal use and may not know how much of their expenses represents cost of doing business and how much, income in kind. A precise separation would require a more careful accounting system than would be profitable for them to maintain. In practice, in the Survey of Consumer Finances, income in kind is ignored.

Although the above problems are most common among owners of unincorporated businesses, they may also be present for professional men and owners of small corporations. A few of the latter even report that they do not keep separate bank accounts for their businesses. The solution adopted is to count among the individual's liquid assets as a householder the full amount in any combined accounts. This solution is unsatisfactory from the theoretical point of view, but it is difficult to achieve any more satisfactory approach in practice.

Farm operators present the same type of problem. A farmer's bank account and his car or truck often are used for both farm business and personal activities. Farmers also frequently receive income in kind, especially food. The practical approach adopted is to ignore income in kind and deal only with cash income, but to count as personal holdings the full value of farmers' liquid assets. Even within these limitations some difficulties remain. Interviewers ask farmers to itemize their cash receipts and their cash expenses for farm purposes. Farmers are asked to include as farm expenses only that part of their outlay for fuel, tires, and repairs for their cars which was for farm business, but there is no assurance that they make any but the crudest distinction between farm business and other uses of their cars. If a farmer drives to town on Saturday and, while there, sells produce and then goes to the movies, how should he allocate the cost of the gasoline? The other items of farm expenses are usually, but not always, readily separated into outlays for consumption and for farm business.

The preceding discussion has indicated some of the difficulties and arbitrary elements in the definition of a spending unit. These problems are inherent in the complexity of the real world. While other units than the spending unit as defined in the Survey of Consumer Finances may be appropriate for special studies of particular problems, the spending unit is as close an approximation to a household as it is possible to attain, using a single multi-purpose definition.

*The time span of analysis.* For agricultural incomes in the temperate zone the progression of the seasons makes a year a natural period of analysis. Even for nonagricultural incomes in the United States the reports required of most of the population by the Bureau of Internal Revenue make one calendar year the logical period of analysis. Seasonal fluctuations in purchases of large household items such as refrigerators and automobiles also suggest one year as a natural period to use in studying major purchases by consumers.

The general question, how did consumers dispose of their income, can best be answered from a body of data, each item of which refers to the same period of time. For example, it would not make sense to study an individual's savings for a period different from that used in studying his income. Accordingly, interviewing for the Surveys is always conducted in January and February (with some few interviews made early in March), and the data collected on income, purchases made, and amounts saved refer to the preceding calendar year (though some information is gathered for the time period extending backward from the date of the interview to "a year ago").

### THE FREQUENCY OF SPECIFIC ECONOMIC ACTIVITIES
### AMONG HOUSEHOLDS

The basic tools developed by accountants for analyzing the affairs of businesses are also useful in studying households. The balance sheet, income statement, and statement of sources and uses of funds all have proved useful in connection with the Surveys of Consumer Finances. They provide a framework within which to classify the financial affairs of households. The preparation of financial statements for households, however, should not be regarded as an end in itself, any more than should the preparation of statements for businesses. The information assembled in this section is intended to show in some detail what transactions households engage in, what assets they possess, and what debts they owe. The following section considers alternative objectives in the study of consumers' affairs and the varying combinations and elaborations of detailed accounts to which these objectives may lead.

*Balance sheet.* A basic item of information in the study of any asset owned by consumers is the proportion of the population who own it. A table in the form of a balance sheet showing, for the items covered by the Surveys, the approximate proportion of the population who own each type of asset or have each type of debt appears as Table 2. This table, like the two following tables, is intended only to convey the rough order of magnitude of the statistics shown. Statistics from more than one year have been included in a single table when their inclusion makes the table more complete, but for the most part Tables 2 and 4 are based on the 1950 Survey, and Table 3 on the 1951 Survey. The amount of detail shown in the tables depends upon the degree of detail with which the items have been covered in the Surveys. More extensive investigations would make it possible to include more items and to show more subdivisions of the items included.

While a few assets are owned by a substantial proportion of the population, Table 2 shows that many are owned by only a few. Over

TABLE 2

"BALANCE SHEET"[a]

*Approximate proportion of all spending units holding various assets or liabilities*

| Assets | Percent | Liabilities and Net Worth | Percent |
|---|---|---|---|
| Liquid assets—all types | 61 | Debts—all types | 51 |
| Checking accounts | 41 | Charge accounts | 26 |
| Savings accounts | 42 | Borrowed from insurance | |
| Series A-F bonds | 39 | company | 3 |
| Other U. S. Government bonds | 3 | | |
| Life insurance | 77 | | |
| Interests in business enterprises | | | |
| Stock in publicly held corporations | 7 | | |
| Stock in privately held corporations | 1 | | |
| Interests in unincorporated businesses | 8 | | |
| Loans to private individuals (1953) | 12 | | |
| Real estate | | | |
| Home | 39 | Debt on home | 18 |
| Farm | 9 | Debt on farm | 2 |
| Other real estate—all types | 16 | Debt on other real estate | 3 |
| Other one- or two-family house | 4 | | |
| Apartment house | ..[b] | | |
| Summer or weekend home | 1 | | |
| Commercial or rental property | 2 | | |
| Other farm or farm land | 4 | | |
| Lot (excluding cemetery lots) | 4 | | |
| Other types | ..[b] | | |
| Durable consumer goods | | | |
| Automobile | 55 | Installment debt (1952) | 38 |
| Refrigerator (1952) | 68 | Debt for medical services | |
| Television set (1952) | 30 | (1952) | 19 |

[a] Data from the 1950 Survey of Consumer Finances except as indicated.
[b] Less than 0.5 percent.

75 percent of the population own life insurance, but only one percent, stock in privately held corporations. Half the population owe debts of some kind, but a mere three percent owe money to an insurance company. Some of the assets held by small proportions of the population, however, involve large sums of money and are of major economic importance. For example, although only about three percent of the population own U. S. Government bonds other than savings bonds, the estimated median holding is approximately $2,000.

A number of assets and liabilities of consumers have not been covered by the Surveys, and do not appear in the table. Among these items are the following: interests in patents, copyrights, and trademarks; interests in estates and trusts; stocks of nondurable consumer goods such as clothing and food; stocks of durable consumer goods such as furniture, jewelry, washing machines, stoves, and the like (only stocks of automobiles, television sets, and refrigerators have been investigated, and of these only automobiles have been studied in detail); interests in retirement and pension funds; and securities of state, local, and foreign governments. An attempt was made to obtain information concerning holdings of currency, but the results seemed to suffer from underreporting on the part of people with larger cash holdings.[6] No attempt has been made to estimate the present value of consumers' future income or liabilities. For example, the personal balance sheet of a consumer in 1950 might include an entry for the discounted value of his future earnings, but no such entry appears in Table 2.

*Income statement.* Another set of basic statistics concern the frequency with which different members of the population receive income from various sources. Table 3 shows the proportion of the population receiving income of different types. The types of income are listed in order of frequency, from wages and salaries to income from roomers and boarders. The estimate that 12 percent of the population receive income from interest, dividends, trust funds, and

[6] See "Surveys of Liquid Asset Holdings," *Federal Reserve Bulletin,* Sept. 1945, p. 7.

royalties is too low in view of the proportions of the population known to hold savings bonds and savings accounts (see Table 2). Many people whose income from these sources is trivial do not mention it when asked if they have received income of this type in the past year. Even allowing for the fact that many people do not consider interest accruals on savings bonds as income until they are realized, the estimate of 12 percent seems low.

TABLE 3

"INCOME STATEMENT"[a]

*Proportion of all spending units reporting income in 1950 from various sources*

| Type of Money Income | Percent |
|---|---|
| Wages and salaries | 78 |
| Transfers (veterans' pensions, school allotment, family allotment, or bonus from a state; unemployment benefits, retirement pay, old age pensions, annuities, alimony, regular contributions, welfare) | 25 |
| Income from professional practice, other self-employment, farming | 16 |
| Rent (exclusive of receipts from roomers and boarders) | 13 |
| Interest, dividends, trust funds, royalties | 12 |
| Income from unincorporated businesses | 7 |
| Income from roomers and boarders | 4 |

[a] 1951 Survey of Consumer Finances.

*Sources and uses of funds.* Every consumer engages in a very large number of transactions over a year. A minute statement of uses of funds theoretically would include, for example, an entry for purchases of each type of clothing bought. Table 4 covers, instead, only selected major transactions. It excludes entirely purchases of non-durable consumer goods and services.

In analyzing the affairs of a spending unit, there are two basic methods of obtaining information about sources and uses of funds. One can ask directly for the information about a source (or use): "How much has the balance in your checking account changed?" One can also ask separately for the spending unit's holdings a year ago and now, and obtain the difference by subtraction: "How much money did you have in your checking account a year ago? How

TABLE 4

TYPES OF SOURCES AND USES OF FUNDS—1949

*Proportion of all spending units who receive funds from each source and who allocate funds to each use*

| Sources | Percent | Uses | Percent |
|---|---|---|---|
| Money income | 99 | Loss (negative income) | 1 |
| Withdrawals from liquid assets | 31 | Payment of Federal income tax | 66 |
| Borrowing | | Additions to liquid assets | 26 |
| Mortgage taken out to finance purchase of home (nonfarm) | 3 | Purchases of real property and durables | |
| Mortgage taken out to finance purchase of other real estate | 1 | Home | 3 |
| Borrowed to finance additions or repairs to home (1950) | 3 | Other real estate | 2 |
| Borrowed to finance cars and durables | 23 | Additions and repairs to home (nonfarm) | 35 |
| Receipts from sale of assets | | Car | 22 |
| Securities (excluding Federal) | 1 | Other durable goods | 39 |
| Real estate | 3 | Payments on loans owed | |
| Business (sale or liquidation) | 1 | Mortgage (on nonfarm home) | 17 |
| Decrease in farm inventory | 3 | Debt (on other real estate) | 3 |
| Receipts from settlement of claims, etc. | | Payments into retirement funds | 12 |
| Repayment of loans | 4 | Purchase of securities (excluding Federal) | 2 |
| From insurance company | 3 | Life insurance premiums | 74 |
| Inheritance | 3 | Loans made to others | 5 |
| | | Purchases of farm equipment | 4 |
| | | Increase in farm inventory | 2 |
| | | New investment in own business | 3 |
| | | Profit left in own business | 2 |

much do you have now?" Both approaches are used in the Surveys, depending on the item under study.

Income is a source of funds for almost every spending unit. Borrowing is frequent, especially borrowing to finance purchases of cars and durables. Withdrawals from liquid assets are also frequent.

The most common use of funds covered by the data is the payment of life insurance premiums, followed by purchases of cars and durables, additions to liquid assets, and additions and repairs to houses. Of the uses of funds of particular interest to economists, some involve small proportions of the population. For example, only three percent invest new money in a business of their own. In general, the larger the proportion of the population who engage in a transaction in a given year, the easier it is to investigate the transaction by interviewing a cross section of the population.

## ALTERNATIVE SYSTEMS OF ACCOUNTS FOR HOUSEHOLDS

*Potentialities of surveys.* All too frequently economists find themselves forced to make use of statistics gathered without regard to their individual needs. Organizations gathering statistics may have in mind a particular purpose, which need not coincide with the purposes of the analyst. Or they may have in mind several different uses to which their data may be put, and effect some kind of compromise when conflicting interests would lead to diverse methods of gathering and processing the data.

It is an advantage of the survey method that the whole body of statistical material in a survey is collected in one operation. The question of splicing material originally gathered by several organizations does not arise.

The survey method also possesses potential flexibility. The same basic raw data may be processed first in one manner and then in another to meet particular objectives. Essentially the problem of definition is one of classifying the multiplicity of economic facts into an internally consistent set of categories which can be manipulated for the purposes of particular investigations. The same definitions are not likely to be appropriate for all possible research.

*Three topics of investigation.* In this section, three broad research objectives are considered, and the implications of these objectives for problems of definition are developed. Although there are other possible objectives of research, the three following are main areas of economic investigation involving consumers: (1) economic welfare, that is, the economic well-being of the population; (2) contributions by consumers of savings to business enterprises for the development of the productive resources of the economy; and (3) contributions by consumers to the level of economic activity. Directly, the study of any one objective may involve only a balance sheet, income statement, or statement of sources and uses of funds for consumers. But it is impossible to specify one of these three accounting statements without indirectly imposing restrictions on the other two. Internal consistency of the accounts requires that the investigator specify a complete system of accounts simultaneously. We may consider, first, the system of accounts required for each of the three objectives, and second, the system actually used in the Survey in its relation to these three types of objectives.

*Economic welfare.* For the study of consumers' welfare, the following equation is appropriate:

$$\text{Income} = \text{Savings} + \text{Consumption}$$

Here the income of a spending unit should include any income in the form of goods, services, or cash received by the unit within a given period, including gifts and inheritances as well as receipts on income account, narrowly defined. In addition to changes in claims by or against the unit, savings should include any increase or decrease in its stocks of goods of all kinds during the given period, including stocks of nondurable consumer goods. Consumption thus would include the value of all goods and services actually consumed during the period. That is, consumption should refer literally to consuming —the eating of food, wearing of clothing, and so forth. If a consumer purchased a suit of clothes out of income for $100, wore it for two years, and then threw it away, in the first year he would be regarded as having saved $50 and consumed $50, and in the second year as having engaged in negative saving of $50 and consumption of $50.

Stocks of nondurable goods may be of great importance to the economy as a whole in time of war. A nation may devote the resources of the clothing industry, for example, to military purposes, forcing the population to wear garments that become increasingly threadbare. A system of accounts that ignores the reduction in these stocks misses an item of negative saving. Fluctuations in consumers' stocks of nondurables for the nation as a whole are not restricted to wartime, but may occur from periods of depression to periods of prosperity. Fluctuations in the affairs of individuals undoubtedly lead to similar changes.

The preparation of estimates of income, savings, and consumption which followed rigorously the above definitions, however, would require very extensive and detailed information. The greatest difficulties would arise with the nondurable and semidurable consumer goods. In a period when the stocks of such goods in the hands of consumers do not vary systematically, the expenditure of time and money in order to obtain such extensive information may not be warranted.

A balance sheet for consumers to correspond to these income and flow concepts would require information about stocks of all kinds of consumer goods, durable and nondurable, as well as debts and claims of all descriptions.

*Contributions to productive resources.* A second topic of investigation is the contribution of consumers to the increase in the productive resources of the economy in the hands of business enterprises. A typical problem, especially in underdeveloped economic areas, is how to increase the proportion of the national income which is devoted to investment in producers' goods. How much of their "income" do different consumers "save" in the sense of making it available for such investments?

Saving in the sense previously described includes both changes in consumers' holdings of consumer goods and changes in their indirect holdings of producers' goods, if we may speak of consumers as indirectly holding producers' goods in their capacity as ultimate owners of the business enterprises which own these goods. Either an increase in consumers' holdings of consumers' goods or an increase in their claims against the business sector can improve their welfare. But, if it is the main objective of economic policy to increase the stock of producers' goods in an economy, it is obvious that an increase in the stock of consumer goods will not achieve the goal.

Indeed, one way of financing an *increase* in productive facilities is by *negative* saving in the welfare sense. That is, a nation may reduce the stocks of goods in the hands of consumers and thus maintain consumption (in the sense defined earlier) while at the same time increasing the proportion of newly produced goods and services devoted to productive investment.

We may use the preceding definitions to cover this situation only if we divide "saving" into two components: (1) increase (or decrease) in stocks of consumer goods in the hands of consumers; (2) increase (or decrease) in other assets of consumers. Then (1) would include changes in holdings of houses, durable goods, and nondurables; and (2) would include changes in investment in businesses (both unincorporated and incorporated), liquid assets, debts, insurance, etc. Thus we have the following identity:

$$\text{Income} = \text{Savings (1)} + \text{Savings (2)} + \text{Consumption}$$

If the investigation of consumers' contribution to productive resources is conducted in circumstances where stocks of consumer goods in the hands of consumers are not expected to vary, or where the probable variation is not considered important, more restricted definitions may be satisfactory. Then income can be restricted to cash received by consumers. Savings of type (1) may be classified as a part of consumption, which would be defined to include cash outlay for houses and durables as well as for other consumer goods and services. The term savings would then be applied only to savings of type (2), that is, to funds directly or indirectly made available for productive investment. Distinctions could be drawn between savings directly made available for such investment by direct transfer to business enterprises, and savings only potentially made available, by transfer to financial intermediaries or to the government.

A balance sheet in a system of accounts drawn along the latter lines could exclude stocks of consumer goods but would require a detailed breakdown of interests in and claims against business enterprises and financial intermediaries.

*The level of economic activity.* For the study of the third topic, the impact of consumers' behavior upon the level of economic activity, in the United States we may ignore transactions in kind. Short term fluctuations in the level of activity in the American economy are not the result of changes in the amount of home-grown food or rent imputed to home owners. The major concerns become, first, the flow of money to consumers and the division which they make of it between spending it for goods and services of all types and not spending it; and, second, the uses made by consumers of stocks of liquid assets and money borrowed to finance spending for goods and services of all types.

The appropriate identities then become:

> Income in Cash + Miscellaneous Cash Receipts = Liquid Savings + Cash Outlay for Durable Goods and Housing + Cash Outlay for Consumption

Here income is restricted to cash income, while to it must be added an item for miscellaneous cash receipts, primarily gifts and inheritances of cash. Savings include cash additions to or withdrawals from liquid assets, including cash receipts from realized capital gains from the holding of securities. Money borrowed or repaid is also part of liquid savings. Outlay for durable goods and housing includes cash spent for durables and real estate. Outlay for consumption includes cash spent for all other consumer goods and services. Since the last two terms in the identity are always positive, receipts of cash from the sale of durable goods, housing, or other consumer goods appear as miscellaneous cash receipts. (If no provision were made for such receipts, the accounts of individual spending units would not balance.)

The corresponding balance sheet would need to include only marketable assets. Stocks of consumer goods would be important only to the extent that they might be sold. The calculation of depreciation on these stocks would be unnecessary.

#### CONCEPTS USED IN THE SURVEYS OF CONSUMER FINANCES

*Income, savings, and consumption.* The Surveys of Consumer Finances have been built on a system of accounts which represents a compromise among the requirements of different objectives, taking into account considerations of cost and the peculiar limitations and potentialities of the survey method. A single system is used for most of the analysis, primarily for reasons of cost, though from time to time modifications have been introduced for particular purposes. It may be of interest first to describe the system regularly used, and then to compare it with the systems that would be appropriate for each of the objectives just outlined.

TABLE 5

COMPONENTS OF SAVING IN THE REGULAR DEFINITION USED
IN THE SURVEYS OF CONSUMER FINANCES[a]

| *Component* | *Saving Component Breakdown* |
|---|---|
| Miscellaneous saving | Amount paid in year for purchase of house less mortgage and other borrowing at time of purchase (entered for home buyers only) |
|  | Additions to the house (entered for home owners only) |
|  | Deduct any borrowing to finance additions and repairs |
|  | Amount of own money put into purchase of real estate other than own home |
|  | Deduct amount realized from sale of real estate other than own home |
|  | Excess of purchases over sales of securities |
|  | Deduct excess of sales over purchases of securities |
|  | Deduct receipts from cashing of insurance |
|  | Amounts loaned by spending unit |
|  | Deduct amounts repaid to spending unit |
|  | Deduct inheritance of money and bonds |
|  | Miscellaneous |
| Consumer indebtedness | Deduct borrowing for purchase of car in current year |
|  | Deduct borrowing for purchase of durables in current year |
|  | Deduct other borrowing during the year[b] |
|  | Amount of debt repaid by the spending unit |
| Change in liquid asset holdings | Holdings at end of year of U. S. government bonds, savings accounts, and checking accounts |
|  | Deduct holdings at beginning of year |
| Business saving | Profits left in business or business loss |
|  | Liquidation of business investment, or new investment in business |
| Contractual saving | Regular payments on principal of debt on home (lump sum settlements are counted as miscellaneous saving) |
|  | Life insurance premiums |
|  | Payments to retirement or pension funds |

[a] Strictly speaking, the items shown are those included in saving in the 1951 Survey, but differences from year to year are of minor importance.

[b] By "other borrowing" is meant borrowing for purposes other than the purchase of real estate, cars, or durables.

Consider again the identity:

$$\text{Income} = \text{Savings} + \text{Consumption}$$

Income in the Survey includes cash income only. The components of income are shown in Table 3. Thus, income in kind is not included. No attempt is made to impute income, for example, to home owners.

The components of saving are shown in Table 5. Since income is on a cash basis, saving also is largely on a cash basis. Thus, no entry is made for depreciation on owner-occupied homes, and no entries are made for changes in stocks of consumer goods, with the single exception of real property. Sums invested in one's own business, including retained profits, are also considered saving.

The components of consumption, for the most part, are not estimated directly in the Survey. The largest exception to this rule is the estimation of outlay for selected durable goods. If we regard income tax as a deduction from income, the identity becomes:

Cash Income − Federal Income Tax = Cash Savings + Savings in Real Property and Investments in Own Business + Outlays for Selected Durables + Residual Expenditures.

How do the Survey accounts measure up to the three sets of "ideal" accounts just described? First, for the study of consumers' welfare the Survey accounts are incomplete. For this purpose income in kind should be added to income. Savings would include a sixth major component, namely, additions to stocks of all kinds of consumer goods less allowances for use. Consumption would not consist as at present of cash outlay for consumer goods but of actual using-up of consumer goods. Evidently, income would be larger than under the present system, and the total of savings plus consumption would be larger, but the division of this increased total between savings and consumption might lead to an increase or decrease in either, depending on the course of events.

Second, for purposes of studying the contribution of consumers to the supply of producers' goods in the hands of business enterprises, a different set of accounts would be appropriate. Here the essential item of information is the amount of transfer of assets to and from the business sector and financial intermediaries. Since the financial intermediaries *may* transfer funds from consumers to the government rather than to business, if they do not lend them back to other consumers, it would become important to reorganize the components of saving to make this distinction between the business sector and financial intermediaries. Also, changes in holdings of real property by consumers would no longer be savings at all. To build a home is not to increase the nation's supply of producers' goods. Outlay for this purpose should appear, therefore, as consumption instead of saving as it does in the present system.

Third, for the purpose of studying consumers' contributions to the level of economic activity, yet another set of accounts is appropriate. Income should be restricted to cash income. It should not include, as income in the Survey now does include, undistributed profits of unincorporated enterprises. Savings also should be restricted to cash savings; it should exclude two items now included—changes in holdings of real estate and undistributed profits of unincorporated enterprises. Consumption should cover cash outlays for goods and services of all types, including real estate, durable goods, nondurables, and services. For this purpose, then, both the Survey definition of income and the definition of saving cover too many items.[7]

Theoretically it would be possible to set up an identity broken down into enough components to make possible the calculation of income, savings, and consumption for all three purposes. Only practical—but weighty—considerations stand in the way of such a formulation as the following:

[7] The data in the Survey covering income and saving in 1949 and 1950 have been reworked according to definitions of the type suggested here. See John B. Lansing and E. Scott Maynes, "Inflation and Saving by Consumers," *Journal of Political Economy,* LX (October 1952), 383–91.

Income in cash + Undistributed profits of unincorporated enterprises + Imputed income from owner-occupied dwellings − Depreciation on owner-occupied dwellings + Other income in kind = Undistributed profits of unincorporated enterprises + Changes in claims against other businesses + Changes in claims against the government + Changes in claims against financial intermediaries + Changes in holdings of real estate + Changes in inventories of durable goods and other consumer goods + Consumption of consumer goods and services.

The reader may be reminded that when one is dealing with aggregate statistics, the arithmetic of such a formulation need be worked out only once. When one is dealing with a sample survey, it must be done for each spending unit in the sample. But if it could be done, any of the concepts outlined above could be constructed from the same data.

*Durable goods.* Once the main outline of a system of accounts for consumers has been set, there remain numerous problems to be settled within the general framework. Some of these questions are sufficiently important to warrant mention here. One is the definition of durable goods.

A classification of goods according to their durability would be a straightforward operation, requiring extensive information as to the mean length of life of each item purchased by consumers. The logical procedure then would be to rank the goods in order of durability, and classify as "durable" those whose life extends more than some interval—say, a year.

No such precise procedure is followed in the Surveys of Consumer Finances. Considerations of economy of questions have led to the restriction of the list of "selected" durables to the following:

Furniture (including pianos)
Radios
Television sets
Phonographs, record players
Refrigerators, ice boxes, and deep freeze units
Washing machines

Clothes driers and ironers

Stoves

Vacuum cleaners

Toasters

Sewing machines

Movie projectors

Air conditioning units (when not a permanent part of the heating
  system)

Space heaters and imitation fireplaces (when purchased by renters)

Other electrical appliances

A problem arises for some items in distinguishing between durable
goods and additions to a house. Goods which become a permanent
part of the dwelling are not counted as durable goods but as additions. For example, Venetian blinds, storm windows, furnaces, air
conditioning units when they are built in all are classified as additions to the house.

*Liquid assets.* There is no simple, definitive answer to the question
of what is a "liquid" asset. Ordinarily deposits in checking accounts
and currency are regarded as liquid and may be taken as a standard
of liquidity. (Even here, of course, problems may arise in connection with closed banks, foreign banks, exchange control, etc., but
these problems are not of importance for consumer surveys in the
United States in the postwar period.)

Accepting this standard, one may rank assets according to the
time and expense or loss involved in converting them into cash. Since
time and expense are not identical, the ranking may present problems,
but some rank order can be achieved. One may then classify as
"liquid" assets all items rated over a more or less arbitrary rank.
We may refer to these assets as "objectively" liquid.

Alternatively, instead of classifying all amounts in certain types of
assets as liquid, one may attempt to discover how people regard
their individual assets. One individual may regard a sum of money
in a savings account as a liquid reserve to be kept intact except in
an emergency. Another may regard a savings account as a repository

for funds which he is accumulating to finance certain purchases. For the latter, the deposits may be said to be more liquid than for the former. Thus it may become a problem for research to determine to what extent particular assets are "subjectively" liquid.

In the Surveys of Consumer Finances the procedure has been to classify as liquid all holdings of consumer units in checking accounts, savings accounts, shares of savings and loan associations, Series A-F bonds, and other U. S. government bonds. The question of the purposes to which these liquid assets may be devoted and thus of the extent to which they are subjectively liquid has been treated as a separate topic of investigation. The selection of these four classes of assets as "liquid" involves the exclusion, obviously, of other assets. Holdings of currency are certainly objectively liquid, but, as noted previously, information about them is not obtained in the Surveys. The exclusion from "liquid" assets of bonds of governmental bodies other than the U. S. government and of all private bonds and stocks undoubtedly involves an arbitrary element. These assets are, for the most part, almost as liquid if not fully as liquid as U. S. government bonds.

On close examination, then, the question of what items should be classified as "liquid assets" proves to be difficult. The definition adopted in the Surveys represents one choice among a number of possibilities; the choice can be defended as reasonable, but the possibility must remain that for some purposes other choices would be more appropriate.

Given the Survey list of items classified as "liquid assets," the further question arises of how to separate consumers' personal holdings from those of businesses with which they may be associated. As noted in the discussion of spending units, the rule adopted is to exclude all holdings which are kept separate in business accounts earmarked as such. A possible alternative would be to include all accounts held by owners of unincorporated businesses, in the case of partnerships ascribing to each partner a share of the firm's accounts. Even if he has separate accounts, a man may maintain what he regards as a single liquid reserve, which can be used, if need be, either for personal or business expenditures. It may be a matter of indifference in which bank account he holds this reserve. He may even hold it in Series E Bonds. Thus the decision to include as holdings of consumers all funds not kept in separate business accounts and no part of any separate accounts represents, again, one reasonable choice among several which might be made.

*Debts.* The question, what is a debt owed by a spending unit, does not present major difficulties. On the fringes of the concept of debt, however, there are minor questions. Does a pledge to a charitable organization constitute a debt? Although some consumers regard such pledges in the same way as, say, payments on an installment loan, pledges are not enforceable in the courts and it does not seem proper to consider them debts. The legal definition of debt is also helpful in drawing the line between valid and invalid claims: if a claim is legally enforceable, it should be considered a debt, otherwise not.

The distinction between current bills and debts may occasionally present difficulties. So also may loans made within a family. Sometimes it is not intended that such "loans" should be repaid, or repayment is in part at the option of the borrower. Such debts do not represent a claim of the same burden as claims of regular lending institutions, but, nevertheless, it seems proper to regard them as debts as long as they are so regarded by the borrower.

The distinction between loans for business purposes made against business assets and loans for consumption is much more of a problem. Any borrowing by the owner of a business may be a source of funds to be used for business purposes. For example, the owner of a small business which is showing a profit may choose to reinvest a part of the profit in his business and to purchase a new house, financing it with a large mortgage. Or he may borrow money on a house which he at one time owned clear of debt, and invest the money in his business. The analyst who wishes to disentangle loans for business and loans for consumption purposes must ascertain the purpose for which each loan was made: he cannot rely on information as to the lending agency and the nature of the security for the loan. If he does, he will be lumping together loans actually obtained and used for divergent purposes. His only "easy" choice is to lump together all loans made to business owners, sacrificing the distinction between business and nonbusiness borrowing.

### COMPARISON OF CONCEPTS USED IN THE SURVEY WITH CONCEPTS USED ELSEWHERE

From the point of view of the analyst, ideally the entire body of current economic statistics for the United States should form a consistent and integrated unit. Distributions from such sources as the Surveys of Consumer Finances should correspond exactly to aggregate statistics independently estimated. It would then be possible to study jointly aggregates and the corresponding distributions, carrying the investigation back to the behavior of individuals falling in the sample from which the distributions were estimated, and making possible the integration of psychological study of the behavior of individuals with the study of aggregate statistics.

As matters at present stand, these possibilities can be realized but not fully, for the available aggregate and survey statistics fit together imperfectly. The bulk of this section is devoted to a discussion of the conceptual differences between the Survey statistics and those in the statistics of national income prepared by the National Income Division of the Department of Commerce. The latter have been selected for comparison because of their importance and wide acceptance, though the Survey concepts also can be compared to a variety of other important bodies of economic data. Among the latter the series on liquid saving maintained by the Securities and Exchange Commission is particularly worthy of mention.

While the discussion here is restricted to conceptual differences, errors of measurement are important. Survey data are subject to sampling error, and both survey and aggregate data are subject to systematic errors of measurement. The analysis of these errors is beyond the scope of this discussion, but on many items they probably equal or exceed in importance the conceptual differences treated here. If the collection of statistical data involved neither error nor expense, problems of conceptual differences would disappear. One could always adjust any set of statistics to any desired basis.

*Income.* Table 6 presents a comparison of the components of Personal Income, as that term is used in the statistics of national income, with income as defined in the Survey, in some detail. As a first approximation both types of income include the current income received by persons, but some important items are treated differently. All of the following items are included in Personal Income but not in the Survey: income in kind; income of persons other than natural persons (trusts, nonprofit institutions, estates); income of natural persons not included in the Survey universe (migratory workers, the institutional population, residents of transient hotels, persons living on military reservations, Americans resident abroad employed by American organizations); changes in farm inventory; and imputed interest and rent. Thus the most important differences are, first, that the Survey definition is on a cash basis, with the single addition of undistributed profits of unincorporated enterprises, while Personal Income includes several noncash items; and second, that the Survey universe is restricted to natural persons living in more or less permanent dwelling units, while Personal Income is not.

In one sense, any such comparison is misleading because of basic differences between the methods used in the collection of the two sets of statistics. In the Survey of Consumer Finances the income of a spending unit is, basically, the sum of the amounts mentioned by the respondent in answer to a series of questions. These answers are edited in the central office when there is clear evidence from the interview that the respondent misunderstood the questions. He may have included in his answer sums which he said came to him from a source not considered income in the Survey, such as the sale of a business. He may have excluded from his answers to the questions about income but clearly described elsewhere in the interview receipts

## TABLE 6

COMPARISON BETWEEN INCOME IN THE SURVEYS OF CONSUMER
FINANCES AND PERSONAL INCOME IN THE STATISTICS OF
NATIONAL INCOME

| Components of "Personal Income" | Income Components in the Survey of Consumer Finances |
|---|---|
| Wage and salary receipts | Cash receipts of wages and salaries by consumers, in general, are included |
| Total employer disbursements | Total employer disbursements |
| Includes income in kind, for example, of servants, soldiers, farmers, employees of institutions who "live in," rental value of parsonages, and board received by Catholic clergy | Excludes all income in kind |
| Includes tips | Includes tips |
| Deducts employee contributions for social insurance | Employee contributions for social insurance *not* deducted |
| Adds excess of wage disbursements over wage accruals (resulting from retroactive payments) | Counts cash receipts by employees, which include the excess of disbursements over accruals |
| Includes all wages paid to members of armed forces | Includes only payments to members of armed forces who fall within the sample universe, which excludes personnel living on military reservations or overseas. Also includes regular contributions to domestic spending units by all soldiers |
| | Includes only residents of the U. S. |
| Includes payrolls of employees stationed abroad who are citizens of the continental U. S. | |
| Includes transient and institutional population | Transient and institutional population excluded from sample universe |
| Other labor income | Most other labor income items are not included |
| Includes compensation for injuries (benefits under accident compensation laws) | Excludes compensation for injuries |
| Includes contributions by employers to private pension and welfare funds | Excludes contributions by employers to private pension and welfare funds |
| Includes various miscellaneous components, such as the following: | The miscellaneous items in the adjacent column are not covered explicitly in the questions asked in the Survey. A few are clearly excluded; others are included to the extent reported |
| pay of military reservists | Included |

TABLE 6 (*Continued*)

| *Components of "Personal Income"* | *Income Components in the Survey of Consumer Finances* |
|---|---|
| government payments to enemy prisoners of war | Excluded |
| payments arising from merchant marine war risk | Excluded |
| life and injury claims | Excluded |
| directors' fees | Included |
| jury and witness fees | Excluded |
| compensation of inmates of prisons | Excluded |
| marriage fees to justices of the peace | Included |
| Proprietors' and rental income | Proprietors' and rental income is included only to the extent it accrues to individuals. Income of nonprofit institutions, private trust funds, and private pension and welfare funds is not included in the Survey |
| Income of unincorporated enterprises | Income of unincorporated enterprises is included, though the definition of "unincorporated business" used in the Survey excludes income of professional practitioners and farmers, which appear under their own headings |
| Income of independent professional practitioners | Included |
| Income of business enterprises | Included |
| Net income of farm proprietors | Included, in general, but see the following: |
| Includes net change in value of farm inventories | Excluded |
| Includes value of home consumption of farm produce | Excluded |
| Includes gross rental value of farm homes less depreciation | Excluded |
| Deducts as expenses taxes on farm property (real estate and personal property taxes) | No such deduction is made |
| Inventory valuation adjustment | No inventory valuation adjustment is made |
| An adjustment is made to arrive at the same result as if a uniform system for measuring change in value of inventories had been used by all unincorporated enterprises | |
| Rental income of persons | Rental income of persons is included in part |

TABLE 6 (*Continued*)

| Components of "Personal Income" | Income Components in the Survey of Consumer Finances |
|---|---|
| Rented nonfarm property | Included, but not distinguished from income from rented farm property |
| Personal net rents from rented dwellings | Included[a] |
| Personal net royalties | Included (though not referred to as income from rents) |
| Personal net rents from business and industrial property | Included |
| Imputed income from owner-occupied nonfarm dwellings | Excluded |
| Net rent from farm property | Included |
| Dividends | Included |
| Personal interest income | Included, in part |
| Monetary interest | Included |
| Imputed interest (arising out of transactions of financial intermediaries) | Excluded |
| Net interest paid by government (includes interest accrued but not paid) | Included, except that interest accrued and not paid is excluded |
| Transfer payments | Included, in part[b] |
| Government transfers | Included (to the extent made to individuals) |
| Business transfers (consumer bad debts, personal injury payments by business other than to employees, etc.) | Excluded |

[a] In the Survey, income of landladies from roomers and boarders is taken to be equal to the gross receipts where four roomers and boarders or fewer are involved.

[b] As noted earlier in this chapter, the Survey also includes as income transfer payments from one person to another—notably in the form of regular contributions.

which are considered income in the survey. Such interviews are exceptional. In the great majority, the respondent's income is taken to be the sum of the amounts he mentions in answer to the questions on income. Precisely how he interpreted the questions in matters of detail must remain uncertain. For example, there is no certain way of discovering whether respondents who received income from jury and witness fees did in fact include those fees in their answers. A question specifically mentioning this type of income could be added to the schedule, though the amounts involved hardly seem to justify such a question. In its absence, one can say that the presumption is that such income is not included since it is not asked for.

In the statistics of national income, on the other hand, there are fewer uncertainties as to what is included and what is not included when one speaks on the conceptual level. The difficulties arise in the process of estimation, which is far more elaborate and complex than that in the Surveys of Consumer Finances. In the statistics of national income one enjoys a maximum of conceptual precision at the price of an involved and occasionally even shaky estimating procedure. In the Surveys of Consumer Finances one enjoys a much more straightforward estimating procedure at the price of a lack of precision on the fringes of the concept. To say that a component is included in income in the Survey usually means that it is explicitly mentioned in a question, but sometimes only that it is implied.

*Saving.* The comparison of Personal Saving and saving as measured in the Surveys is a complex matter. The difficulty arises from the fact that both the statistics of national income and the Survey take advantage of the celebrated identity relating income, saving, and consumption, but in different ways. In the Survey, income and saving are estimated directly; consumption, by subtraction. In the statistics of national income, income and consumption are measured directly; saving, by subtraction. One can compare the concepts of income by looking at the detailed lists of components, as has been done in Table 6. One must compare the concepts of saving indirectly, by such procedures as preparing a list of items included as Personal Income but not as Survey income, and determining whether these items are counted as consumption and deducted from Personal Income in arriving at Personal Saving. Even more elusive are items, such as changes in holdings of currency, which are not treated explicitly in either set of statistics. (The Survey does not include them as saving, but the Department of Commerce does include them implicitly). The published reconciliation between Personal Saving and Liquid Saving (as estimated by the Securities and Exchange Commission) is helpful in this connection, though it adds yet a dimension of complexity to the task. Table 7 purports to make the comparison between Personal Saving and saving in the Survey, but it is presented with the caution that it may not be perfect.

TABLE 7

COMPARISON BETWEEN SAVING IN THE SURVEYS OF CONSUMER FINANCES AND PERSONAL SAVING IN THE STATISTICS OF NATIONAL INCOME

| Item | Comment |
|---|---|
| Items included in Personal Saving but not in Saving in the Surveys: | |
| Changes in holdings of currency by individuals | |
| Retirements of corporate bonds held by individuals | |
| Changes in charge account debt | |
| All savings of nonprofit institutions, private trust funds, private pension and welfare funds, and estates | |
| All savings of individuals excluded from the Survey universe (transient population, institutional population, persons living on military reservations, Americans overseas who are employed by American agencies or who are in the armed forces) | |
| Depreciation on owner-occupied homes, both farm and nonfarm, and on farm buildings and equipment | |
| Net change in value of farm inventories | |
| Purchase of passenger automobiles for farm use | |
| Inventory valuation adjustment for unincorporated enterprises | |
| Items wholly included in the Survey but included in Personal Saving in part or not at all: | |
| Insurance premiums | Survey Saving includes the full value of premiums paid on life insurance less lump sum settlements. Personal Saving includes the increase in the value of reserves against life insurance. Personal Saving thus excludes the expense of handling life insurance but includes income of life insurance companies from property |
| Premiums paid by individuals on government insurance | Excluded from Personal Saving |
| Payments made by individuals to government retirement funds | Excluded from Personal Saving |

TABLE 8

COMPARISON BETWEEN "SELECTED DURABLE GOODS" IN THE SURVEYS
OF CONSUMER FINANCES AND "DURABLE GOODS" IN THE
STATISTICS OF NATIONAL INCOME

| Coverage | Item |
|---|---|
| Included in both concepts | Furniture<br>Refrigerators<br>Washing machines<br>Sewing machines<br>Miscellaneous electrical appliances<br>New cars and net purchases of used cars[a] |
| Wholly included in "Durable Goods" but included in the Surveys in part only | Cooking and portable heating equipment (stoves are included in the Survey, but space heaters, and imitation fireplaces are counted only when purchased by renters. Pots and pans are excluded)<br>Radio and television receivers, phonographs, parts, and records (parts and records are excluded in the Survey)<br>Pianos and other musical instruments (pianos are included under furniture. Other musical instruments are excluded) |
| Included in "Durable Goods" but excluded from the Surveys' "Selected Durable Goods" | Jewelry and watches<br>Floor coverings<br>China, glassware, tableware, and utensils<br>Durable house furnishings<br>Products of custom establishments not elsewhere classified<br>Writing equipment<br>Opthalmic products and orthopedic appliances<br>Monuments and tombstones<br>Tools<br>Tires and tubes (for automobiles)<br>Parts and accessories (for automobiles)<br>Luggage<br>Books and maps<br>Wheel goods, durable toys, and sport equipment<br>Boats and pleasure aircraft |

[a] Included in the Survey, but usually separated from other selected durables.

Table 7 may suffice at least to establish that differences between the two concepts are substantial even though there is a broad similarity between the two definitions—both include as savings such items as purchases of homes and sums invested by individuals in their own businesses and both exclude purchases of consumers' durable goods.

*Durable goods.* A comparison between the list of "selected" durable goods covered by the Surveys of Consumer Finances and "Durable Goods" in the statistics of national income appears as Table 8. The items in "selected" durable goods are for the most part the large durables purchased by substantial numbers of spending units. Items which typically represent smaller outlays per transaction (e.g., tires and tubes for automobiles) and items which tend to be purchased by a small proportion of the population in any year (e.g., boats and pleasure aircraft) are not included in the Survey definition.

### NOTE ON REPEATED INTERVIEWS AND REINTERVIEWS

The usual practice in the Surveys of Consumer Finances is to interview successive cross sections of the population. The chance that the same person will fall in two successive samples, selected independently from each other (although by means of the same sampling methods), and therefore will be interviewed twice, is very small. A large part of the analysis consists in the study of differences and similarities between these successive samples of the population of the United States taken at intervals of one year.

In the Survey conducted in early 1949, covering income, savings, etc., for the year 1948, a special attempt was made to interview again some of the respondents interviewed in 1948. For purposes of procedure in sampling, a distinction is drawn between people living in cities and towns and people living outside of such places in what is called the open country. Reinterviews were not attempted in the open country in this survey. In the cities and towns the regular procedure is to send interviewers to dwellings which are designated by street and number and, when necessary, by further information, such as apartment number. The procedure used to provide for reinterviews was to send interviewers to the same address for two successive years. The addresses selected to be sent out twice constituted a random sample of dwelling units exclusive of dwelling units in the open country and included about one-half of the urban addresses used early in 1948.

The reinterviews actually obtained, however, fall short in some respects of a random cross section of spending units living in urban areas. Any reinterview survey will tend to fall short of a perfect cross section for three main reasons. First, some spending units who should have been interviewed in the first survey will not be interviewed, mainly because the interviewers cannot find some potential respondents at home, or because some potential respondents refuse to be interviewed. Second, some of the spending units who were interviewed at an address in the first survey have moved away before the second survey. Third, some of the spending units who are interviewed in the first survey and who are still living at the same address during the second survey will not be interviewed the second time for one of the usual reasons—the respondent will not be at home after repeated calls or he will refuse to be interviewed again. Some respondents may be interviewed in the second survey who did not respond in the first, but these interviews obviously cannot be reinterviews.

The effect of these losses is cumulative, and the result is certain to make reinterviews less satisfactory as a cross section than interviews from a single survey. In the present example, 1,321 spending units were located during the first survey at addresses in the portion of the sample under discussion. Of the 1,321, 1,070 or 81 percent were interviewed. Of the 1,070, about 17 percent moved away before the second survey began. Of the remainder, about 27 percent were not interviewed, leaving 655 actual reinterviews taken. In other words, about half of the original group of 1,321 spending units were successfully interviewed twice. In contrast, the usual proportion of successful single interviews on the Surveys of Consumer Finances is about 85 percent.

When the effective response rate on a survey is as low as that for this reinterview survey, a comparison of the distributions from this sample with distributions from samples of the same population with higher response rates becomes important. Such comparisons are made in Table 9. The data in this table indicate that the reinterviews include too few young people and too few secondary spending units

## TABLE 9

COMPARISON OF CHARACTERISTICS OF THE POPULATION AS ESTIMATED
FROM REINTERVIEWS AND FROM ALL INTERVIEWS
IN URBAN AREAS—1949

*Percentage of spending units*

|  | Reinterviews (*percent*) | All Interviews in Urban Areas (*percent*) |
|---|---|---|
| *Spending Unit Composition* | | |
| Primary spending units | 90 | 79 |
| Related secondary spending units | 9 | 15 |
| Unrelated secondary spending units | 1 | 6 |
|  | 100 | 100 |
| *Number of Children in Spending Unit* | | |
| 0 | 58 | 59 |
| 1 | 17 | 19 |
| 2 | 15 | 13 |
| 3 | 5 | 4 |
| 4 | 2 | 2 |
| 5 | 1 | 1 |
| 6 | 1 | 1 |
| 7 or more | 1 | 1 |
|  | 100 | 100 |
| *Occupation of Head of Spending Unit* | | |
| Professional | 9 | 8 |
| Self-employed and managerial | 14 | 13 |
| White collar employees | 17 | 18 |
| Skilled or semi-skilled workers | 28 | 30 |
| Unskilled and service workers | 13 | 14 |
| Protective service workers | 1 | 1 |
| Farm operators | . . [a] | . . [a] |
| Housewives | 5 | 4 |
| Students | 1 | 2 |
| Retired | 7 | 6 |
| Unemployed | 4 | 4 |
|  | 100 | 100 |
| *Age of Head of Spending Unit (Years)* | | |
| 18–24 | 5 | 12 |
| 25–34 | 19 | 22 |
| 35–44 | 24 | 21 |
| 45–54 | 24 | 20 |
| 55–64 | 15 | 14 |
| 65 or over | 13 | 11 |
|  | 100 | 100 |

[a] Less than 0.5 percent.

TABLE 9 (*Continued*)

|  | Reinterviews (*percent*) | All Interviews in Urban Areas (*percent*) |
|---|---|---|
| *Education of Head of Spending Unit* | | |
| Grammar school (any level) | 35 | 34 |
| High school (any level) | 41 | 43 |
| College (any level) | 21 | 20 |
| None | 2 | 2 |
| Not ascertained | 1 | 1 |
|  | 100 | 100 |
| *Race of Head of Spending Unit* | | |
| White | 89 | 90 |
| Negro | 10 | 9 |
| Other | 1 | 1 |
|  | 100 | 100 |

but about the proper proportion of spending units headed by individuals in various occupations and of different education, race, and parental status.

For some purposes of analysis, reinterviews have important advantages, which have led to the use of data from the reinterviews taken in 1949 in the investigations described later in this volume. Briefly, these advantages include the following: (1) Reinterviews make it possible to relate attitudes at the *beginning* of a year to the behavior of the same persons during the year. Without reinterviews the investigator must measure attitudes at the close of the period. (2) Reinterviews one year apart make it possible to study behavior for two years without requiring respondents to remember and report their behavior for more than one year in a single interview. (3) For studies of savings in a single year, reinterviews eliminate memory errors which tend to occur when respondents are asked to report on such magnitudes as their holdings of liquid assets at a date one year prior to the interview. In general, we may say that reinterviews suffer from larger errors of overall nonresponse than single surveys but benefit from reductions in reporting error for certain variables and from the additional information available about each spending unit which is interviewed twice.

# II: VARIABILITY OF CONSUMER BEHAVIOR AND THE SURVEY METHOD

## by George Katona

The basic considerations that have been responsible for setting up the Economic Behavior Program of the Survey Research Center may be summarized in the following three points:

(1) Consumers play a great and active role in the present-day American economy. Because of the current high supernumerary incomes, substantial liquid assets, and the great variety of postponable expenditures, consumer spending and saving are not rigidly tied to income.

(2) Fluctuations of spending and saving are influenced by people's motivations, attitudes, and expectations. Quantitative studies of these psychological variables and the determination of their differences among different groups and their changes over time are possible and promise to contribute to an understanding of economic processes.

(3) Aggregate economic statistics—on national income, total amount of bank deposits, and the like—need to be supplemented by information on the distribution of these variables. It is necessary to determine, for instance, the proportion of families whose income or bank deposits have increased or decreased in a given year, as well as the characteristics of these groups of families. Such microeconomic data represent the link to psychological variables, since the latter can be determined only in the case of individual economic units.

These general assumptions are derived from a broader framework which, when implemented and developed, may represent a theory of consumer behavior. The outline of such a theory will be presented first.

### OUTLINE OF THEORY OF CONSUMER BEHAVIOR

Traditionally, two forms of money outlays by consumers are distinguished—expenditures and amounts saved. This distinction, although of utmost importance, is not the only useful way of classifying consumer money outlays. We shall introduce here a second distinction, one between "outlays of choice" or "variable outlays" and "habitual outlays."

The major consideration that enters into the distinction between spending and saving concerns the different economic effects of the two forms of money outlays. Amounts spent do not interrupt the money flow, while amounts saved may do so unless "used" promptly by the savings institutions. In addition, it is possible to distinguish between spending and saving from the point of view of the decision makers: money outlays which serve to provide for immediate needs are called spending; money outlays which serve to provide reserves for future needs, saving.

Neither set of considerations yields definite rules that would enable the student to classify all outlays into either spending or saving. Particular difficulties arise regarding the classification of payments for consumer purchases of durable goods. Although some of the analysis in this volume will make use of alternative definitions, in this chapter the definitions used in the Surveys of Consumer Finances, as described in the preceding chapter, will be adopted. Accordingly, payments made for the purchases of durable goods are classified as expenditures, while payments made for the purchases of homes are classified as amounts saved.

A second form of classifying consumer money outlays is the result of an analysis of the decision-making process itself. Not all transactions undertaken by consumers are deliberately planned and carefully considered. Only in certain instances do consumers weigh alternative courses of action and choose among them. In the absence of such genuine decision making, we find, most commonly, habitual behavior.[1] Certain things are done, and money outlays are made, because they have been done repeatedly before in similar circumstances. Routine characterizes also a variety of money outlays which ensue in consequence of decisions previously made. Fulfilling contractual obligations in paying premiums on life insurance policies or in paying rent belongs in that category.

In analyzing the behavior of individual decision makers it appears possible to classify each money outlay according to whether it has been based on deliberate choice or not. If, however, an attempt is made to classify the various important types of consumer money outlay into the two categories so that the classification should be valid for all or most consumers, certain difficulties arise. All that can be done is list broad groups of money outlays which usually or most commonly, but not necessarily in every instance, fall into the one or other classification. Such a rough classificatory scheme will, however, prove to be of value because money outlays of choice are relatively variable while habitual outlays are relatively stable over short periods of time, both for individual consumers and for the economy as a whole.

A rough scheme of classification of consumer money outlays will be presented first. It makes use of both classifications, the one distinguishing between spending and saving, and the second distinguishing between habitual outlays and outlays of choice.

SCHEME OF CLASSIFICATION OF CONSUMER MONEY OUTLAYS

|  | *Spending* | *Saving* |
|---|---|---|
| Habitual outlays | I. Food, certain clothing items, rent, interest, taxes, etc. | II. Life insurance premiums, payments into retirement funds, repayment of debt, etc. |
| Outlays of choice (Variable outlays) | III. Durable goods, repairs of houses, vacation trips, luxury expenditures, many forms of services, etc. | IV. Additions to liquid assets, investments in securities and real estate, etc. |

[1] The distinction between genuine decision making and habitual behavior was introduced, and its psychological basis discussed, in George Katona, *Psychological Analysis of Economic Behavior* (New York: McGraw-Hill, 1951).

*Habitual money outlays,* that is, outlays which usually or most commonly are not based on deliberate choice, are regular expenditures on necessities as well as fixed charges and contractual obligations previously entered into.

Which of the money outlays fall into this classification will vary somewhat from family to family, and may vary within the same family over time. On the whole, however, it appears to hold true for most American families at the present time that most expenditures on food and clothing—except expenditures on food which may be classified under the heading of entertainment and money spent on luxury clothing items—fall into this category and are also classified as spending. These outlays, then, belong in cell I, above, just as payments of rent (on the part of families who do not own their homes), interest on mortgage debt (on the part of home owners) and on other debts. Payment of taxes and of social security contributions belong in the same category if the starting point of the analysis is income before taxes and if rights acquired through contributions to social security are not classified as savings.

From the point of view of the decision-making process, the outlays just enumerated do not differ from certain other outlays which, however, are classified as savings. Important examples are payments on mortgage principal, repayment of other debts, premiums paid on life insurance, and payments into a retirement fund. Payroll deductions for the purchase of U. S. Savings Bonds fall conceptually into the same group.

It is clear from the examples given that the term "deliberate choice" is used here only if a decision was made in the period immediately preceding the money outlay. The purchase of a new life insurance policy or the signing of an installment debt contract on the occasion of buying an automobile are not habitual forms of behavior. Yet after a purchase or debt contract have been entered into, the payments of premiums or of installments become contractual obligations which most commonly do not require the making of new genuine decisions. While the purchase of an automobile is usually not habitual, the purchase of gasoline—used for commuting to work—may be so considered. Expenditures on gasoline during a vacation trip, however, represent a different kind of money outlay because taking or not taking a vacation, and how much to spend on vacation, are usually matters of deliberate choice.

Certain other kinds of money outlay by consumers are usually made on the basis of deliberation and choice. These outlays are postponable and vary greatly within the same family over time.

Some of the *outlays of choice* are classified as expenditures. Among them payments for the purchase of durable goods (automobiles, furniture, appliances, etc.) are usually of great importance. Money spent for repairs of houses owned, for vacation trips, for entertainment and the purchase of luxury items, as well as payments for many forms of services, fall in the same category.[2]

Among the discretionary outlays which are classified as amounts saved are liquid saving—additions to bank deposits, purchase of government bonds and of other securities. (But purchases of savings bonds may be habitual, as noted earlier, and additions to bank deposits, especially to checking accounts, may occur because of the absence of certain decisions rather than as the result of deliberate choice.) Investments of all kinds, especially purchase of real estate, as well as purchase of and additions to homes owned, are likewise variable forms of saving. Variable saving of a family, and also of the economy as a whole, in contrast to variable money outlays, may of course be negative; bank deposits may be reduced, savings bonds cashed, and securities or real estate sold; also, money may be borrowed in order to enable the borrower to make money outlays.

The most fundamental difference between habitual money outlays and outlays of choice is found in the degree of latitude or discretion of the consumers. To be sure, consumers also have some latitude in

---

[2] Payments for some visits to physicians may be classified among money outlays of choice, while expenditures due to accidents and acute illness belong conceptually among the expenditures which are not made on the basis of deliberate choice. Yet the latter expenditures are undoubtedly variable (for individual families). This is one of the difficulties of the model presented here.

changing their habitual outlays even in the short run. The most radical change, default of contractual obligations, may be neglected in a first approach because it can be assumed to be rare except under conditions of great hardship. But expenditures on necessities may fluctuate. The thesis to be presented here is, first, that these fluctuations are slow and gradual, much slower and much smaller in extent than the fluctuations of outlays of choice. This is the case because changes in the cultural norms or patterns of living, in taste and technology, or in the composition of the population, which affect the habitual money outlays, may be neglected if economic fluctuations over short periods are considered. Secondly, it may be postulated as a first approximation that changes in habitual money outlays are a function of income—of its level, its distribution, and its changes—and of other traditional economic and demographic variables (possibly with a time lag). Fluctuations in outlays of choice are, on the other hand, dependent to a much greater extent on consumer attitudes—on changes in motivations, opinions, perceptions and expectations. To be sure, sometimes the purchase of a durable consumer good may be "inevitable" and not based on deliberation and choosing; yet on the whole such expenditures by individual families as well as the entire economy may be greatly increased or reduced at any given time according to people's attitudes.

It is hereby assumed that substantial changes in attitudes often occur at about the same time among very many people. Furthermore, that such changes are not fully determined by prior changes in the economic environment (in incomes, assets, and the like). Consumers have some latitude in changing their behavior because they are not slaves of underlying conditions but react to stimuli according to their past experiences and attitudes as well as to their group belonging. They use their discretion primarily to change the composition of their money outlays of choice. These outlays, therefore, have a much greater "residual variance" (variance unexplained by a few such traditional variables as income and assets) than the habitual outlays. This does not mean that outlays of choice are not predictable while habitual outlays are, but implies differences in the explanatory variables that need to be taken into account.

## Variable versus Habitual Outlays

From the point of view of short-term economic developments the choice of consumers between variable expenditures and variable saving (the choice between cells III and IV in the scheme, above) is of paramount importance. Before turning to that problem, a few words need to be said about the factors which add to the importance of variable money outlays in contrast to the habitual ones (the question of how cells I and II differ from III and IV).

Four factors may be singled out which contribute to the relative importance of variable money outlays. The first is income level. If we think of an economy in which all income receivers use their entire income for mere subsistence (and no reserve funds exist), the absence of supernumerary incomes will restrict the economy to habitual money outlays. On the other hand, in an economy with a substantial number of receivers of supernumerary incomes and with large amounts of such incomes, habitual outlays will represent a smaller proportion of total money outlays.

The second factor to be considered is the level of assets held and especially that of liquid assets. In an economy in which a substantial proportion of families own sizable assets that can be readily transformed into cash, people have it in their power to step up their expenditures beyond their income. It is here postulated that this power is exercised, primarily, to increase variable rather than habitual money outlays. Availability of substantial assets of the inventory type—automobiles, furniture, and the like—may likewise influence the fluctuations of variable money outlays, because large inventories may make those outlays still more postponable than they otherwise are.

An institutional setup which facilitates borrowing may be listed next. In the absence of a possibility to borrow, money outlays must be financed out of income or assets. On the other hand, convenient and simple arrangements to purchase on installment, for instance, enable people to purchase goods even though they have insufficient funds available.

Finally, technological progress has added substantially to the importance of variable outlays. The present-day American economy differs from that which prevailed, say, fifty years ago in this country or prevails today in many other countries not only in the spread of institutional credit arrangements and the relative level of liquid assets and supernumerary incomes, but first of all in the fact that many more consumer goods of enduring value are manufactured today than at earlier times or elsewhere. The present importance of automobiles, refrigerators, radios, television sets and many other durable or storable consumer goods is, of course, not simply a matter of technology; these articles have become necessities for many consumers.

### Variable Spending versus Variable Saving

Variable spending and variable saving are alternatives. Consumers have the greatest latitude in shifting from variable spending to variable saving, or vice versa. In this area they can choose between satisfying their immediate needs or accumulating reserves for later needs. When expenditures on durable goods and the like are bunched, the rate of variable saving will be relatively low. When desires for higher savings are strong, the rate of supernumerary expenditures will be relatively low.

This proposition applies not only to individual families but to the economy as a whole. The choice of individual consumers is, to some extent at least, subject to group influences. If, as is postulated here, shifts from the one type of behavior to the other occur at the same time among very many people, periods of high rate of variable spending may alternate with periods of high rate of variable saving.

It is a very important task of a short-run theory of business cycles to establish which variables promote either higher rates of variable saving or a bunching of variable expenditures.

We may distinguish between two kinds of factors by asking the following two questions.

First: Suppose an economy saves (spends) a high proportion of its income in one period (a year or a quarter of a year) and spends (saves) a high proportion of its income in the next period; what factors may account for the change? [3]

Second: Suppose we find that an economy saves a much higher or lower proportion of its income in one year or decade than several years or decades earlier; what factors may account for the difference?

Although this chapter will concentrate on the discussion of problems raised by the first question, which alone relates to short-run economic fluctuations, some of the variables that need to be considered in seeking an answer to the second question will be enumerated first.

(1) Distribution of the population by age, marital status, and number of children. These factors must be considered because in the younger age group—shortly after marriage and when there are young children in the family—a tendency to spend may be prevalent while in older age groups, prior to retirement, a tendency to save may be more powerful.

(2) Business and farm ownership. From recent findings that owners of businesses and farms save a higher proportion of their income than non-owners, the hypothesis may be derived that in a period or in a society with widespread business and farm ownership the rate of saving may be higher than in a period or society with a low rate of such ownership.

(3) Desire to save and appreciation of saving as a virtue. In comparing different periods or different societies, it is possible that the fundamental attitudes toward saving will differ greatly and that such differences may account for high or low rates of saving.

---

[3] In asking this question it is not necessary to specify that spending and saving take the form of outlays of choice; since habitual and contractual outlays are assumed to be relatively stable, short-run shifts from spending to saving (or from saving to spending) must be accounted for by changes in the relation of variable expenditures to variable saving.

(4) Ownership of liquid assets. If a period or a society with widespread ownership of substantial liquid assets is compared with another period or society in which only relatively few people own liquid assets, differences in the needs for saving may be postulated. It does not necessarily follow, however, that the rate of saving will be larger in the second case. For it may easily be that the existence of liquid asset holdings is the result of high rates of saving in the recent past, and that the factors making for high rates of saving continue to prevail.

This list may be continued at some length, especially with regard to possible effects of different institutional arrangements (such as social security legislation). It is presented here first of all to explain the exclusion of certain variables from the subsequent analysis. If we center our attention on short-run variations from high rates of spending to high rates of saving, or vice versa, we can hardly use any of the variables just listed as explanatory factors. Naturally, the composition of the population and the prevalence of business ownership will not change radically in the short run. Basic attitudes toward saving are known to fluctuate rarely and slowly. Differences in the ownership of liquid assets will usually be very small if two short successive periods are compared. Finally, we should also mention that differences in levels of income or its distribution, which usually are great if two distant periods or societies are compared, will usually be relatively small in two successive short periods.

Turning now to variables which may influence the consumer choice between supernumerary spending and saving in the short run, we shall list three sets of factors. Regarding the first two, hypotheses derived from psychological considerations have been subjected to numerous tests during the last few years. We are therefore in a position to present hypotheses that spell out the influence of these variables in some detail. Regarding the third set of variables, however, only relatively vague assumptions can be presented.

(1) Income expectations and economic outlook. Optimism about one's own income prospects, expectation of income increases in the

near future, and a feeling of security regarding one's job and income tend to promote spending. Recent past income increases, if considered to be enduring rather than temporary, operate in the same direction. Optimism about business cycle developments in the near future, the expectation of higher production and employment in the country, adds significantly to the feeling of security.

On the other hand, fear of income declines or unemployment as well as apprehension about the general economic outlook and a feeling of uncertainty and insecurity promote saving. If a person has a satisfactory income but believes that the prevailing good times will soon come to an end, his incentives to create reserves for the future become powerful.

(2) Past and expected price changes. Perceptions of recent price movements and price expectations influence consumer behavior only when substantial price changes have occurred or are expected. In that case dissatisfaction with past price increases coupled with an expectation of price stability tends to reduce spending, while anticipation of rapid price increases as well as of shortages tends to increase spending.

(3) Inventory situation. It may be assumed that after a period in which unusually large quantities of durable consumer goods have been purchased the rate of spending will be retarded and, conversely, that in a period following low rates of purchases the rate of spending will be relatively high. The widespread practice of installment purchases may be thought to accentuate that trend: after large purchases have been made on installment, the debt incurred must be repaid, while in the absence of such purchases in the recent past the capacity to incur new debt is relatively high.

No clear-cut evidence exists at present for the validity of the assumptions regarding the influence of the inventory situation. It is conceivable that certain psychological factors such as habits and levels of aspiration operate in the reverse direction, and also that effects of high or low inventories are overshadowed by other considerations. "Saturation" with goods or "felt need" for a variety of goods may be viewed as psychological states, depending on motives, attitudes, and expectations, rather than as functions of the number, age, and quality of the goods owned. It seems doubtful that the timing of reversals in economic trends is initiated by nothing but a high or low rate of consumer purchases in the preceding period.

## THE FUNCTIONS OF SURVEY RESEARCH

In order to clarify the propositions embodied in the theoretical model just presented and to develop the theory further, a vast array of data is needed. The required information on consumer behavior and its underlying causes might be grouped under three headings. The interrelationships among three groups of variables are of primary interest.

(1) Consumers' situation and balance sheet. This area includes demographic data (age, occupation, education, size of family, etc.), data on incomes and income changes, assets and debts.

(2) Consumers' actions and transactions. In this area belong consumer money outlays, especially for the purchase of houses, automobiles, and other durable goods, as well as amounts saved and invested (amounts added to or withdrawn from liquid assets, amounts borrowed, etc.).

(3) Consumers' attitudes and intentions. The subjective feeling of being better or worse off, expectations regarding future incomes, prices and general economic trends, preferences among several investment outlets, and intentions or plans to buy houses, automobiles, and other durable goods are examples of data which belong in this area.

Concerning the first two groups, researchers may rely to some extent on records assembled for legal or practical purposes rather than for the sake of understanding consumer behavior. In that case, however, some difficulties may arise because unsuitable definitions of concepts may be used in the records, and especially because most available records refer to aggregates only and need to be supplemented by information on distributions. Quantitative data regarding the third area cannot be obtained by means other than by interrogating the people whose actions are studied, that is, by means other than surveys of representative samples of the population. In order to study the interrelation among variables belonging in all three areas, it is necessary to assemble all the data concerning the same people. This requirement poses an important practical question: Is it possible to obtain all the information needed in one survey?[4]

The survey method is a powerful tool, greatly developed during the last decade and useful for a multitude of purposes. But it has limitations which restrict its use. The scope of the surveys is restricted by the impossibility or inadvisability of extending the interview time beyond a certain point and by the fact that the survey method is not suitable for obtaining reliable data about some of the items desired. This latter consideration was paramount in the selection of topics considered in the surveys conducted by the Survey Research Center. Some major limitations of the survey method may be presented by listing the following points:

(1) Information which is not known to the respondents cannot be obtained in surveys. Examples: Annual increases in the value of life insurance reserves (on policies owned by individual families) and amounts of depreciation on houses or automobiles owned would be needed for the sake of an exact determination of amounts saved by individual families; such information, however, is not available to individual policy holders or owners of homes and automobiles.

(2) Information which is not salient to the respondents cannot be obtained in a reliable way. Examples: Most people have not given any thought to the amounts spent on food or clothing, or on most individual food and clothing items, over a year; therefore, annual surveys are not suitable for determining these amounts. Past data are often forgotten or falsified in memory; measurement of income earned, or of the size of bank deposits held, several years ago is not a suitable topic for surveys.

(3) Asking for information that is considered secret must be

---

[4] Successive surveys made with the same people or even with matched population groups represent other possibilities which have not yet been sufficiently explored.

avoided; interrogation that appears to check upon the honesty of the respondents should not be made. Examples: Questions about income from gambling or about currency hidden in mattresses or locked in safety deposit boxes are not fruitful; references to tax returns filed may endanger the interview.

(4) Information about activities that are shared by a very small proportion of the population cannot be obtained in a reliable way in cross section surveys. It was found in the Surveys of Consumer Finances, for example, that during each of the last few years less than three percent of the population purchased publicly traded common stock, while about 75 percent of all families paid life insurance premiums. Surveys of representative samples of the population, therefore, are suitable to obtain information about the distribution of premium payments, but surveys of a different kind, based on different samples, would be needed in order to analyze the distribution of common stock purchases.

(5) Data which can be obtained only with very great sampling errors do not constitute proper topics of sample surveys. The previous point could have been presented in terms of sampling errors, which increase greatly when the number of cases decreases. Here a related point is implied, which can be explained by stating that it is impossible to determine through sample surveys what the highest income in a given year was. Futhermore, it is a matter of mere chance whether a small sample survey finds one, two, several, or no families with an annual income of more than $100,000. Considering a much larger proportion of the population, it remains true that the sampling error of such a finding as, "The mean income of families making more than $10,000 was in 1950 $........" is rather high. It is much higher than the error of such a finding as, "The proportion of families making more than $10,000 was in 1950 ... percent." Similarly, survey data on aggregate incomes, bank deposits, or savings of all families are much less reliable than data on the frequency distribution of incomes, bank deposits, or savings (because the distributions of all these items are greatly skewed). Fortunately, data of the first

kind are available from nonsurvey sources, while the latter cannot be obtained except through surveys.

(6) Information obtained from one single survey is less reliable than trend data derived from two or more consecutive surveys that use the same methods. The occurrence of reporting errors can be minimized but not excluded. Most reporting errors are, however, similar in consecutive surveys that make use of the same methods, so that comparisons of data from several surveys are more reliable than findings from one single survey. If, for instance, it were true that some high-income people tend to understate their income, a finding such as, "Families with over $10,000 income obtained ... percent of the aggregate income in 1950," will represent an understatement. A finding such as, "The share of aggregate income obtained by families with an income of over $10,000 increased by ... percent from 1949 to 1950," will, however, not be subject to the same bias.

(7) Surveys cannot be aimed at obtaining exact quantitative forecasts of things to come. If people are asked, for example, about their plans to purchase houses or automobiles during the next twelve months, their answers to these questions do not supply a measure of the number of houses or cars that will be purchased. Unexpected developments—in the country as a whole or in one's personal situation—may make people change their plans. Expressed intentions represent attitudes which shed light on the willingness to buy at the time of the survey. By comparing these intentions with those obtained in previous surveys for previous times, trends of the urgency of demand can be obtained. Such trends do have predictive value unless underlying conditions change radically. Furthermore, analysis of the relation of attitudes to behavior—for instance, of income expectations to saving—may yield generalizations which likewise have predictive value.

On the basis of these considerations it is possible to list the most legitimate objectives of annual surveys in which representative samples of consumers are interviewed and thus to understand the selection of topics studied in the Surveys of Consumer Finances. To be sure, surveys can never yield exact values; because of sampling and reporting errors they can only present information about the order of magnitude of the values. But the order of magnitude obtained is most reliable if the surveys concentrate on the following topics:

(1) Determination of distributions (e.g., distributions of income or income changes among all families or the skilled workers);

(2) Information on large or unusual transactions in which a substantial proportion of the people participate (e.g., prices paid for automobiles purchased or amounts of savings bonds bought and cashed, as well as the characteristics of purchasers and bond redeemers);

(3) Information on people's economic motives, attitudes, and expectations (e.g., motives to save, preferences among investment outlets, income expectations, intentions to purchase durable goods);

(4) Establishment of the relationships prevailing among different variables (e.g., the relation between income and liquid asset holdings or between income increases and purchases of durable goods);

(5) Establishment of trends over time through successive surveys (e.g., changes in the share of income received or in the share of liquid assets held by skilled workers during the last few years).

This analysis of the respective merits and limitations of different kinds of survey data yields conclusions which appear to be favorable for attaining the objectives in which we are here interested. In order to develop and verify the basic propositions of our theoretical model, interrelationships between large or unusual transactions and psychological factors are of primary interest, and in these respects the restrictions imposed on researchers by the survey method are relatively small.

Among the manifold tasks that need to be undertaken to give the hypotheses previously presented the status of empirical generalizations, two loom largest. First, it is necessary to provide evidence about the habitual nature of certain actions and transactions, to show that certain other forms of behavior are usually based on deliberate choice, and that the habitual money outlays are much less variable than outlays of choice. Second, the role and function of motives, attitudes, and expectations in influencing the choice between variable expenditures and variable savings needs to be demonstrated.

At this point, only some contributory evidence will be presented in regard to these complex issues. To discuss the psychological foundations of the distinction between habitual behavior and genuine decision making, as well as to apply that distinction to economic behavior, has been one major objective of this writer's book, *Psychological Analysis of Economic Behavior*. What remains to be done, and what will be undertaken in the next section of this chapter, is to present information about differences in the variability of the two forms of behavior.

Detailed analysis of the role of some major factors in contributing to fluctuations of consumer saving and consumer expenditures on durable goods represents the major topic of some of the later chapters in this book. That task is undertaken by an analysis of findings made over several postwar years in which shifts from saving to spending and from spending to saving were relatively minor. In order to point specifically to the function of psychological variables in promoting such shifts, and to relate these data to the basic hypotheses previously presented, the last section of this chapter will discuss some findings made in the years 1950 to 1952, in which substantial shifts have occurred.

### VARIABILITY OF DIFFERENT FORMS OF CONSUMER BEHAVIOR DURING TWO CONSECUTIVE YEARS

The concept of variability of consumer behavior may have several different meanings. It may, for instance, be understood to denote the variations in reactions to greatly changed environmental conditions. Thus, in contrasting periods of economic prosperity with those of depression, the question may be raised about the forms of consumer behavior that differ greatly or slightly. In a different sense, variability of consumer behavior may mean changes in the behavior in the course of the life cycle of individuals or families. In that case, the questions raised may be about the kind of activities—buying houses or durable goods, amounts saved, etc.—which are typical among the young or the middle-aged or the old.

In this section, variability of consumer behavior is considered in a third sense. Suppose we take two consecutive years in which general economic activity has not changed substantially (and which, representing a short and consecutive period, are not affected by changes in the life cycle of families). By definition, then, aggregate amounts spent on the purchase of houses, durable goods, life insurance, savings bonds, etc., have remained substantially stable. Does it follow that individual families have acted in the same way in the two periods? Or would we find that certain activities of individual families have remained fairly constant while certain other activities have changed substantially?

This problem may be formulated from the point of view of the psychologist and on the basis of the theoretical assumptions previously presented as follows: It is known that habits play a large role in human behavior; certain activities accomplished repeatedly and successfully are continued habitually. Which of the important economic activities of the households are habitual in the sense of being repeated under similar circumstances by the same people, and which activities are those regarding which few people develop habits?

The problem of repetitiousness versus variability of household activities is too broad to be fully studied in this chapter. It may be assumed a priori, and has been confirmed by occasional observations, that activities which occur rarely in one's lifetime (e.g., buying a house) are less frequently habitual than constantly repeated activities such as purchasing groceries or small items of clothing. The available empirical data, restricted to two consecutive years, do not encompass, however, all kinds of household activities. We shall concentrate our investigation on an analysis of the repetitiousness of certain forms of consumer saving and of purchases of durable goods.

The investigation must be based on a study of the behavior of identical families over two consecutive periods. Such data are available from a "reinterview study." A sample of over 3,000 spending units, representative of all spending units in the country, was interviewed in the Survey of Consumer Finances of January and February, 1948, in regard to its activities in 1947; 655 of the previously interviewed spending units, a representative sample of urban spending units (who had not moved in 1948) were reinterviewed in January and February, 1949, in regard to their activities in 1948.

Concerning the general economic developments in the years 1947 and 1948, it may suffice to recall that these were years of high production, employment, and consumption. National income, as computed by the Commerce Department, rose in 1947 by approximately 10 percent against the previous year, and in 1948 again by almost 10 percent against the year 1947. Personal savings were relatively small in both years (about 5 percent of aggregate income) and consumer expenditures substantial. Expenditures on consumer durable goods were somewhat higher in 1948 than in 1947.

The distribution of incomes by size was rather similar during the two years, but the reinterview study showed that there were frequent shifts both upward and downward in the incomes of identical families.[5] About one-third of the urban spending units had an income increase in both years, while almost the same proportion had an increase in one but a decrease in the other year.

People's financial attitudes resembled each other closely at the end of both years. Measures are available about the subjective evaluation of spending units' financial situation ("Would you say that you people are better or worse off financially than you were a year ago?") and about the distribution of income expectations and of people's general economic outlook ("Concerning the country as a whole, do you think we will have good times or bad times or what

[5] Data on the stability in the distribution and concentration of income during the two years on the basis of the reinterview study have been presented in an article by George Katona and Janet A. Fisher in *Studies in Income and Wealth,* Vol. XIII (New York: National Bureau of Economic Research, 1951); see especially pp. 72–74.

during the next twelve months?"). They show not only that changes in the distribution of these attitudes for the entire population were small, but that the opinions expressed by identical people were much more often unchanged than reversed. Moreover, unexpected favorable or adverse developments were not too frequent during the year 1948. When, for instance, income expectations determined at the beginning of 1948 were compared with actual income trends (as determined at the beginning of 1949), it was found that most spending units predicted their prospective income trend quite correctly. Only 15 percent of the units were "disappointed" in the sense that they expected their income to go up although it actually went down, or that they expected it to go down although it actually went up. Regarding the general economic outlook, only two of every ten spending units reversed their opinion between the beginning of 1948 and the beginning of 1949 by saying at one date that they expected good times to come and at the other date that they expected bad times to come.[6]

We next turn to a comparison of consumers' savings performance during the years 1947 and 1948. Table 1 shows that in this respect again consumers as a whole behaved in substantially the same manner in both years. The proportion which saved and the proportion which dissaved and even the proportions of large savers and dissavers resembled one another closely during both years. Moreover, as the last column of Table 1 shows, the savings performance of all urban spending units during the 24-month period covering both years 1947 and 1948 was very similar to their performance in each year.

Similar data are presented in Table 2 regarding the distribution of expenditures on durable goods (automobiles, furniture, and larger items of household equipment). Again the proportion of urban consumers who purchased durable goods, as well as the proportions of those who spent a smaller or larger share of their income on durable

---

[6] Data on the relative stability of financial attitudes were presented in the article by the author, "Expectations and Decisions in Economic Behavior," in *The Policy Sciences,* edited by Lerner and Lasswell (Stanford University Press, 1951); see especially pp. 224–27.

## TABLE 1

### PROPORTION OF INCOME SAVED BY IDENTICAL SAMPLE OF URBAN SPENDING UNITS IN TWO CONSECUTIVE YEARS

| SAVINGS IN PERCENT OF INCOME BY CLASS INTERVALS[a] | PERCENTAGE DISTRIBUTION OF URBAN SPENDING UNITS | | | | | |
|---|---|---|---|---|---|---|
| | 1947 | | 1948 | | 1947 and 1948[b] | |
| −25 or more | 9.2 | | 7.8 | | 7.6 | |
| −10–24 | 8.6 | | 6.3 | | 6.2 | |
| −1–9 | 12.1 | | 13.4 | | 16.4 | |
| All negative | | 29.9 | | 27.5 | | 30.2 |
| 0.0 | | 5.0 | | 4.0 | | 2.4 |
| +1–9 | 30.6 | | 32.4 | | 33.6 | |
| +10–19 | 14.2 | | 16.4 | | 17.9 | |
| +20–29 | 10.1 | | 9.2 | | 9.1 | |
| +30–49 | 6.4 | | 8.3 | | 5.3 | |
| +50 or more | 3.8 | | 2.2 | | 1.5 | |
| All positive | | 65.1 | | 68.5 | | 67.4 |
| Total | | 100.0 | | 100.0 | | 100.0 |

[a] Income before taxes.
[b] Amounts saved during the 24-month period in percent of 24-month income.

goods, are almost identical in both years. But in this respect the performance during the 24-month period differs from the annual performances. A much larger proportion of units purchased durable goods during the twenty-four months than in either of the two single years.

## TABLE 2

### PROPORTION OF INCOME SPENT ON AUTOMOBILES AND OTHER DURABLE GOODS BY IDENTICAL SAMPLE OF URBAN SPENDING UNITS IN TWO CONSECUTIVE YEARS

| DURABLE GOODS EXPENDITURES IN PERCENT OF DISPOSABLE INCOME | PERCENTAGE DISTRIBUTION OF URBAN SPENDING UNITS | | |
|---|---|---|---|
| | 1947 | 1948 | 1947 and 1948[a] |
| 0.0 | 57 | 55 | 37 |
| Under 5 | 9 | 10 | 22 |
| 5–9 | 13 | 13 | 15 |
| 10–19 | 9 | 10 | 14 |
| 20–29 | 6 | 5 | 7 |
| 30–39 | 3 | 3 | 2 |
| 40–49 | 1 | 1 | 1 |
| 50 or more | 2 | 3 | 2 |
| | 100 | 100 | 100 |

[a] Expenditures made during the 24-month period in percent of 24-month disposable income.

Tables 1 and 2 form the background for an investigation of the variability or repetitiousness of the behavior of individual consumer units. To turn first to a discussion of the variability of amounts saved: in each of the years 1947 and 1948 about three out of every ten units were dissavers; were these the identical units? If that were true, we would find that about 30 percent of the units were dissavers in either year. If, on the other hand, all those who dissaved in one of the two years saved in the other year, we would find that not less than 60 percent of the units spent more than their income in one of two consecutive years. The findings, as can be seen from the summary of Table 3, are between the two extremes; 47 percent dissaved in the first or the second year. Moreover, we find that 62 percent of the units "repeated" their performance, namely,

    49 percent saved both years
    2 percent neither saved or dissaved both years
    11 percent dissaved both years.

On the other hand, 33 percent reversed their performance by saving the first and dissaving the second year, or by dissaving the first and saving the second year.[7]

The detailed presentation of the savings performance of identical consumer units during the two consecutive years in Table 3 reveals one further significant fact. Repetitiousness, which is more frequent in positive than in negative saving, appears to be concentrated among people who save a small percentage of their income. We find that over 13 percent of all units saved between 1 and 9 percent of their income in both years, and over 25 percent between 1 and 19 percent in both years.

How do people whose saving performance was similar in the two years differ from those who reversed their savings activities from one year to the next? Level of income does not appear to be a rele-

---

[7] Since some of these units saved more in the year in which they saved than they dissaved the other year, only about one-half of them appear as dissavers for the 24-month period, as shown in the last column of Table I. Some of these data, as well as those referring to durable goods, have been presented earlier by the author. See *Psychological Analysis of Economic Behavior,* p. 164.

## TABLE 3

## RELATION OF 1947 SAVINGS TO 1948 SAVINGS OF IDENTICAL SPENDING UNITS

*Percentage distribution of urban spending units interviewed at the beginning of 1948 and 1949*

| SAVINGS IN PERCENT OF INCOME BY CLASS INTERVALS, 1947 | SAVINGS IN PERCENT OF INCOME BY CLASS INTERVALS, 1948 | | | | | | | | | |
|---|---|---|---|---|---|---|---|---|---|---|
| | −25 or More | −10–24 | −1–9 | 0.0 | +1–9 | +10–19 | +20–29 | +30–49 | +50 or More | Total |
| −25 or more | 1.7 | 1.0 | 1.1 | 0.7 | 2.0 | 1.5 | 0.6 | 0.6 | | 9.2 |
| −10–24 | 1.0 | 0.4 | 1.6 | 0.1 | 2.9 | 0.9 | 1.0 | 0.4 | 0.3 | 8.6 |
| −1–9 | 0.7 | 0.7 | 2.6 | | 3.7 | 2.4 | 1.6 | 0.4 | | 12.1 |
| 0.0 | 0.4 | 0.5 | 0.7 | 2.4 | 0.7 | 0.1 | 0.2 | | | 5.0 |
| +1–9 | 1.9 | 1.1 | 5.3 | 0.2 | 13.2 | 5.2 | 1.8 | 1.7 | 0.2 | 30.6 |
| +10–19 | 0.7 | 1.5 | 1.0 | | 4.7 | 2.5 | 1.7 | 1.5 | 0.6 | 14.2 |
| +20–29 | 0.7 | 0.5 | 0.7 | 0.2 | 3.1 | 1.9 | 1.6 | 1.1 | 0.3 | 10.1 |
| +30–49 | 0.4 | 0.4 | 0.4 | 0.4 | 0.7 | 1.7 | 0.6 | 1.2 | 0.6 | 6.4 |
| +50 or more | 0.3 | 0.2 | 0.4 | 0.4 | 1.4 | 0.2 | 0.1 | 1.4 | 0.2 | 3.8 |
| Total | 7.8 | 6.3 | 13.4 | 4.0 | 32.4 | 16.4 | 9.2 | 8.3 | 2.2 | 100.0 |

SUMMARY

| 1947 | 1948 | | Percentage of Urban Spending Units |
|---|---|---|---|
| − | − | Repetitive | 10.8 |
| 0 | 0 | Repetitive | 2.4 |
| + | + | Repetitive | 49.2 |
| 0 | ± | Nonrepetitive | 2.6 |
| ± | 0 | Nonrepetitive | 1.6 |
| + | − | Nonrepetitive | 15.1 |
| − | + | Nonrepetitive | 18.3 |
| | | | 100.0 |

vant factor. The proportion of people with high, middle, and low incomes is quite similar in both groups. Age of the heads of the households shows, however, an interesting relationship: among those who reversed the direction of their saving, people in the age range from 25 to 34 appear to be particularly frequent. Direction of income change from 1947 to 1948 is related somewhat to changes in savings performance, but does not suffice to explain the differences obtained.

TABLE 4

DIRECTION OF SAVING IN THREE FORMS DURING TWO CONSECUTIVE
YEARS BY IDENTICAL SPENDING UNITS

| Saving Performance | Contractual Saving (percent) | Change in Liquid Assets (percent) | Change in Consumer Debt (percent) |
|---|---|---|---|
| No saving | 10 | 19 | 50 |
| Saved both years | 80 | 12 | 2 |
| Dissaved both years | | 17 | 9 |
| Saved first year, dissaved second | | 16 | 3 |
| Dissaved first year, saved second | | 16 | 7 |
| Saved first year, no change second | 5 | 1 | 4 |
| No change first year, saved second | 5 | 9[a] | 5 |
| Dissaved first year, no change second | | 2 | 6 |
| No change first year, dissaved second | | 8[a] | 14 |
| | 100 | 100 | 100 |

[a] These figures are overestimated because change during the first year was determined by asking for recollection at the end of the first year; change during the second year was determined by the more exact method of comparing findings from two surveys in each of which questions were asked about "current" asset holdings. The "recollection" method always yields a high proportion of "no change" answers.

The problem of repetitiousness or reversal in the saving behavior needs to be studied by analyzing different forms of saving during the two consecutive years. Table 4 shows the beginnings of such an analysis regarding three important forms of saving. The data refer first to what is called contractual saving—life insurance premium payments, payments into retirement funds, and repayments on the principal of mortgage debts. Secondly we consider changes in liquid assets—government bonds and various types of bank deposits—both

additions to and withdrawals from them. Finally, changes in consumer indebtedness are analyzed, including all forms of borrowing
and repaying except repayments on mortgage principal.

Contractual saving, in contrast to other forms of saving, can only
be positive. We find in Table 4 that 80 percent of the urban spending
units saved in contractual forms in both consecutive years. Of the
80 percent, about one-half saved less than $200 in each of the two
years (this is not shown in the table). A further substantial group
shows identical or very similar performances in both years. Less
than one-tenth of the group shows substantial differences in the
amounts saved during the two consecutive years. It appears further
that a high proportion of those units who put the same relatively
small amounts in contractual forms of saving in 1947 and in 1948
saved exclusively in those ways (and did not change their liquid
assets, debts, etc.).

Regarding changes in liquid assets, the differences in the performance during the two consecutive years are much larger. The
direction of performance was identical in the two years only on the
part of 29 percent of the units. Adding to the liquid assets in one of
the two years and reducing them in the other year occurred, however, on the part of 32 percent of the units.

It is interesting to note that with respect to one component of the
liquid asset holdings, U. S. Government E-bonds, repetitiousness of
behavior is much more frequent than in regard to all other types of
liquid assets. Among the people who either bought or cashed savings
bonds during the two years considered, we find only three types of
activities performed with any great frequency: buying in both years
(most usually through payroll deduction), buying in one year and
not doing anything in the other year, and cashing in one year and
not doing anything in the other year.

Neither level of income nor size of liquid asset holdings appears to
be correlated with the performance regarding liquid assets in the two
consecutive years. People who added to their liquid assets in both
years, who reduced their liquid assets in both years, and who re-

versed their performance are found in similar proportions in all income levels (except that the first group is found somewhat more frequently among those with very high incomes). When the size of liquid asset holdings at the beginning of the two-year period is studied regarding its relation to the three kinds of performance, we find no confirmation of the hypothesis that steady or occasional reductions are made preponderantly by people who have large liquid assets at the beginning of the period.

It can be seen in Table 4 that one-half of all urban spending units had some activity in consumer debts (borrowing or repaying) during either of the two years. Only a very small proportion repaid debts in

TABLE 5

EXPENDITURES ON AUTOMOBILES AND OTHER DURABLE GOODS BY
IDENTICAL SPENDING UNITS DURING TWO CONSECUTIVE YEARS

|  |  | Percent |
|---|---|---|
| Bought in both 1947 and 1948 |  | 25.1 |
| Spent similar amounts each year | 12.2 |  |
| Spent greatly different amounts each year | 12.9 |  |
| Bought in one of the two years only |  | 37.6 |
| In 1947 but not in 1948 | 17.7 |  |
| In 1948 but not in 1947 | 19.9 |  |
| Bought in neither 1947 or 1948 |  | 37.3 |
|  |  | ——— |
|  |  | 100.0 |

each of the two years or added to their debts in each of them. As expected, the variability of the performance is very substantial in this respect. The same appears to be true in regard to investments in securities, businesses, and houses, although the relatively few cases available do not permit detailed analysis of the data.

The study of the variability of expenditures on durable goods should not be carried out in regard to expenditures on individual goods. For our purposes it is not of great significance that only relatively few spending units have been found to have bought an automobile or furniture or a refrigerator in both years. We study the changes in the expenditures of identical consumer units for all types of durable goods taken together. Table 5 shows that almost two-thirds of all units spent some money on durable goods during either of the two years. Of these units, however, more spent money on durable goods in only one of the two years than spent money in both consecutive years. The variability of behavior regarding expenditures on durable goods appears to be larger than that regarding saving. Interestingly enough, the data presented in Table 5 do not show great changes if they are computed for upper income units alone. In that case there are many fewer in the last row of the table (those who have not spent any money in either year), but one-year purchasers remain more frequent than buyers in each of the two consecutive years.

Finally, we present some calculations about the performance of identical consumer units in regard to their "residual expenditures." No questions were asked in the survey regarding these expenditures, but it is possible, for each individual unit, to deduct from money income received the total amount saved and the amounts spent on durable goods as well as a (calculated) amount for income taxes. What remains are the expenditures for food, clothing, rent, services, and diverse other purposes. It appears from Table 6 that in regard to these expenditures the variability of performance in the two consecutive years was small. About one-third of all units spent the same percentage of their income on "residual expenditures" in both years —percentages being calculated in brackets—and another third spent relatively similar proportions of their income in both years.

An attempt was made to test the hypothesis about the inverse relationship between variable spending and variable saving.[8] Suppose we divide the population into three groups according to the extent of their variable or discretionary saving in one year. The first group consists of those who saved substantial amounts in such discretionary ways as adding to liquid asset holdings, securities, and business or real estate investments; the second group did hardly anything in these respects (either small additions or small withdrawals), and the third dissaved substantial amounts. Could we predict anything about the

[8] The author is indebted to James N. Morgan for the considerations and calculations presented below.

differences in the spending–saving performance of the three groups during the next year? If it were true that substantial amounts of variable saving in a given year coincide with small amounts of variable expenditures (or, specifically, that they coincide with the absence of larger durable goods purchases) and, conversely, negative

TABLE 6

RELATION BETWEEN "RESIDUAL EXPENDITURES" IN 1947 AND IN 1948 BY IDENTICAL SPENDING UNITS

*Percentage distribution of urban spending units interviewed at the beginning of 1948 and 1949*

| RESIDUAL EXPENDITURES AS A PERCENT OF INCOME— 1947 | RESIDUAL EXPENDITURES AS A PERCENT OF INCOME—1948 | | | | | | | |
|---|---|---|---|---|---|---|---|---|
| | *Under 50* | *50–59* | *60–69* | *70–79* | *80–89* | *90–99* | *100 or Over* | *Total* |
| Under 50 | 1.8 | 1.0 | 0.9 | 0.6 | 0.6 | 1.6 | 0.7 | 7.2 |
| 50–59 | 0.6 | 0.5 | 0.5 | 0.7 | 0.3 | 0.5 | 0.3 | 3.4 |
| 60–69 | 0.8 | 0.8 | 0.7 | 0.8 | 1.8 | 1.2 | 0.8 | 6.9 |
| 70–79 | 1.0 | 0.8 | 1.5 | 2.0 | 2.4 | 2.2 | 2.3 | 12.2 |
| 80–89 | 0.5 | 1.0 | 1.3 | 3.0 | 4.5 | 6.4 | 2.0 | 18.7 |
| 90–99 | 0.6 | 0.3 | 1.4 | 2.0 | 4.2 | 10.8 | 7.2 | 26.5 |
| 100 or over | 0.4 | 0.3 | 1.8 | 1.6 | 2.1 | 7.7 | 11.2 | 25.1 |
| | 5.7 | 4.7 | 8.1 | 10.7 | 15.9 | 30.4 | 24.5 | 100.0 |

SUMMARY

| | Percentage of Urban Spending Units |
|---|---|
| Same bracket | 31.5 |
| One-bracket difference | 36.2 |
| Two-bracket difference | 14.3 |
| Three-bracket difference | 9.6 |
| More than three-bracket difference | 8.4 |
| | 100.0 |

amounts of variable saving coincide with substantial amounts of variable expenditures (or expenditures on durable goods), and if it were true that one year of restraint in variable spending is commonly followed by another year of large-scale variable spending, we could make certain predictions. We could expect that our first group would in the second year increase its durable goods expenditures and reduce its variable savings, while the third group would reduce its durable goods expenditures and increase the amounts it saves in variable forms.

The first assumption just made is, of course, known to be not quite correct. Dissaving may be due to many causes and not exclusively to large durable goods expenditures. Furthermore, some people may spend much on durable goods and nevertheless save substantial amounts in variable forms. Therefore, in recording the changes our three groups have made from the first to the second year in their expenditures on durable goods, we proceed to test our underlying hypotheses under rather unfavorable conditions. If we had recorded all kinds of variable expenditures, we should expect greater differences among our three groups than were actually obtained.

Nevertheless, the results are quite striking. The changes in the spending–saving performance of the three groups were found to be substantial from 1947 to 1948. The first group, on the whole, saved substantially less in 1948 than in 1947, the third group substantially more. Similarly, the first group increased its expenditures on durables and the third group decreased them. The direction of changes in saving and in durable goods expenditures is shown in the following table:

| Saving Patterns of Three Groups of Urban Spending Units during 1947 | Change in Total Saving from 1947 to 1948 (mean amounts in dollars) | Change in Durable Goods Expenditures from 1947 to 1948 (mean amounts in dollars) | Number of Cases |
|---|---|---|---|
| I. Total saving larger than contractual saving | −529 | +111 | 147 |
| II. Total saving about equal to contractual saving (both in same bracket) | −11 | +44 | 159 |
| III. Total saving smaller than contractual saving (negative variable saving) | +635 | −146 | 155 |
| All three groups | +40 | +2 | 461 |

Note: These calculations were made from the reinterview survey after excluding business owners; in contrast to the other tables, they represent unweighted data. The amount of changes in durable goods expenditures cannot be taken as representative of the amount of changes in variable expenditures.

Although the number of cases available in each of our three groups is so small that further breakdowns are hardly justified, we may call attention to at least one important factor that has not yet been considered. In setting up our groups we should have considered, in addition to differences in the first year's saving performance, income changes from the first to the second year (and also income expectations). Would the changes recorded above hold good irrespective of whether the spending units in each group had an increase or a decrease in their income from the first to the second year? Tentative calculations, based on very few cases, seem to indicate that this was the case. Even spending units in Group III who suffered a sizable decline in income from 1947 to 1948 (there were 36 such units in our sample) saved considerably more in 1948 than in 1947. Needless to say, further studies are needed to assess the respective strength of various factors that may influence people's spending–saving performance during two consecutive years.

## Conclusions

The data about the performance of identical consumer units during two consecutive years, as available from the reinterview study, are not in the form most suitable for testing the underlying assumptions presented in the first section of this chapter. No information is available about various types of consumer expenditures that have been postulated as volatile (luxury expenditures, vacation trips, services, etc.), and the separation between habitual and variable forms of saving is incomplete. Nevertheless, certain clear-cut conclusions emerge.

Repetitiousness of the saving performance, insofar as it occurs, is overwhelmingly due to contractual forms of saving. A substantial proportion of those spending units who saved in both years the same relatively small proportion of their income saved exclusively in contractual forms. Contractual saving has been found the only clearly repetitive form of saving. Two years are, of course, a relatively short period for such an investigation. In the light of available data it appears probable that consumer saving exclusive of contractual saving would be found highly variable if the performance of identical units over three or four years were analyzed.

Saving is variable because, first, some of it depends on the extent of durable goods purchases, which are highly variable. Buying durable goods is one factor—not the only one, but an important one during the last few years—which makes people dissave (or save little). The relationship between durable goods expenditures and dissaving is more pronounced over a period of twelve months than over a period of twenty-four months. In each of the years 1947 and 1948, 35 to 37 percent of the units who bought durable goods have dissaved; in the twenty-four months covering both years, only 25 percent of buyers of durable goods dissaved. The reason is clear: a substantial proportion of units bought durable goods in only one of the two years and saved the other year.

Yet occasional dissaving, or reversal in the direction of the saving performance by identical units, cannot be explained by the purchases of durable goods alone. Some people themselves, when asked, explain dissaving by reference to emergencies and income declines. Illness, hospitalization, temporary unemployment are listed as having occurred in one of the two years; references to unusual expenditures—trips, purchase of home furnishings, house repairs, etc.—also occur, but less frequently, possibly because of inadequate procedures of questioning.

While expenditures on durable goods and liquid forms of saving were found to be highly variable from one year to the next, contractual saving and "residual expenditures" appeared to be relatively stable. These findings confirm our assumption that people change their behavior year after year in regard to such decisions as buying a car, other durable goods, or securities more commonly than in regard to paying rent and buying food or clothing. Residual expenditures are, of course, a misnomer. Most of them represent the first charges on income, namely, constant expenses of running the household, which appear to change little from one year to the next—under relatively stable conditions.

After having discussed the differences in the variability of consumer money outlays, we turn to the problem of factors responsible for shifts in the composition of the variable outlays. During the years considered in the preceding section (1947–48), individual families have shifted from spending to saving or from saving to spending but, on the whole, these changes have canceled each other out, and consumer attitudes likewise remained relatively stable. In the years 1950–52, however, there occurred substantial changes in the economy. A period of spending waves and substantial price increases from June, 1950, to February or March, 1951, was followed by a period of high rates of saving and stable or declining prices. At the same time financial attitudes underwent rapid and substantial changes. It can be shown that such changes in attitudes and in spending–saving behavior were closely related and even that changes in attitudes could be determined in advance of changes in behavior.[9]

Before discussing the relation of consumer attitudes to behavior, we may point out that overall statistical data provide support to some basic assumptions presented before. The two periods, that of inflation and that of stabilization, were characterized primarily by a shift from durable-goods purchases to liquid savings, that is, from variable spending to variable saving. According to the data compiled by the Securities and Exchange Commission and the Commerce Department during the nine months from July 1, 1950, to March 31, 1951, liquid savings (in currency, bank deposits, shares of savings and loan associations, and securities) amounted to 3,500 million dollars and consumer expenditures for durable goods to 23,800 million dollars. During the following nine months, up to December 31, 1951, liquid savings rose to 12,200 millions and durable goods expenditures fell to 19,300 millions. In terms of the proportion of

[9] For a detailed discussion of the contents of this section, see George Katona and Eva Mueller, *Consumer Attitudes and Demand, 1950–1952* (Survey Research Center; 1953).

national income spent on durable goods, the reduction of durable-goods purchases was quite small. But the reduction occurred at a time of rising national income and had substantial effects on the sellers of durable goods and the price level in general.

## Economic Trends as Revealed by Attitudinal Data

Something more drastic and shocking occurred in 1950 than the outbreak of war in Korea, namely, military setbacks. In summer 1950 we learned that our troops were almost driven out of Korea; in winter 1950, after the intervention of the Chinese Communists, we learned that our troops were driven back several hundred miles from the Yalu River. Scare buying on the part of both businessmen and consumers occurred in two waves, coincident with the two items of adverse military information. What made such news lead to accelerated buying was fear of a third world war and recollection of such domestic effects of war as shortages of civilian goods and inflation.

In August, 1950, the great majority of the American people expected prices to go up. Still more importantly, at that time one out of every four people expected substantial price increases (increases of more than 10 percent within a year), whereas in the preceding years, as well as in 1951–52, very few of those who expected prices to rise thought that price increases of that magnitude were probable.

In 1951 the American people no longer appeared to face an acute threat of military defeat and did not expect an early outbreak of a third world war. They learned that a stalemate had developed. Most commonly, the prospects were seen as many years of cold war. Conflict and strain in international relations were not associated with high employment and good times at home. The most generally perceived domestic economic effects of cold war were high prices and high taxes, both involving hardship. Moreover, the unknown prospects of a long-enduring cold war generated uncertainty.

When, in January and February, 1951, the 1951 Survey of Consumer Finances was conducted, scare buying and inflationary pressures were still prominent. Nevertheless, the survey provided indications that consumer action would result in a weakening of inflationary pressures. It was found that "fewer consumers were planning to buy at least one major durable good (automobile, television set, furniture, etc.) at the beginning of 1951 than a year earlier." In the light of these and similar findings it was concluded that "there may be somewhat less urgency in consumer buying in the automobile and major appliance markets this year." [10]

By June, 1951, when the first of a new series of surveys was conducted, consumer demand had fallen off and experts described the situation as a "buying lull." The prevailing interpretation was that people had bought too much before and therefore reduced their rate of spending for a short while. In view of rising government expenditures and deficits, experts generally thought that the period of restrained spending would be short-lived and would be followed soon by renewed inflationary fever.

In June, 1951, however, the proportion of consumers who thought that it was a bad time to purchase household goods was twice as large as the number who thought that it was a good time. Among the factors that brought this notion about, the following were important:

(1) People on the whole were aware of the fact that prices had gone up sharply in the recent past; they thought the price increases unjustified and resented them. Although they also believed that prices would continue to advance a little, they hesitated to pay the "high" prices.

(2) The expectation of shortages in civilian goods was relatively infrequent.

(3) Because of the price increases the number of people who felt that they were worse off exceeded the number of those who felt that they were better off.

(4) People most commonly evaluated their financial situation in a cautious way and expressed uncertainty about their future.

(5) Past and expected price increases did not shake people's trust

[10] Quotations from the *Federal Reserve Bulletin* (April, 1951).

in the value of the dollar; government bonds and bank deposits remained the favored forms of saving.

These and similar findings formed the basis of the conclusion that a return to scare buying was not to be expected; the buying lull or, more correctly, the restraint in spending would continue unless major unfavorable developments were to occur.

The changes registered from June to November, 1951, were not substantial. Again more people considered the present a bad time to buy consumer goods than considered it a good time, and again the expected (small) price increases were not seen as a threat to the purchasing power of the dollar. Furthermore, hesitation and uncertainty about political and economic trends prevailed. Several indications pointed, however, toward a greater concern with inflation. The proportion of those whose attitudes toward spending and whose investment preferences were influenced by the expectation of price increases rose somewhat and the proportion of families who said they were better off increased.

The 1952 Survey of Consumer Finances, conducted in January and February of that year, indicated that "consumers were planning, as in early 1951, to purchase durable goods in moderate volume in relation to income." Intentions to purchase automobiles and houses showed small increases from 1951 to 1952, while those for some other major durable goods were slightly lower. Also, "approximately six in every ten consumers with opinions expressed the view that the current year [1952] is a bad time to make large purchases, such as automobiles or refrigerators." [11]

Although in several fundamental respects there was no change in the economic position of consumers during the first half of 1952, there were in June, 1952, indications of a somewhat greater inclination to spend. First, the majority of those with opinions believed that prices of household goods would remain stable during the next twelve months. Second, the majority thought that those prices had not gone up during the past six months and complaints that prices were

[11] Quotations from the *Federal Reserve Bulletin* (April, 1952).

too high were voiced less frequently than in 1951. Third, the proportion of consumers who believed that this was a good time for buying had increased considerably from June, 1951, to June, 1952. Nevertheless, somewhat more consumers considered the present a bad time to buy household goods than considered it a good time. The major conclusion derived from this survey was therefore expressed in the cautious statement that "it is too early to infer that people are getting accustomed to the present level of prices."

Subsequent developments showed that retail sales picked up in fall 1952, corresponding with the greater inclination of consumers to spend. However, the proportion of consumer income spent remained far below that experienced before the Korean conflict.

## TABLE 7

OPINIONS OF CONDITIONS TO PURCHASE LARGE HOUSEHOLD GOODS[a]

*Percentage distribution from consecutive surveys, each conducted with different representative samples*

|  | January–February 1951 (percent) | June 1951 (percent) | November 1951 (percent) | June 1952 (percent) |
|---|---|---|---|---|
| *Opinions* | | | | |
| Good time to buy | 32 | 22 | 27 | 33 |
| Uncertain | 16 | 23 | 27 | 24 |
| Bad time to buy | 50 | 53 | 42 | 41 |
| Not ascertained | 2 | 2 | 4 | 2 |
|  | 100 | 100 | 100 | 100 |
| *Major Reasons Why Good Time to Buy* | | | | |
| Expected shortages | 20 | 6 | 7 | 3 |
| Prices going up | 16 | 11 | 11 | 10 |
| *Major Reason Why Bad Time to Buy* | | | | |
| Prices are high | 40 | 48 | 40 | 32 |
| Number of Cases | 3,415 | 999 | 957 | 929 |

[a] In the last three surveys, the question was: "Do you think this is a good time or a bad time to buy such large household items (furniture, house furnishings, rugs, refrigerators, stove, radio, and things like that)? Why do you say so?" The data for early 1951 are from the Survey of Consumer Finances. There the question read: ". . . looking at things in general, do you think it's a good time or a bad time to buy autos and large household items? Why do you say so?"

The preceding discussion has made use of survey findings about changes in several financial attitudes. It may suffice to illustrate the extent of these changes by presenting data regarding the changes in consumers' opinions of conditions to purchase durable household goods. These opinions were closely related to several other attitudes, especially to expected purchases of durable goods, as well as to buying behavior in the months preceding the interview. It appears from Table 7 that the inclination to buy was particularly low and that dissatisfaction with the prevailing prices was particularly high in June, 1951.

## Test of Underlying Hypotheses

Two basic hypotheses presented earlier have related shifts from variable spending to variable saving, or vice versa, to changes (a) in income expectations and the general economic outlook and (b) in the perception of past price movements and in price expectations (see pages 58–59 above). These hypotheses were subjected to tests in 1951–52. In regard to the validity of the first hypothesis, we shall present data about the relation of people's general economic outlook to their inclination to spend on durable goods. Answers to questions about the probable course of economic activity during the following year, as well as during the following five years proved among the most revealing.

In 1952 expressions of optimism about the economic outlook were more frequent than expressions of pessimism. At the same time, uncertainty about the future course of the economy was widespread —much more so than before 1950. As Table 8 shows, there was a marked correlation between optimism (pessimism) regarding the business outlook and the opinion that the present was a good (bad) time to purchase durable goods. Furthermore, we find that uncertainty about the business outlook was associated with opinions about spending that resembled opinions of the pessimists much more closely than those of the optimists. The relationships shown in Table 8 proved to hold good in all income groups.

TABLE 8

RELATION BETWEEN GENERAL ECONOMIC OUTLOOK[a] AND
OPINIONS OF BUYING CONDITIONS

| OPINIONS OF BUYING CONDITIONS[b] | GENERAL ECONOMIC OUTLOOK | | | | | |
| | GOOD TIMES AHEAD | | UNCERTAIN | | BAD TIMES AHEAD | |
| | During Next Year (percent) | During Next 5 Years (percent) | During Next Year (percent) | During Next 5 Years (percent) | During Next Year (percent) | During Next 5 Years (percent) |
|---|---|---|---|---|---|---|
| Good time to buy | 41 | 42 | 21 | 25 | 18 | 23 |
| Uncertain | 24 | 25 | 36 | 31 | 21 | 24 |
| Bad time to buy | 35 | 33 | 43 | 44 | 61 | 53 |
| | 100 | 100 | 100 | 100 | 100 | 100 |
| Number of Cases[c] | 1,025 | 968 | 785 | 1,342 | 218 | 482 |

[a] The questions were: "Do you think that during the next twelve months we'll have good times or bad times, or what?" and "Now looking ahead a little, which would you say is more likely—that we will have continuous good times during the next five years or so, or that we will have periods of widespread unemployment or depressions, or what?"

[b] For question, see Table 7.

[c] Data on one-year expectations are based on two surveys conducted in June, 1952, and November–December, 1952; data on five-year expectations are based on three surveys conducted in November, 1951, June, 1952, and November–December, 1952. A few "not ascertained" cases were omitted from this tabulation.

In 1951–52 it was not possible to test the effects of substantial changes in past and expected prices. (Some data collected in the fall of 1950 were mentioned before.) Small expected changes in prices did not appear to have a great influence on spending although from June, 1951, to June, 1952, when the frequency of the opinion "this is a good time to buy" rose (see Table 7), the proportion of those who expected price increases declined. There was, however, another attitudinal measure which was correlated strongly with spending behavior.

People's subjective evaluation of changes in their financial situation was measured by asking them whether they thought they were better off or worse off financially than a year ago. It appears that the answers to this question are influenced both by changes in income and by changes in the cost of living (as felt by the respondents). It was found in several surveys and in all income groups that the opinion "this is a good time for buying" prevailed more frequently among those who felt they were better off, and the opinion "this is a bad time for buying" more frequently among those who felt they were worse off. Table 9 illustrates the relationship as established in 1951 and 1952.

TABLE 9

RELATION BETWEEN EVALUATION OF CHANGES IN FINANCIAL
SITUATION[a] AND OPINIONS OF BUYING CONDITIONS

| OPINIONS OF BUYING CONDITIONS[b] | CHANGES IN FINANCIAL SITUATION | | |
|---|---|---|---|
| | Better Off Now (percent) | The Same (percent) | Worse Off Now (percent) |
| Good time to buy | 34 | 27 | 23 |
| Uncertain | 29 | 29 | 25 |
| Bad time to buy | 37 | 44 | 52 |
| | 100 | 100 | 100 |
| Number of Cases[c] | 970 | 1,772 | 1,207 |

[a] The question was: "Would you say you and your family are better off or worse off financially now than you were a year ago? Why do you say so?"

[b] For question, see Table 7.

[c] Based on four surveys conducted in June and November, 1951, and in June and November–December, 1952. A few "not ascertained" cases were omitted from this tabulation.

The relationships shown in Tables 8 and 9, as well as the preceding discussion of economic trends in 1951 and 1952 as revealed by studies of financial attitudes, serve to support our theoretical assumptions. It hardly needs to be said that the approach to business cycle studies used here is a partial approach. It is meant to supplement the traditional economic time series—of national income, retail sales, government expenditures and deficits, etc.—and must be supplemented by surveys of business activities (especially of past and planned capital expenditures). Furthermore, the evidence about the influence of consumer attitudes on behavior is far from complete. But the findings presented in this chapter indicate that the Survey Research Center's program of economic behavior holds the promise of clarifying important problems of economics.

# III: FACTORS RELATED TO CONSUMER SAVING WHEN IT IS DEFINED AS A NET-WORTH CONCEPT

*by James N. Morgan*

INTRODUCTION

This and the following chapter discuss an analysis of saving behavior using a different definition of saving from that ordinarily used in the Surveys of Consumer Finances. Further, they are based on "unweighted" data, that is, each interview is taken as a single observation, regardless of the fact that the proportion of the population represented by that interview may differ from that represented by others because of the differing sampling and response rates. The results indicate what factors and patterns of factors are important but are not intended to measure the exact relationships in terms of coefficients that could be applied to the whole population.

There are two ways of approaching an analysis of this sort. We may investigate which factors, or patterns of factors, among the many possible ones are related to the variables we are trying to explain; or we may concentrate on testing for the significance of explanatory factors suggested by previous studies or theoretical considerations. The second of these approaches, when applied to data such as those from the Surveys of Consumer Finances, makes it necessary to maintain the representative nature of the sample and to select statistical methods which will actually provide estimates of population parameters. The first approach, the one we have taken, treats each household as an experimental observation and tests for significance of relations without measuring their exact intensity. While both methods start with some theoretical model and a number of hypotheses, our model is rather general, and the approach is somewhat more inductive.

### THE ANALYSIS PLAN

*The definition of an individual's saving.* While it is possible to start out with an investigation which is directed toward discovering which definition of saving is best, on the basis of how well it correlates with other variables, it seems better to choose a definition based on theoretical considerations. As Lansing has explained in Chapter I, alternative definitions are possible. The major dimension in which they vary can be described somewhat as follows: We can emphasize the inflationary or deflationary impact of consumer behavior in the aggregate and define saving to be money not spent, not even for investments in physical assets. In these terms, saving consists of the accumulation of money or dollar claims (stocks, bonds), real estate (if we do not include real estate prices in our inflation analysis), and the repayment of debts. On the other hand, we can emphasize the change in the net worth of the individual spending unit. This can only be done imperfectly, of course, because it is impossible on an individual basis to do an adequate job of estimating depreciation, or investments in certain intangibles such as education. But a net worth definition has the great advantage that it may be closer to the goals and motivation of the consumer, since it represents greater security through increased economic resources.

Ideally, saving as optimally defined, should be perceived and defined similarly by distinguishable groups of spending units, if not by all spending units. Or, at least, people must make decisions about components which make up what we call saving, or make decisions with an eye to what effect they have on saving. If households only made decisions about specific commitments, some of which affected saving one way, and some another, with no regard to their overall effect on saving, then we should examine these decisions and not saving. Much further research needs to be done in this area. Do consumers really have any concept of saving? Do they pay any attention to changes in their overall net worth?

In our analysis we have assumed that consumers do have some idea of what is happening to their net worth, and that while they make specific decisions to buy things, or to save in certain contractual forms, some awareness of their overall position monitors each of these decisions. We have some slight evidence, which will be presented later, that this is true.

In the endeavor to use a definition of saving which approximates change in net worth, we have assumed that consumers do not think of purchases of durable goods as an equivalent reduction in their net worth but rather as an investment of assets in a more specific and perhaps somewhat less liquid form. Hence, in the analysis reported here, we have departed from the Survey of Consumer Finances definition of saving by treating purchases of durable goods as an asset accumulation—a positive component of saving. Saving then includes life insurance payments; payments on mortgage principal; reduction in other debt; increase in liquid assets; net purchases of stock, houses, and other real estate and durable goods; annuity payments; and some miscellaneous items. The chief result of this change is that people who buy durable goods by using other assets or on credit no longer appear as dissavers. Since there is a high negative correlation between age and purchases of durable goods, the effect of age on "saving" is affected by the specific definition used. Younger people not only buy more durables but also spend more money buying houses or making additions to them; hence a definition of saving that excluded *all* these expenditures would result in a still different relation between age and saving.[1]

We have not attempted to add the estimated value of current services of houses and durable goods to income, or to subtract their

[1] See, e.g., the discussion by J. B. Lansing and E. S. Maynes, "Inflation and Saving by Consumers," *Journal of Political Economy*, LX (October 1952), 383–91.

depreciation from saving, largely because of the difficulty in estimating such magnitudes, particularly in inflationary periods. As a partial substitute we have separated home owners and non-owners for most of the analysis. We do not treat a house or car as consumed during the year of purchase nor do we estimate depreciation, so that we never introduce the consumption involved. Our rationale is that depreciation is present everywhere, and to count it only for those who made a purchase, and only at the time of purchase, seriously distorts interpersonal comparisons. Insofar as most durable goods are purchased by younger people, treatment of durable-goods purchases as consumption seriously understates their saving in the net-worth sense. Insofar as physical assets are accumulated through the life cycle, reaching a maximum, say, at about the age of sixty, most definitions have a gradually increasing overstatement of saving up to the age of sixty and beyond, because of this disregard of depreciation.

Our separation of home owners from non-owners, and, in the later analysis, of renters from people who neither own nor rent, tends to separate groups with different levels of holdings of physical assets subject to depreciation. The home owner has his home and, in most cases, more durable goods. The renter has probably more durable goods than someone who neither owns nor rents. Depreciation on these assets should be added to consumption and subtracted from saving.

Another problem concerning the definition of saving arises because of the fact that the consumer is constrained in the short run by infrequent decisions which commit him to contractual payments, often components of saving in whole or part. Such things as life insurance premium payments, annuity payments, mortgage payments, etc., are usually only flexible in an upward direction and sometimes not even in that direction. We have made some preliminary investigations of the relation between current expenditures (income minus taxes, saving, and durable goods expenditures) and residual income (after deducting taxes and contractual saving payments), but these are not reported here.

At any rate, in the subsequent analysis, we shall use a definition of saving which is somewhat closer to a change-in-net-worth concept and, we hope, somewhat closer to a concept which might have relevance to the consumer.

*The general theoretical framework.* Our overall theory of consumer behavior is largely inductive and exploratory. We assume that the spending unit is a relevant decision-making unit, or at least that the decisions of the members of the unit are affected by consideration of their effect on (and the current status of) the unit's saving. We assume that there are forces acting on the spending unit which can be indicated by objectively measurable variables and that there are some basic differences between spending units (needs, attitudes toward saving, security, etc.), which differences can be indicated by scaled responses to survey questions.

We assume that the spending unit has certain felt needs, partly related to such empirical facts as the number of people in the spending unit, the stage reached in the life cycle, accustomed standard of living, size of city, etc., and partly to less easily measured things such as aspiration levels. We assume also that there are certain resources available to satisfy these needs: income, assets, credit.

Certain additional hypotheses were partly established at the outset and have been confirmed by examination of the data. First, there are important interactions among the forces affecting behavior, and there are complexes or patterns of factors which have effects on consumer behavior disproportionately greater than the separate effects of each element. For instance, income change, expected income, and assets have effects on saving which are certainly not additive. Such relations are called interaction effects in variance analysis, or can be represented by cross-product terms in multiple correlation.

Second, many forces produce significant effects on saving behavior only when they take extreme values—e.g., income change, city size, and age seem to have but little effect through the whole central range of values but are quite important at the extremes. Finally, the spending unit has only a limited degree of freedom as to what it can do. The chief limitations are contractual commitments, the amounts "needed" to pay for what the individuals perceive as minimum daily living, and the availability of assets or credit, particularly where there is pressure to dissave.

*Specification of explanatory variables.* The following major variables have been used, and we present these general interpretations of what they measure:

The variable "disposable income" is an estimate of total money income from all sources, as derived from a series of questions,[2] minus an estimate of federal income taxes based on taxable income and the number of exemptions. This is taken to represent the main resource available for current disposition—either for consumption or for saving. Of course, assets and credit are also available, and, on the other hand, contractual commitments may limit the freedom to dispose of income.

Liquid assets at the beginning of the year consist of bank deposits and U. S. Government bonds but exclude currency. They are taken to indicate both additional resources available for use, and—excluding possible gifts or inheritances—past income and past saving behavior as well. They may also indicate accumulations purposefully made for planned expenditures. Consequently, liquid assets are both a predetermined variable and a resultant or indicator of other, more basic, variables.

Home ownership status is taken to indicate both a certain stability of location and even of income and the existence of (imputed) rental income and depreciation which have not been included in our income variable or subtracted from saving. Those with mortgages have also a contractual commitment to save. The subsequent separation of renters from those who neither own nor rent is made because of the fact that the second (small) group consists largely of related sec-

[2] See Table 6, Chapter I.

ondary spending units or of domestic servants living where they work. They receive large proportions of their income in kind or in the form of intrafamily transfers which are not treated as income.

The distinction between farmers, business owners, and the "others" is intended to separate those who need funds for their business or farm operation—funds which can be obtained easily and without loss of control solely by their own saving. The entrepreneurial groups are assumed to have very strong needs for investment funds, needs which may often seem absolute. They may also expect a very high rate of return on the investment of these funds. Furthermore, business or farm losses involve involuntary dissaving as well as problems for the analyst in the treatment of negative income. The entrepreneur also has complex affairs—debts and assets which are partly business and partly personal, and many transactions the recorded details of which may exist only in the business records at the office, if at all. Furthermore, the interview schedule is not directed toward getting the details of business affairs. The interview secures household data and, for unincorporated business, profits reinvested in the business. This attempt to separate business and household affairs is always difficult and sometimes—particularly where no separate books are kept—practically impossible. Difficulties arise with the treatment of inventory accumulation and debt payments in determining business profits, the handling of depreciation on business or farm equipment, sources of money for new investment, and the estimation of liability for federal income tax. For farmers there is also the problem caused by the omission of any adjustment for changes in inventories. The omission is justified by the manifest difficulty of getting any accurate estimate of change in farm inventory, even if we could agree on the proper valuation of the inventory in periods of rapid price changes. The most important reason for the separation of these entrepreneurial groups from the rest of the population is not, however, the difficulties with the data but the hypothesis that their motivation is quite different from that of people who do not have business needs for funds, nor expectations of high profit yields from invested savings, nor "forced" investment in inventories or equipment. In all the subsequent analysis, except for a few preliminary comparisons, the data refer only to the nonentrepreneurial segment of the population.

This exclusion of the entrepreneurs is a crucial decision insofar as we want to translate our findings into conclusions about the behavior of aggregate saving, since businessmen account for amounts of saving out of proportion to their number or their incomes.[3]

Income change is a variable of obvious importance, particularly in allowing investigation of dynamic effects in a cross-section study. Drastic changes of income in one direction or another are clearly associated with other events in many cases, but the concept of the "dynamic marginal propensity" to spend or save refers to the impact of changes in income. There are several qualifying considerations which must be kept in mind, however:

First, income change has its greatest relevance when considered jointly with expectations for future income. Whether the change is considered temporary, permanent, or the prelude to continued changes in the same direction is clearly important.[4]

Second, the group whose income has changed less than 5 percent includes a larger proportion of people whose incomes are fixed over long periods and whose spending–saving behavior is affected by this income stability. They may, for instance, save less than those whose incomes have fallen a little, because of their higher overall stability of income, and perhaps also because their income has not been rising in recent years.

The variable "place," or size of city where the individual lives, should be related to saving behavior for several reasons: on the one hand, "cost of living" is higher in the larger cities; on the other, there is good reason to believe that people's "standards of living" are also higher in the larger cities. If people in larger cities save less,

[3] See my articles, "The Structure of Aggregate Personal Saving," *Journal of Political Economy,* LIX (December 1951), 528–34, and "Individual Savings in 1947 and 1948," *American Economic Review XL* (June 1950), 381–88.

[4] G. Katona, "Effect of Income Changes on the Rate of Saving," *Review of Economics and Statistics,* XXXI (May 1949), 95–103. See also Klein's tabulations in Chapter V.

we are never quite sure whether it is because everything they buy costs them more, or because they are "forced" by the situation or the community standards to live a more expensive type of life, or because they have a "reference group" (as distinct from the whole community) with higher standards of consumption.

"Demographic structure" is a combination of age, marital status (indicated by the presence of two or more adults in the spending unit), and number of children. Each of these variables is used separately, with rather clear interpretation. The combination is intended as a rough approximation of what the sociologists call the "life cycle" of the typical family : young single people, young married people without children, young people with children, older people with children, older people without children ("the empty nest"), and old single people (widows and widowers). Some people of course do not go through this cycle, but enough do to make "demographic structure" a useful construct.

Similarly, each of the other variables we have used is assumed to have relevance either to the psychological or economic forces acting on the spending unit or to the meaning of these forces to the spending unit. In some cases the meaning of a variable is not clear. An example of this is income expectations in January–March 1951 as related to saving during 1950. If the same expectations have existed for the past year, they may be useful variables in explaining spending–saving decisions of the spending unit during the year as a whole. But these expectations may actually reflect an optimism–pessimism which *results from* the recent past expenditures of the spending unit. Also, an income decline combined with an expectation of future decline often means that some catastrophic event has occurred during the year, such as the death of the wage earner, and that its full consequences have yet to be felt.

We shall attempt, as we present results indicating the relations of these and other variables to saving behavior, to interpret their meaning in terms of the probable motivation of the consuming units involved.

*The sample included for analysis.* In keeping with our previous comments about the difficulty both with the data and with their interpretation for spending units involved in some entrepreneurial activity, we decided to exclude from the sample farmers and those who owned a business.[5]

In any survey, there are some interviews where a relevant item of information is not obtained, e.g., income, assets, or some component of saving. When, as in the Surveys of Consumer Finances, it is intended to publish data and relations pertaining to the nation as a whole, it is best to assign values to these cases by matching these spending units with others in the sample who are like them in as many respects as possible. The alternative would be to eliminate these interviews entirely, throwing away all the other information, and implicitly assigning them the mean sample values of all the variables (by reweighting the other interviews). However, for our purposes, where we are interested in detailed patterns of relationships and levels of significance, it seemed better to eliminate all these cases and any possibility of spurious relations resulting from the assignment procedure. Hence, we removed from the samples all cases where the amount of income, assets, or saving had been assigned. For the relevant tables we also eliminate the cases where such things as income change, occupation, etc., were not ascertained.

Finally, we made two other types of exclusion: First, we excluded a few cases where there seemed good reason to suspect the reliability of the information. For instance, we took out cases where saving was so large as to leave very small amounts for living expenses, or so small as to indicate a level of expenditure out of proportion with the general economic position of the spending unit. The latter cases usually involved some large transactions where all the money did not seem to be accounted for. Second, there were some cases where

---

[5] In the course of investigating individual cases which deviated widely from expected patterns, we discovered some additional borderline cases which had not been coded as business owners or farmers but which seemed best so treated. These cases were recoded, and hence eliminated from the nonentrepreneurial group studied in the remainder of the analysis.

extreme saving behavior was clearly present, but it was so extreme and so unusual as to require separate treatment.

The main reasons for "reasonable" extreme saving behavior were severe illness with attendant huge medical bills, death, and combinations of circumstances such as divorce, loss of job, moving, starting on a new job, interfamily transfers of money, or a very large income (over $25,000).

The distribution of saving is not only skewed, but even if saving is transformed to reduce the size of the extreme items, there are a few cases which remain many standard deviations away from the mean. These cases are interesting, but cannot be included in a statistical study using individual cases from a small sample. In any detailed analysis, they would dominate the average of any cell into which they happened to fall.

Many of these cases, as well as those reclassified "business" or "farmer," were discovered by rereading interviews where the saving behavior seemed unreasonable. Consequently, excluding them tends to reduce the variance and, probably, to give a spurious increase in the correlation in the remaining cases between saving and income. An attempt was made to make the investigation systematic by deciding on levels of saving beyond which all cases were checked.

To some extent, these exclusions, and the cases reclassified as business, farm, or not ascertained on some variable, were discovered and eliminated from the sample during the process of investigation. Also, different investigations require exclusions of different groups of those for whom some variables were not ascertained. Hence the frequencies behind the tables keep changing slightly. However, the large body of exclusions—the "not ascertained" and assigned cases and the farmers and businessmen—was made early in the process. The frequencies involved are given in Table 1. The last two lines of this table will become clear when we explain the derivation and use of $D/\sigma$ and $NDH$ (Chapter III, p. 128, and Chapter IV, p. 165).

There is a basic paradox here which faces anyone who wishes to investigate data of this sort. Aggregates and least-squares relationships are affected markedly by the extreme behavior of a few spending units and also by the behavior of a fairly small group of people, in this case upper income people. If we exclude the unusual cases, we obtain better information on the motivations and behavior patterns of the majority, but we may miss factors which affect the aggregates by operating through a few extreme cases. As we shall see later, the same problem arises in a different guise when we have to decide on the best statistical method to use, since the "best" statistical methods weight down the importance of the (high asset and income) groups whose behavior may have a dominant effect on aggregate saving.

TABLE 1

CASES EXCLUDED FROM THE SAMPLE

|  | 1947 | 1948 | 1949 |
|---|---|---|---|
| Excluded for most of analysis |  |  |  |
| Farmers | 390 | 392 | 343 |
| Business owners | 327 | 339 | 321 |
| Not ascertained cases | 395 | 414 | 482 |
| Unreliable or unusual | 49 | 63 | 15 |
| Remaining in sample | 2,302 | 2,401 | 2,351 |
| Excluded from these for relevant tables |  |  |  |
| N.A.[a] on demographic structure | 15 | 38 | 25 |
| Extremes of $D/\sigma$ | 11 | 5 | 0 |
| Extremes of $NDH$ | 1 | 0 | 17 |

[a] "Not ascertained" cases.

Our "solution" to this paradox has been to exclude the extreme cases, with a brief summary about the causes of their extreme behavior. As to the choice between analyzing what the majority of the people do as against what people do who account for most of the saving, we have analyzed the data in two ways, one of which allows the wealthy their full influence, and one which weights them down because their behavior is more variable and finds what factors affect the majority of the spending units. The latter is done by "homogenizing" the data, i.e., dividing them by an estimate of their own variance. This will be explained below; here we want only to note that the differences in results between the unadjusted and the "homogenized" data may indicate that some factor is effective chiefly at high, or low, income levels.

*Statistical procedure.* Our statistical procedure was based on the fact that many of our variables were not measurable, or not measured accurately enough to treat as continuous variables; that many of the relations were not linear; and that the effects of the different variables on saving were not additive. Such a situation would ordinarily lead to a straightforward analysis of variance. Several conditions argued against this, however. The existence of one dominant variable, i.e., income, with a powerful effect on saving, would have necessitated the preservation in every variance analysis of some six to ten income groups, and even then some of the income effect would have been hidden within the income groups. With this as a start, it is easy to see how complicated the analysis would become and how few other variables could be used without having empty cells in some of the tables. In a manifold classification using customary groupings for each variable, the number of cells grows rapidly as seen in the following tabulation:

|  | Number of Brackets | Total Number of Subcells |
|---|---|---|
| Income | 7 | 7 |
| Assets | 6 | 42 |
| Age | 6 | 252 |
| Occupation | 6 | 1,512 |

Since it is impossible in sampling for a survey to control on all the relevant variables and still preserve an unbiased sample, the cell frequencies are disproportionate and frequently become zero for cells which represent extremes on several variables. For instance, the number of spending units where the head is less than twenty-five years old, has an income over $7,500, assets of $5,000–$7,500, and is an unskilled worker, is bound to be small. Hence a variance analysis design with 1,512 subcells would have to have a sample of 10,000 to 30,000, depending on the particular variables and their distributions, in order to avoid empty cells. Of course it is possible to assign values to a few empty cells using some variant of the Yates missing-plot technique,[6] and we have done this in a few cases, but there are limits to the amount of assigning that can be done. It is also possible to combine some of the groups used, but this reduces the amount of information available. A better alternative was clearly to reduce the number of subcells by taking out the effects of a few major variables first, and use variance analysis on the residuals.

If there were a single income effect which was the same for everyone, we could use covariance, or rather—in an investigation of this sort, where we are not sure which other variables are important—we could compute deviations from an overall saving–income regression and analyze these deviations. However, there is a real problem whether the income effect is really the same for all groups. If one group had uniformly higher saving than the others at all income levels, this would not be a serious problem because this group would have positive deviations from the overall regression at all income levels, and these would show up in the later analysis. The problem arises if the regression *ratios* (slopes of the saving–income lines) vary among groups, that is, if there is an interaction effect between income and some other variable with respect to their effects on saving. If, for instance, one group has much lower saving than most at low income levels, and much higher than most at high income levels, then the average residual from an overall regression line will be close to zero for this group, yet the group is clearly different from the rest. This difference would be masked if we used a single overall regression of saving on income and then analyzed the residuals from this regression. Consequently, it was essential to discover whether there were real differences between subgroups of the population in the slopes of their saving–income relations.

*Factors affecting the saving–income slope.* We searched for these differences by determining mean saving by income groups for each

---

[6] F. Yates, "The Analysis of Replicated Experiments when the Field Results are Incomplete," *Empire Journal of Experimental Agriculture,* I (1933), 129–42.

of the subgroups of other variables, e.g., age, occupation, etc. It is not possible to present all the detailed data here, but we tested the following:

> Age of head of spending unit
> Occupation of head of spending unit
> Number of people in the spending unit
> Family composition (primary, related secondary, unrelated secondary)
> Family composition (primary with or without secondaries)
> Race
> Income change
> Size of city
> Home ownership
> Liquid assets at the beginning of the year
> Rent level of dwelling (for block cities of 50,000 or over only)
> Rent level of block (for block cities of 50,000 or over only)

There is, of course, a slight possibility that in examining these individually, we might fail to find certain three-way interactions with income, but the danger does not seem very great. The only dimensions in which the saving–income slopes were clearly different were home ownership and liquid assets. Income change did not seem to have important differences in slope but turned out later to have them, for reasons we shall explain below. Some variables, notably size of city, involved different levels of saving at all income levels but similar slopes; hence they were left to the analysis of the residuals. Data for the farmers and businessmen were also computed, and these people would clearly have had to be treated separately even had we not already decided to exclude them (see Table 2).

While mean saving by income groups is a rather crude analytical device, which hides the distribution within the income brackets and frequently involves averages of rather small groups, it was sufficient at this stage to indicate whether the differences in income–saving slopes were great enough to require separate regression lines in "re-

## TABLE 2

### MEAN SAVING BY INCOME CLASSES FOR DIFFERENT ENTREPRENEURIAL ACTIVITIES OF HEAD OF SPENDING UNIT (DOLLARS) [a]

| Disposable Income[b] (dollars) | 1947 | | | 1948 | | | 1949[c] | | | 1950[c] | | |
|---|---|---|---|---|---|---|---|---|---|---|---|---|
| | Business | Farm | Other | Business | Farm | Other | Business | Farm | Other | Business | Farm | Other |
| 0–999 | −584[d] | −46 | −168 | −1,632[d] | −8 | −144 | −682[e] | −622 | −161 | −2,765[e] | −451 | −96 |
| 1,000–1,999 | 305[e] | 291 | 74 | 111[e] | −52 | 54 | −9[e] | 202 | 51 | 379[e] | 292 | 107 |
| 2,000–2,999 | 465 | 871 | 250 | 332[e] | 914 | 252 | 445 | 718 | 293 | 416[e] | 584 | 250 |
| 3,000–3,999 | 926[e] | 1,572[e] | 443 | 1,081[e] | 1,378[e] | 475 | 562 | 1,505[e] | 543 | 809 | 1,305 | 563 |
| 4,000–4,999 | 708[e] | 1,866[e] | 844 | 1,514[e] | 1,999[e] | 834 | 1,073 | 1,799[e] | 809 | 1,014[e] | 1,888[e] | 849 |
| 5,000–7,499 | 2,132 | 2,909[e] | 1,300 | 1,679 | 2,287[e] | 1,059 | 2,216 | 2,955[e] | 1,149 | 1,835 | 1,739[e] | 1,443 |
| 7,500 or more | 6,000[e] | 4,765[d] | 4,082 | 4,508 | 4,765[e] | 2,487 | 4,925 | 5,006[e] | 3,290 | 7,596 | 3,292[d] | 3,280 |

[a] In this and subsequent tables of chapters III and IV, means are unweighted unless otherwise specified.

[b] In all tables in this and the next chapter "income" means disposable income after deduction of estimated Federal income taxes.

[c] Added later for comparison purposes.

[d] Fewer than 10 cases.

[e] Only 10–49 cases.

moving" the income effect. Further, since in most cases the means were computed separately for 1947 and 1948, consistency of patterns for the two years gave us confidence in our findings (see Tables 3–4). Later years were added to Table 3 as they became available. We then computed saving–income regressions for each of the

TABLE 3

SAVING BY INCOME AND HOME OWNERSHIP—1947–50 (DOLLARS)[a]

| Disposable Income | 1947 | | 1948 | |
|---|---|---|---|---|
| | Home Owners | Non-owners | Home Owners | Non-owners |
| 0–999 | −247 | −110 | −238 | −90 |
| 1,000–1,999 | 52 | 83 | 29 | 50 |
| 2,000–2,999 | 295 | 216 | 335 | 194 |
| 3,000–3,999 | 511 | 385 | 635 | 340 |
| 4,000–4,999 | 986 | 698 | 962 | 676 |
| 5,000–7,499 | 1,417 | 1,169 | 1,114 | 975 |
| 7,500 or more | 4,065 | 4,140[c] | 2,754[c] | 1,941[c] |

| Disposable Income | 1949[b] | | 1950[b] | |
|---|---|---|---|---|
| | Home Owners | Non-owners | Home Owners | Non-owners |
| 0–999 | −195 | −135 | −152 | −39 |
| 1,000–1,999 | 13 | 69 | 83 | 119 |
| 2,000–2,999 | 376 | 233 | 311 | 215 |
| 3,000–3,999 | 667 | 421 | 642 | 484 |
| 4,000–4,999 | 951 | 604 | 1,002 | 649 |
| 5,000–7,499 | 1,299 | 857 | 1,542 | 1,294 |
| 7,500 or more | 3,679 | 1,940 | 3,580 | 2,370 |

[a] Only the nonfarm, nonbusiness population is included.
[b] Added later for comparison.
[c] Only 10–49 cases.

detailed asset groups for home owners and non-owners separately. Details are given in Tables 5–7. In addition to the general testing for the minimum number of different regression groups, we were able to check our procedure in some other ways:

By adjusting liquid assets for security holdings, as in Table 5, we discovered that this was an unnecessary refinement. There were almost no cases where the spending unit had securities without also having a substantial amount of liquid assets.[7]

[7] That this is also true in eary 1950 is seen in Table 25 of "The Distribution of Assets, Liabilities and Net Worth of Consumers, Early 1950," Federal Reserve Bulletin, XXXVI (December 1950), 1,601.

By making the computations with and without the top income group, we could also test roughly for linearity and for domination of the regression by the top income group. There did not seem to be a serious problem in either case. However, when we reduced the number of groups to seven on the basis of similarity of the regression ratios, and actually computed the parabolic regression

$$\text{Saving} = b_0 + b_1 \,(\text{Income}) + b_2 \,(\text{Income})^2$$

as in Table 7, we found that in one case the correlation was significantly higher, the $b_2$ coefficient was of appreciable size, and a separate test of curvature of array means gave a significant F-ratio. Hence we used a parabola for this group—the non-owners with \$1–499 in liquid assets at the beginning of the year. Further, in one case—the

TABLE 4

SAVING BY INCOME AND BEGINNING-OF-YEAR LIQUID ASSETS—
1947–1948 (DOLLARS)[a]

| Disposable Income | LIQUID ASSETS—1947 | | | |
|---|---|---|---|---|
| | *None* | *1–499* | *500–1,999* | *2,000 or More* |
| 0–999 | 25 | 9 | −128[b] | −365[b] |
| 1,000–1,999 | 124 | 94 | 51 | −62 |
| 2,000–2,999 | 255 | 311 | 254 | 296 |
| 3,000–3,999 | 427 | 469 | 441 | 607 |
| 4,000–4,999 | 619[b] | 994[b] | 783 | 900 |
| 5,000–7,499 | 813[c] | 1,458[b] | 1,228 | 1,629 |
| 7,500 or more | | | 3,733[b] | 4,016 |

| Disposable Income | LIQUID ASSETS—1948 | | | |
|---|---|---|---|---|
| | *None* | *1–499* | *500–1,999* | *2,000 or More* |
| 0–999 | 44 | −19 | −273 | −288[b] |
| 1,000–1,999 | 134 | 104 | 1 | −54[b] |
| 2,000–2,999 | 303 | 311 | 294 | 305 |
| 3,000–3,999 | 460 | 562 | 415 | 610 |
| 4,000–4,999 | 646[b] | 919 | 764 | 993 |
| 5,000–7,499 | 916[c] | 840[b] | 1,269[b] | 1,368 |
| 7,500 or more | | | 2,498[b] | 2,852[b] |

[a] Nonentrepreneurial population only.
[b] Only 10–49 cases.
[c] Fewer than 10 cases.

high asset home owners—there seemed to be a difference between the two years, and separate regressions were used. In both cases— use of the parabola and separation of the two years—there was no theoretical explanation or justification, and the variation in method was a simple statistical matter of trying to remove as much as possible of the effect of income and assets on saving, in order to be able to see what other variables were important.[8]

The reader should interpret these regressions with caution. They are not estimates of population parameters, nor are any of the usual tests of significance actually strictly applicable. They are not representative of the whole population because of the exclusions from the sample, and because the weights were not used. Even with income, assets, and home ownership as variables, there may be some differences between the groups which were sampled at different rates— though the weights are chiefly correlated with income. Also, since the variances are not homogeneous among different income groups, these are not maximum likelihood estimates. While we do not know whether this would cause bias, it does mean that the estimates of the parameters are not the most efficient in the statistical sense.

There are several reasons why the usual tests of significance do not apply, even though we have used some of them as rough indicators. First, we excluded some cases, among them some of extreme behavior. Second, the variances are not homogeneous. Third, the data came from a multistage sample which is clustered at each of several stages.[9] There may well be intraclass correlation within clusters, which would mean that the actual number of degrees of freedom is smaller than the number of interviews. Finally, there is not only skewness, but also kurtosis or peakedness in the distribution of saving and even for residuals from the regressions, and this has

[8] In Chapter V, Klein estimates savings equations with nonlinear relationships between saving and income, but he uses the customary definition of saving from the Surveys of Consumer Finances and does not add expenditures on durable goods as we have done. Other apparent differences between his findings and these of this chapter are also largely due to the choice of the savings concept used.

[9] See "Methods of the Survey of Consumer Finances," *Federal Reserve Bulletin,* XXXVI (July, 1950), 795–809, for a description of the sample design.

TABLE 5

INCOME-SAVING RELATION FOR GROUPS WHICH DIFFER IN
REGRESSION COEFFICIENTS

Saving $= a + b$ (income)

### 1947

EXCLUDING INCOMES OF $7,500 OR OVER

| LIQUID ASSETS AT BEGINNING OF YEAR[a] (DOLLARS) | Regression Value of Saving at Zero Income $a$ (dollars) | Slope of Regression Line $b$ | Square of Correlation Coefficient[b] $r^2$ | Standard Error[c] of $b$ | Number of Cases |
|---|---|---|---|---|---|
| HOME OWNERS | | | | | |
| 0 | −170 | 0.2295 | 0.32 | 0.026 | 167 |
| 1–499 | −300 | 0.2787 | 0.31 | 0.026 | 255 |
| 500–1,999 | −320 | 0.2638 | 0.25 | 0.027 | 295 |
| 2,000–4,999 | −490 | 0.3349 | 0.29 | 0.040 | 175 |
| 5,000 or more | −1,070 | 0.5177 | 0.49 | 0.051 | 106 |
| All asset classes | −560 | 0.3139 | 0.32 | ..[d] | 998 |
| NON-HOME-OWNERS | | | | | |
| 0 | −50 | 0.1069 | 0.15 | 0.013 | 386 |
| 1–499 | −190 | 0.1827 | 0.18 | 0.020 | 389 |
| 500–1,999 | −420 | 0.2577 | 0.21 | 0.026 | 371 |
| 2,000–4,999 | −510 | 0.2959 | 0.22 | 0.046 | 155 |
| 5,000 or more | −420 | 0.3038 | 0.19 | 0.064 | 93 |
| All asset classes | −360 | 0.2258 | 0.23 | ..[d] | 1,394 |

### 1948

| | | | | | |
|---|---|---|---|---|---|
| HOME OWNERS | | | | | |
| 0 | −100 | 0.2341 | 0.29 | 0.027 | 190 |
| 1–499 | −160 | 0.2481 | 0.25 | 0.026 | 274 |
| 500–1,999 | −350 | 0.2892 | 0.25 | 0.032 | 251 |
| 2,000–4,999 | −740 | 0.3743 | 0.35 | 0.041 | 156 |
| 5,000 or more | −680 | 0.3653 | 0.26 | 0.060 | 110 |
| All asset classes | −290 | 0.2942 | 0.28 | ..[d] | 981 |
| NON-HOME-OWNERS | | | | | |
| 0 | −30 | 0.0961 | 0.18 | 0.025 | 446 |
| 1–499 | −160 | 0.1656 | 0.18 | 0.017 | 403 |
| 500–1,999 | −430 | 0.2291 | 0.17 | 0.028 | 337 |
| 2,000–4,999 | −640 | 0.3169 | 0.19 | 0.052 | 148 |
| 5,000 or more | −260 | 0.2642 | 0.11 | 0.093 | 65 |
| All asset classes | −380 | 0.1982 | 0.18 | ..[d] | 1,399 |

[a] Adjusted for security holdings.
[b] All correlations were positive.
[c] Not a valid statistic here but used as an indicator.
[d] Not computed.

TABLE 5 (*Continued*)

## 1947

ALL INCOME GROUPS INCLUDED

| LIQUID ASSETS AT BEGINNING OF YEAR[a] (DOLLARS) | Regression Value of Saving at Zero Income a (*dollars*) | Slope of Regression Line b | Square of Correlation Coefficient[b] $r^2$ | Standard Error[c] of b | Number of Cases |
|---|---|---|---|---|---|
| | | HOME OWNERS | | | |
| 0 | −170 | 0.2295 | 0.32 | 0.026 | 167 |
| 1–499 | −420 | 0.3299 | 0.40 | 0.025 | 256 |
| 500–1,999 | −540 | 0.3438 | 0.34 | 0.028 | 298 |
| 2,000–4,999 | −680 | 0.4022 | 0.45 | 0.033 | 183 |
| 5,000 or more | | 0.3955 | 0.61 | 0.025 | 163 |
| All asset classes | −400 | 0.3768 | 0.58 | 0.010 | 1,067 |
| | | NON-HOME-OWNERS | | | |
| 0 | −50 | 0.1069 | 0.15 | 0.013 | 386 |
| 1–499 | −190 | 0.1827 | 0.18 | 0.020 | 389 |
| 500–1,999 | −460 | 0.2740 | 0.25 | 0.025 | 372 |
| 2,000–4,999 | −460 | 0.2779 | 0.24 | 0.040 | 160 |
| 5,000 or more | −280 | 0.2944 | 0.41 | 0.033 | 108 |
| All asset classes | −280 | 0.2636 | 0.37 | 0.011 | 1,415 |
| | | FARMERS | | | |
| All asset classes | −1,690 | 0.6297 | 0.21 | 0.061 | 389 |
| | | BUSINESSMEN | | | |
| All asset classes | −700 | 0.6416 | 0.61 | 0.030 | 301 |

## 1948

| | | HOME OWNERS | | | |
|---|---|---|---|---|---|
| 0 | −100 | 0.2341 | 0.29 | 0.027 | 190 |
| 1–499 | −340 | 0.3128 | 0.35 | 0.026 | 276 |
| 500–1,999 | −390 | 0.3028 | 0.30 | 0.029 | 254 |
| 2,000–4,999 | −470 | 0.2940 | 0.44 | 0.020 | 168 |
| 5,000 or more | −210 | 0.2765 | 0.41 | 0.029 | 139 |
| All asset classes | −330 | 0.2815 | 0.41 | 0.010 | 1,027 |
| | | NON-HOME-OWNERS | | | |
| 0 | −30 | 0.0961 | 0.18 | 0.025 | 446 |
| 1–499 | −160 | 0.1656 | 0.18 | 0.017 | 403 |
| 500–1,999 | −500 | 0.2535 | 0.24 | 0.025 | 340 |
| 2,000–4,999 | −750 | 0.3514 | 0.28 | 0.046 | 153 |
| 5,000 or more | −560 | 0.3318 | 0.41 | 0.045 | 79 |
| All asset classes | −250 | 0.2535 | 0.32 | 0.010 | 1,421 |
| | | FARMERS | | | |
| All asset classes | −430 | 0.4737 | 0.42 | 0.028 | 391 |
| | | BUSINESSMEN | | | |
| All asset classes | −990 | 0.4202 | 0.55 | 0.021 | 328 |

## Table 6

### Regression Coefficients of Saving on Income by Assets, Year, and Home Ownership[a]

| LIQUID ASSETS A YEAR AGO (DOLLARS) | 1947 HOME OWNERS | | | 1948 HOME OWNERS | | | 1947 NON-HOME-OWNERS | | | 1948 NON-HOME-OWNERS | | |
|---|---|---|---|---|---|---|---|---|---|---|---|---|
| | $b$ | $\sigma_b$ | $N$ | $b$ | $\sigma_b$ | $N$ | $b$ | $\sigma_b$ | $N$ | $b$ | $\sigma_b$ | $N$ |
| 0 | 0.2402 | | 169 | 0.2341 | | 190 | 0.1069 | 0.022 | 386 | 0.1050 | 0.010 | 448 |
| 1–199 | 0.2498 | | 116 | 0.2360 | | 138 | 0.2077 | 0.029 | 193 | 0.1733 | 0.025 | 202 |
| 200–499 | 0.3566 | | 143 | 0.3657 | | 140 | 0.2758 | 0.035 | 201 | 0.1723 | 0.024 | 201 |
| 500–999 | 0.3133 | | 160 | 0.3345 | | 118 | 0.3261 | 0.035 | 205 | 0.2759 | | 180 |
| 1,000–1,999 | 0.3334 | | 159 | 0.2376 | 0.032 | 149 | 0.2866 | 0.038 | 177 | 0.2484 | 0.039 | 166 |
| 2,000–2,999 | 0.3195 | | 90 | 0.2962 | 0.036 | 80 | 0.3709 | 0.057 | 88 | 0.4882 | 0.055 | 77 |
| 3,000–4,999 | 0.4680 | | 99 | 0.3133 | | 86 | 0.2596 | 0.045 | 89 | 0.2218 | | 78 |
| 5,000–9,999 | 0.4126 | | 78 | 0.2865 | | 77 | 0.2759[b] | 0.037[b] | 76[b] | 0.3102[b] | | 69[b] |
| 10,000 or more | 0.3770 | | 53 | 0.2542 | | 49 | | | | | | |

[a] $b$ is the slope of the income-saving line, $S = a + b(I)$; $\sigma_b$ is the standard error of this slope (see note to Table 5); $N$ is the number of spending units (unweighted data).

This table excludes farmers and businessmen. Liquid assets are not adjusted for ownership of stocks or nongovernment bonds.

[b] Combines the two asset groups, $5,000–9,999 and $10,000 or more.

## TABLE 7

### STRAIGHT LINE VERSUS PARABOLA FOR THE SAVING–INCOME RELATION[a]

| GROUP DESIGNATION | | | | LINEAR PARAMETERS | | | | | | PARABOLIC PARAMETERS[c] | | | Increase in Correlation F-test |
| Year | Home Ownership | Liquid Assets at Beginning of Year (dollars) | N | $r^2$ | $a$ | $b$ | $\sigma_b$ | Array F-test[b] | $R^2$ | $b_0$ | $b_1$ | $b_2$ | |
|---|---|---|---|---|---|---|---|---|---|---|---|---|---|
| 1947 and 1948 | Yes | 0–199 | 613 | 0.34 | −146 | 0.2376 | 0.014 | 0.7 | 0.34 | −143 | 0.233615 | 0.000000822 | 0.9 |
| 1947 and 1948 | Yes | 200–2,999 | 1,039 | 0.38 | −413 | 0.3118 | 0.012 | 2.4[d] | 0.38 | −343 | 0.275284 | 0.000003518 | 1.7 |
| 1947 | Yes | 3,000 or more | 230 | 0.62 | −645 | 0.4078 | 0.021 | 0.7 | 0.62 | −949 | 0.512577 | −0.00000506 | 3.7[e] |
| 1948 | Yes | 3,000 or more | 212 | 0.42 | −407 | 0.2931 | 0.023 | 0.9 | 0.45 | −958 | 0.483207 | −0.0000099585 | 10.1[f] |
| 1947 and 1948 | No | 0 | 834 | 0.17 | −48 | 0.1060 | 0.008 | 0.7 | 0.17 | −54 | 0.11254 | −0.00000138 | 0.1 |
| 1947 and 1948 | No | 1–499 | 797 | 0.20 | −231 | 0.2022 | 0.014 | 3.9[f] | 0.24 | 73 | −0.072313 | 0.00050308 | 35.9[f] |
| 1947 and 1948 | No | 500 or more | 1,205 | 0.38 | −576 | 0.3084 | 0.011 | 2.7[d] | 0.38 | −585 | 0.312368 | −0.0000026 | 0.0 |

[a] Only in the case of non-home $1–499 in assets does the parabola increase the correlation *and* have a $b_2$ coefficient of appreciable size *and* give a significant F-test for nonlinearity of regression using array means; hence, we use a parabola for that group only.

[b] See Cyril H. Goulden, *Methods of Statistical Analysis* (New York: John Wiley and Sons, 1939), p. 214.

[c] For the relation, Saving $= b_0 + b_1$ (income) $+ b_2$ (income)$^2$.

[d] Significant at the 5-percent level.

[e] Not significant.

[f] Significant at the 1-percent level.

been shown to affect significance tests in a nonconservative direction.[10]

In spite of this, we also tested the regression coefficients for heterogeneity and found a "significant" degree of difference among them, but it is clear anyway from looking at them that they fall into a pattern and differ widely enough to require separate regressions. The explanations for these differences in regression coefficients, as distinguished from the statistical necessity for taking them into account, might run something as follows.

*Reasons for differences in regression ratios.* The difference between home owners and non-owners may be due partly to the lack of any imputed income or consumption component in our data. If we added an imputed rental value to the income and consumption of home owners, their behavior would look somewhat closer to that of non-owners but would not necessarily be the same. In addition, however, home owners are likely to have contractual saving commitments involved in their mortgage payments when they are young, and free rent through capital consumption when they are older. There may also be other differences, such as number of children, basic attitudes toward patterns of living, stability of employment, ability to dissave if pressed because of ownership of a house as security for debt, or less ability to dissave easily because assets are in nonliquid form, etc.

As for asset level, the theoretical explanation of these differences is much less clear. Explanations may be different at different ends of the income scale. For low income groups, particularly those with income decreases, liquid assets allow dissaving. For the upper income groups, the ownership of large amounts of liquid assets may have an indirect relation to saving through its relation to past saving behavior and hence, assuming continuity of both behavior and income

---

[10] R. C. Geary, "Testing for Normality," *Biometrika,* XXXIV (December 1947), 209–42. He concludes that "in the simplest case of analysis of variance, when the two sample numbers are of the same order of magnitude, the variance is proportional, approximately, to $(\beta_2 - 1)$, so that quite a small measure of universal kurtosis materially changes the probability" (p. 240). See also W. G. Cochran, "Some Consequences when the Assumptions for the Analysis of Variance are not Satisfied," *Biometrics,* III (March 1947), 22–38.

through time, to present saving behavior. High asset people may be high savers, particularly at the margin, and may continue to be so. Indeed, the presence of a large amount of liquid assets may raise the standards of the spending units as to reserve funds and induce them to attempt to accumulate still more.

*Computation of residuals.* At any rate, it is clear that there are substantial differences between the different asset and home owner-ship groups as to their saving behavior at different income levels. If we take each individual spending unit, estimate its "expected" saving on the basis of the income–saving relation for its particular asset and home ownership group, and consider only the deviation of the unit's actual saving from this expected value, we shall have "re-moved" the effect of income, assets, home ownership, year, and all their interactions with one another, on saving. We can then proceed to analyze these deviations to see what other factors account for differences in saving behavior. On IBM machinery the calculation of these individual residuals is quite simple.

Since most of the other variables are not measured on an additive scale, since some others are measured on such a scale but are not precisely accurate, and since some are not linear in their effects, we resort to tabular analysis and to variance analysis of these residuals. In either case the problem arises that the variability of saving among individuals is related to the income and asset levels of the spending units.

For tabular presentations, this means that the average residual for some groups, particularly where the number of cases is not large, may be dominated by the large residuals of a few rich spending units. For variance analysis the problem is even more serious. Variance analysis assumes that the variances of the several subgroups of the population are similar (homogeneous). This assumption of homogeneous vari-ances, or homoscedasticity, is clearly violated by the basic saving data, and equally so for the deviations from regression lines.[11]

[11] As we have indicated, this lack of homogeneity of variances means that simple least-squares methods do not give the most efficient estimates of the true regres-sions, but tests of the saving–income regression coefficients resulting from using

*"Homogenizing" of residuals.* At the suggestion of Professor P. S. Dwyer, we made an investigation of the pattern of variances of the residuals for subcells of the population according to income, assets, income change, and year.

The main results are given in Table 8 and Chart I. It turned out that variability in saving behavior was related both to income and to assets. Additional investigation, not reproduced here, indicated that variability was not related to the year involved, and only slightly to income change. Since we had not used income change as a variable so far in the analysis, any use of income change in "homogenizing" the residuals would have removed some of its effect before we had a chance to assess it. For this reason, and because income change is not one of our most accurate variables, and because income and assets explain so much of the variability in these residuals, we decided to use income and assets alone. Plotting of the data indicated that variability grew within income groups as we moved to higher asset groups, but only up to about $2,500 in liquid assets. Further, the effect of income and of assets on variability among individuals seemed to be additive. Hence, we used the following relation for estimating the variability:

$$\sigma_d = a + b \text{ (income + the first \$2,500 in liquid assets)}$$

From here on, in tables and text, we shall use $D$ as the symbol for deviations (residuals) from the seven regression lines, and $D/\sigma$ for residuals each divided by an estimate of its own standard deviation, i.e., "homogenized."

We computed the actual correlation and obtained the following equation:

$$\sigma_d = -24 + 0.1640 \text{ (income + \$2,500 of assets)}$$

---

weighted data, and saving–income ratio, both of which tend to give more nearly similar variances for all income groups, indicated that the coefficients were not much affected. This was not true of other coefficients, principally those of liquid assets. See: L. R. Klein and J. N. Morgan, "Results of Alternative Statistical Treatments of Sample Survey Data," *Journal of American Statistical Association,* XLVI (December 1951), 442–60.

We also computed the correlations of $\sigma_d$ with income, assets, and the mean saving deviation of the group, as well as the multiple correlation with income and assets, both with and without the top income bracket groups. The results are given in Table 9. They indicate that income plus assets-up-to-$2,500 actually gives a higher correlation than the multiple correlation using income and assets as separate variables. Adding the top income bracket increases the income correlation and decreases the asset correlation, presumably

TABLE 8

STANDARD DEVIATION OF RESIDUALS FROM SEVEN REGRESSION
LINES BY INCOME AND ASSETS (DOLLARS)

| | | INCOME (DOLLARS) | | | | | |
|---|---|---|---|---|---|---|---|
| LIQUID ASSETS (DOLLARS) | 0–999 | 1,000– 1,999 | 2,000– 2,999 | 3,000– 3,999 | 4,000– 4,999 | 5,000– 7,499 | 7,500 or More[a] |
| 0 | 81 | 213 | 334 | 439 | 709[a] | 827[a] | |
| 1–199 | 143 | 225 | 367 | 553 | 737[a] | 957[a] | 1,799[b] |
| 200–499 | 282[a] | 254 | 442 | 540 | 761 | 1,012[a] | |
| 500–999 | 396[a] | 351 | 520 | 615 | 776 | 1,078[a] | 1,953 |
| 1,000–1,999 | 460[a] | 539 | 528 | 740 | 815 | 1,156 | 1,824 |
| 2,000–2,999 | 632[a] | 384[a] | 542 | 970 | 955 | 1,075[a] | 1,655 |
| 3,000–4,999 | 628[a] | 507[a] | 661 | 851 | 1,035 | 1,120 | 2,264 |
| 5,000–9,999 | 545[a] | 534[a] | 811[a] | 960 | 1,016[a] | 1,409[a] | 2,691[c] |
| 10,000 or more | ..[d] | 965[a] | 886[a] | 1,040[a] | 1,079[a] | 1,519[a] | |
| All asset groups | 275 | 324 | 487 | 680 | 854 | 1,168 | 2,288 |

[a] Only 10–49 cases.
[b] Combines the three asset groups, 0, 1–199, and 200–499.
[c] Combines the two asset groups, $5,000–9,999 and $10,000 or more.
[d] No cases.

because the asset effect does not continue to become more powerful as we move to higher income (and asset, since they are correlated) groups. The correlation of the standard deviation of the residuals with their own mean (for the income and asset group) was so low as to preclude the use of any simple transformation such as the square root as a method of making the variances homogeneous.

The reader should note that this process of analyzing the variances of residuals could not have been done as an analysis of the variances of the saving data themselves. The reason is that the range of income,

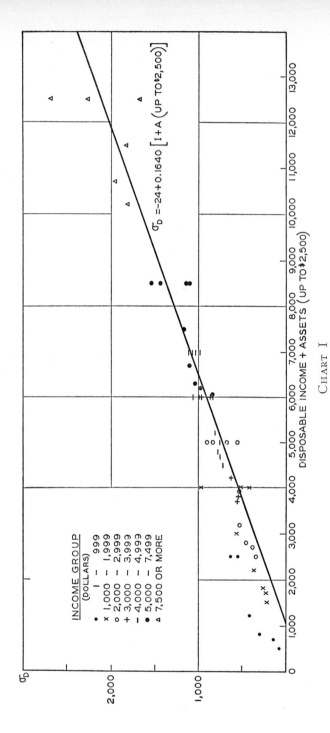

CHART I

Variability in Saving Residuals by Income plus Assets-up-to-$2,500

$$\sigma_D = -24 + 0.1640 \left[ I + A \left( \text{UP TO } \$2,500 \right) \right]$$

DISPOSABLE INCOME + ASSETS (UP TO $2,500)

INCOME GROUP
(DOLLARS)

| | |
|---|---|
| • | 1 — 999 |
| × | 1,000 — 1,999 |
| ○ | 2,000 — 2,999 |
| + | 3,000 — 3,999 |
| − | 4,000 — 4,999 |
| ● | 5,000 — 7,499 |
| △ | 7,500 OR MORE |

and therefore the standard deviation of saving within an income or asset group, depends on the range of income within the group.

We did not make use of detailed dollar-liquid-asset data, since they were not on the IBM cards used, but assigned midpoints of brackets both for the investigation, the correlations, and the subsequent homogenization process. For the open-end group with assets over $10,000 we assigned $17,500.

Since the constant term in the estimating equation was so small, we neglected it and, for each individual, estimated the variance of his saving residual by multiplying 0.164 times (his-income-plus-the-first-

TABLE 9

CORRELATION OF VARIABILITY OF SAVING DEVIATIONS
WITH OTHER VARIABLES

| | CORRELATION COEFFICIENT | |
| VARIABLE | *Omitting Top Income Bracket* | *Including All Income Groups*[a] |
|---|---|---|
| Income | 0.792 | 0.897 |
| Assets | 0.533 | 0.329 |
| Income plus assets-up-to-$2,500 | 0.933 | 0.949[b] |
| Income and assets as separate variables | 0.924 | 0.947[c] |
| Mean saving deviation | 0.142 | 0.225 |

[a] Note that adding the top income bracket increases the income correlation and reduces the asset correlation.

[b] $\sigma_d = -24.275 + 0.1640$ (income + assets-up-to-$2,500).
[c] $\sigma_d = -0.238 + 0.275$ (income) + 0.081 (assets).

$2,500-of-his-liquid-assets), and divided the residual by this estimate of its own standard deviation.

*Tests of the homogenizing process and exclusion of extreme cases.* As a test of the effectiveness of our homogenizing procedure, we checked both the frequency distribution of the homogenized residuals and their standard deviations within income, asset, income change, and expected income groups. If our operation was successful, these standard deviations should range rather closely around 1.0, which they seem to do, ranging from 0.58 to 1.25. In fact, there is little apparent pattern to the standard deviations of the homogenized residuals even by income-change and expected-income groups. This would indicate that there was no necessity for taking these two variables into account in estimating and removing differences in variability. On the surface it might seem that a change in income would create an incentive for extreme behavior and in different directions by different people, but apparently the facilitation of income and assets in allowing variability was more important than the pressures resulting from changing income.

The distribution of the homogenized residuals still departs from

TABLE 10

DISTRIBUTION OF HOMOGENIZED RESIDUALS

| $D/\sigma$ | Expected Frequencies[a] ($f_e$) | Actual Frequencies[b] ($f_a$) |
|---|---|---|
| −14.366 | | 1 |
| −8.989 | | 1 |
| −6.563 | | 1 |
| −5.500 to −5.999 | 1[d] | 1 |
| −5.000 to −5.499 | | 0 |
| −4.500 to −4.999 | | 0 |
| −4.000 to −4.499 | | 2 |
| −3.500 to −3.999 | | 3 |
| −3.000 to −3.499 | 5 | 12[c] |
| −2.500 to −2.999 | 23 | 24 |
| −2.000 to −2.499 | 80 | 45 |
| −1.500 to −1.999 | 213 | 78 |
| −1.000 to −1.499 | 444 | 256 |
| −0.500 to −0.999 | 723 | 754 |
| −0.001 to −0.499 | 924 | 1,436 |
| 0.000 to 0.499 | 924 | 1,072 |
| 0.500 to 0.999 | 723 | 503 |
| 1.000 to 1.499 | 444 | 343 |
| 1.500 to 1.999 | 213 | 151 |
| 2.000 to 2.499 | 80 | 78 |
| 2.500 to 2.999 | 23 | 34 |
| 3.000 to 3.499 | 5 | 17 |
| 3.500 to 3.999 | | 9 |
| 4.000 to 4.499 | | 5 |
| 4.500 to 4.999 | 1[e] | 0 |
| 5.000 to 5.499 | | 2 |
| | | 4,828 |

[a] $f_e$ = In a normal distribution.    [b] $f_a$ = In the sample.
[c] Numbers reading down from 12 through 9 were used in a subsequent analysis.
[d] −3.500 or less.        [e] 3.500 or more.

normality (see Table 10). There is a concentration of cases very close to zero and a few cases—more than in a normal distribution—three and more standard deviations away from zero. It is probable that the former results from the latter, i.e., that the few extreme cases make the standard deviation large, and in dividing by this overly large estimate of the standard deviation, we concentrate many cases near zero. It is possible that we really have two normal distributions: one with a small variance, composed of people to whom nothing unusual has happened, and one with a large variance, composed of people to whom something unusual has happened. At any rate, some of the more extreme cases were excluded from the sample for the analysis which follows, for reasons similar to those we have already given for eliminating some extreme cases in the beginning: they would dominate the means of rather large groups and distort the relations. Further, the kurtosis makes our F-tests nonconservative. The main reason for the appearance of these extremes was a very low level of income and assets (a small divisor), or some unusual circumstance which precipitated unusually large saving or dissaving. Of the 16 cases removed as extreme, 6 were primarily the result of very low income-plus-assets; four of these were the recipients of intra-family transfers, one an old man genuinely consuming assets, and one a sharecropper working on "furnish." Five other cases involved large inter-family transfers; one, the death of the wage earner; and another, a man who had been in business and sold out during the year. Two of the remaining three had some dubious aspects and the third was an unusual person described as "the beginning of an army bum." The exclusion of these 16 cases changed the skewness ($\beta_1$) from $-0.25$ to $0.18$, and kurtosis ($\beta_2$) from 16 to 4, the kurtosis of the normal distribution being 3.

This same sort of leptokurtic distribution of residuals has been found by Klein using multiple correlations and without first eliminating any extreme cases (see Chapter V). We have reduced its importance for our analysis first by removing some cases (see Table

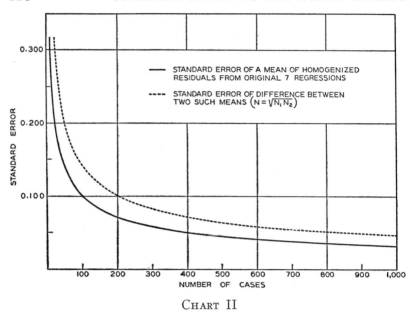

CHART II

Standard Errors of Means of Homogenized Residuals and of Differences
between Two Such Means

*The standard errors are not strictly valid, since the data are unweighted from a
clustered sample with varying sampling rates. They are conservative because actual
errors were reduced 6 percent by removal of 16 extreme cases.*

10), and secondly by using cell means instead of individual cases in
the variance analysis. These means should be normally distributed
even if the basic residuals were still leptokurtic.

Chart II provides a rough method of testing for the significance
of the difference between means of these "homogenized" residuals.
While the formulas do not strictly apply, because of the clustered
nature of the sample, and the presence of some skewness and kurtosis
even after removal of the extreme cases, they provide a rough check,
particularly in light of the following considerations: First they are
conservative because they are based on the estimation of variances
before the removal of the extreme cases. Second, Geary and Cochran
have shown that the two-tailed t-test is not much affected by either

skewness or kurtosis.[12] Finally, while the clustering may easily involve some intra-class correlation of income within the clusters, it is much more doubtful that any significant intra-class correlations of our residuals would exist, i.e., after income, assets, home ownership have been accounted for.

In line with our earlier comments about the effect of the method of homogenizing on the relative weighting of rich and poor spending units, we present results for both homogenized and unhomogenized residuals. Any large differences can be interpreted in the light of this homogenizing effect.

*Appropriateness of variance analysis.* While we are discussing methods, it may be useful to add a few more comments on the appropriateness of the analysis of variance, even though we intend to present some straightforward tabulations first. Variance analysis can be thought of as doing two things. First, it divides the total variation of the dependent variable into pieces. These pieces are the proportions of the variation "explained" by the factors used in grouping the data or by their interactions. The residual variance is generally entitled the "error" variance. Second, it provides a method for converting each of these pieces into an estimate of the population variance and for testing whether these estimates are significantly different from the estimate based on the "error" variance.

If the subgroups were all alike, randomly selected groups from a homogeneous population, then we should be able to estimate the population variance from the group means as well as from individual items, or the individual items within subgroups, and get the same result. If the means of a set of subgroups are significantly different from one another, then we would get an overestimate of the population variance. We should interpret this to indicate that the subgroups are not random groupings from a homogeneous population, i.e., that the criterion by which we chose them is related to the variable we are investigating.

[12] W. G. Cochran, "Some Consequences when the Assumptions for the Analysis of Variance are not Satisfied," *Biometrics,* III (March 1947), 24; R. C. Geary, "Testing for Normality," *Biometrika,* XXXIV (December 1947), 216–17.

The interpretation of interaction variance is more difficult to explain. If two factors have a significant interaction, it means that the combined effect of the two is not a simple addition of the individual effects. It is possible for each of two factors individually to increase saving, but for high levels of both of them to decrease it. Or, more commonly, the level of one may change the degree of influence of the other on saving.

The ability to partition total variance rests on grouping where each basic cell in the table, and hence each subgroup within its own set, has the same number of cases; otherwise the basic theorem on decomposition of total variance does not hold. The ability to test the significance of the difference between the estimates of variance rests also on other assumptions, most important of which is that while subgroups may differ as to their means, they will not differ as to their basic variability.[13] Variance analysis was designed for experimental situations where all the variables could be controlled. That is, in an agricultural plot experiment with different levels of manure, different seeds, etc., the plots could be laid out with, say, three replications of each possible combination of these. Each cell in the table would then have the same number of cases—here three. Recently methods have been worked out for applying variance analysis to cases where the cell frequencies are disproportionate, but the methods involve assuming either that the frequencies are proportionate to those in the population studied (pure random sample) or that the frequencies in the population are actually equal.[14] Neither of these assumptions is met in our data. Our solution to this problem of disproportionate cell frequencies has been, again at the suggestion of Professor P. S. Dwyer, to use cell means as though they were single

[13] For further details, see George W. Snedecor, *Statistical Methods,* 4th ed. (Ames, Iowa: Iowa State College Press, 1946), Chapters 10–13; Cyril H. Goulden, *Methods of Statistical Analysis,* 2d ed. (New York: John Wiley and Sons, 1952), Chapters 5, 9, 14; *Biometrics,* III (March 1947), whole issue.

[14] See particularly Fei Tsao, "General Solution of the Analysis of Variance in the Case of Unequal or Disproportionate Numbers of Observations in the Subclasses," *Psychometrika,* XI (1946), 107–8. See also same author and title, Doctoral Dissertation, University of Minnesota, 1945.

observations. This throws away a certain amount of information but greatly simplifies the analysis. It has the two additional advantages of reducing any remaining kurtosis to negligible proportions and of freeing us from worrying about whether we should reduce the number of degrees of freedom because of clustering of the sample. We certainly have more degrees of freedom than the number of cells, even in the most complicated of our variance analysis designs.

The use of cell means as basic data has another disadvantage, however, in that when the number of cases in the various cells becomes extremely varied, heterogeneity of variances is reintroduced because the variability of an average varies inversely with the square root of the number of cases on which it is based.

*Analysis of the effects of other factors on the residuals.* Since many of the other variables still to be investigated are likely to be interrelated in their effects, tabular presentations cannot simply give main effects one at a time. The effect of age is influenced by the correlation of age with assets, etc. Consequently, we split the sample first by categories we know will be related to the residuals and then proceed to use additional subgroupings to investigate other variables. It was clear even from looking at mean saving by income brackets that saving was related to size of city, or at least to the metropolitan–nonmetropolitan division. Income change also is clearly an important variable but depends on asset holdings for its full effect. Hence, although we had "taken out" the effect of assets directly and through income, we must still take account of the interaction of assets with income change.

Table 11 shows the relation of city size to saving, mean income, dollar residuals from the seven regressions, and the homogenized residuals from these regressions. It is interesting not only in showing the effect of city size but also in indicating how homogenization affects the pattern. Whether these differences between metropolitan areas and the open country are the result of differences in cost of living or differences in standards (reference groups, etc.), we cannot say. While the open-country group differs from the rest, it is so small that we have, in much of the subsequent analysis, merely split the sample into metropolitan and nonmetropolitan, or else omitted the open-country group entirely. At any rate, it is clear that there is a relation here that is not simply the result of differences in average money incomes.

When we examine the effect of income change, we find roughly the type of effect we should expect: people who have suffered declines save less than expected (negative residuals), and people with increases in income have positive residuals because they have not

TABLE 11

INCOME, SAVING, AND SAVING RESIDUALS BY PLACE CODE[a]

| | Number of Cases | Average Income (Disposable) (dollars) | Average Saving (dollars) | D (dollars) | D/σ |
|---|---|---|---|---|---|
| Metropolitan areas[b] | 1,677 | 3,527 | 568 | −49 | −0.061 |
| Nonmetropolitan Cities of 50,000 or over | 858 | 3,103 | 519 | 17 | 0.007 |
| Cities of 2,500 to 50,000 | 1,257 | 2,795 | 447 | 13 | 0.046 |
| Towns under 2,500 | 741 | 2,716 | 441 | 19 | 0.063 |
| Open country nonfarm areas | 395 | 2,148 | 374 | 105 | 0.248 |

[a] In this and subsequent tables, D indicates a mean of pooled residuals from the seven regressions given in Table 7, and D/σ indicates a mean of pooled homogenized residuals from the seven regression lines. For these latter, the standard error is a simple function of the number of cases (see Chart II).

Unless otherwise specified, all tables of D and D/σ are for the years 1947 and 1948 combined.

[b] Includes only the twelve largest metropolitan areas of the United States.

correspondingly increased their expenditures on nondurable goods and services (Table 12). But this is true only for those with some assets. The weighting down of the upper income groups makes the homogenized residuals give more nearly the "expected effect" for the group with less than $500 in liquid assets, but even the homogenized residuals show almost no income-change effect for the group with no liquid assets at all. Partly this is because these people are low income people who consume all their income in any case, have no assets and little credit with which to dissave, and have an abundance of pressing uses for income which can absorb any increase in income immediately. Paying off installment debts also is a sort of forced saving.

The effect of income change on saving depends on what the people expect their future income to be, and in addition this relation seems to differ depending on whether or not the spending unit lives in a metropolitan area (Table 13). These tables do not contradict the findings of Katona that income increases often lead to greatly enlarged expenditures, for the reason that we include durable goods expenditures as well as housing expenditures in saving.[15]

TABLE 12

SAVING RESIDUALS BY INCOME CHANGE AND LIQUID ASSETS
AT BEGINNING OF YEAR[a]

| INCOME CHANGE (PERCENT) | LOW ASSETS ($0–499) | | HIGH ASSETS ($500 OR MORE) | | NO ASSETS |
| | $D$ (dollars) | $D/\sigma$ | $D$ (dollars) | $D/\sigma$ | $D/\sigma$ |
| --- | --- | --- | --- | --- | --- |
| Up 25 or more | 80 | 0.160 | 191 | 0.173 | 0.096 |
| Up 5–24 | 1 | 0.030 | −3 | 0.024 | 0.082 |
| Changed less than 5 | −20 | −0.008 | −64 | −0.022 | −0.037 |
| Down 5–24 | −20 | −0.015 | −61 | −0.039 | 0.177 |
| Down 25 or more | −2 | −0.087 | −210 | −0.318 | 0.068 |

[a] Liquid assets are always as of the beginning of the year.

Table 13 seems to show that people with income decreases tend to save less, and those among them living in metropolitan areas who expect a continuation of low income or a further drop save *still less*. Also, in metropolitan areas, those with increases save more, but those among them who expect a continuation of the high income or a further increase save more than those who expect a subsequent fall. These findings are at variance with what we might expect and with what we find outside the metropolitan areas.

There are several possible explanations of these results: The group with income declines and the expectation of further declines contains a large proportion of spending units to which something drastic has happened, such as death or disability of the wage earner, retirement,

[15] G. Katona, "Effect of Income Changes on the Rate of Saving," *Review of Economics and Statistics,* XXXI (May 1949), 95–103.

etc. The group in metropolitan areas with income increases and the expectation of future increases may well be more inclined than others to purchase durable goods. In addition, however, percentage change in income may not be so relevant in assessing dollar saving as dollar change in income, and it is also possible, as we shall see below, that our regressions inadvertently removed part of the effect of income change on saving.

TABLE 13

SAVING RESIDUALS BY PLACE, INCOME CHANGE,
AND EXPECTED INCOME

| INCOME CHANGE (PERCENT) | EXPECTED INCOME | | | | | | | |
|---|---|---|---|---|---|---|---|---|
| | WILL GO UP | | WILL STAY SAME | | WILL GO DOWN | | DON'T KNOW | |
| | $D/\sigma$ | D (dollars) | $D/\sigma$ | D (dollars) | $D/\sigma$ | D (dollars) | $D/\sigma$ | D (dollars) |
| Metropolitan Area | | | | | | | | |
| Up 25 or more | 0.166 | 198 | 0.042 | 145 | 0.011[a] | 85[a] | −0.230 | −117 |
| Up 5–25 | −0.077 | −39 | −0.099 | −150 | −0.099 | 53 | −0.102 | −55 |
| Changed less than 5 | −0.129 | −87 | −0.180[a] | −127[a] | −0.180 | −126 | −0.172 | −252 |
| Down 5 or more | −0.286 | −42 | −0.290[a] | −10[a] | −0.290 | −236 | −0.227 | −89 |
| Nonmetropolitan Area | | | | | | | | |
| Up 25 or more | 0.139 | 127 | 0.122 | 68 | 0.195 | 207 | 0.217 | 242 |
| Up 5–24 | 0.070 | 47 | 0.017 | 20 | 0.021 | 43 | 0.062 | 59 |
| Changed less than 5 | 0.057 | 52 | 0.041 | 2 | −0.183 | 9 | −0.218 | −101 |
| Down 5 or more | −0.180 | −73 | −0.039 | −29 | −0.039 | −22 | −0.139 | −94 |

[a] 10–49 cases.

Table 14 indicates some relation between the number of people in the spending unit and the mean residual, but the effect seems to disappear and even reverse beyond five people. This is true for all four groups of city size and liquid assets. A possible explanation of this is that the usual demands on income explain the effect up to five people, but that beyond this increasing numbers in the unit signify not only pressures to spend but the existence of a different social group. In any case, the overall effect is small enough to suggest that the spending unit is a good concept and that in analyzing aggregate

# TABLE 14

## SAVING RESIDUALS BY LIQUID ASSETS, PLACE, AND NUMBER IN UNIT

| NUMBER OF PEOPLE IN SPENDING UNIT | NONMETROPOLITAN | | | | METROPOLITAN[c] | | | | ALL GROUPS | |
| --- | --- | --- | --- | --- | --- | --- | --- | --- | --- | --- |
| | LESS THAN $500 IN ASSETS | | $500 OR MORE IN ASSETS | | LESS THAN $500 IN ASSETS | | $500 OR MORE IN ASSETS | | | |
| | D (dollars) | D/σ | D (dollars) | D/σ | D (dollars) | D/σ | D (dollars) | D/σ | D (dollars) | D/σ |
| 1 | 22 | 0.071 | 155 | 0.336 | 12 | 0.053 | 63 | 0.118 | 60 | 0.141 |
| 2 | 24 | 0.063 | 40 | 0.036 | −10 | −0.038 | −93 | −0.073 | −1 | 0.012 |
| 3 | 35 | 0.080 | 46 | 0.021 | −52 | −0.113 | −68 | −0.127 | 4 | 0.006 |
| 4 | 35 | 0.094 | −50 | −0.029 | −8 | 0.061 | −111 | −0.144 | −23 | −0.008 |
| 5 | 12 | −0.006 | −200 | −0.210 | −259[a] | −0.422[a] | −158[a] | −0.280[a] | −111 | −0.162 |
| 6 | 61 | 0.132 | −70[a] | −0.126[a] | −184[a] | −0.289[a] | −161[a] | −0.217[a] | −41 | −0.046 |
| 7 | 31[a] | 0.068[a] | −92[a] | 0.061[a] | −55[b] | 0.024[b] | 284[b] | 0.215[b] | 22 | 0.052 |
| 8 or more | −23[a] | −0.122[a] | 1,290[b] | 1.405[b] | 168[b] | 0.226[b] | −430[b] | −0.584[b] | 9 | −0.076 |

[a] 10–49 cases.　　[b] Fewer than 10 cases.　　[c] Twelve largest metropolitan areas of the United States.

## TABLE 15

### SAVING RESIDUALS BY PLACE, LIQUID ASSETS, AND AGE

| PLACE | LIQUID ASSETS (DOLLARS) | 18–24 | | 25–34 | | 35–44 | | 45–54 | | 55–64 | | 65 OR OVER | | ALL AGES | |
|---|---|---|---|---|---|---|---|---|---|---|---|---|---|---|---|
| | | D (dollars) | D/σ | D (dollars) | D/σ | D (dollars) | D/σ | D (dollars) | D/σ | D (dollars) | D/σ | D (dollars) | D/σ | D (dollars) | D/σ |
| Nonmetropolitan area | Less than 500 | 68 | 0.198 | 92 | 0.173 | 25 | 0.020 | −38 | −0.068 | −25 | −0.008 | −16 | 0.020 | 27 | 0.074 |
| | 500 or more | 166 | 0.334 | 63 | 0.058 | −13 | −0.011 | −23 | −0.016 | 77 | 0.093 | 36 | 0.182 | 32 | 0.062 |
| Metropolitan area | Less than 500 | 40 | 0.082 | 26 | 0.017 | −95 | −0.125 | −100 | −0.205 | −94 | −0.199 | −36[a] | 0.009[a] | −33 | −0.058 |
| | 500 or more | −27 | 0.014 | 90 | 0.023 | −40 | −0.105 | −81 | −0.056 | −121 | −0.065 | −341 | −0.256 | −58 | −0.064 |
| All place and asset groups | | 66 | 0.169 | 73 | 0.088 | −21 | −0.027 | −49 | −0.064 | −14 | −0.003 | −55 | 0.024 | | |

[a] 10–49 cases.

data per-capita data are probably not so good as per-spending-unit data.

Table 15 shows few clear patterns of differences by age groups, except perhaps for the first three, where there is a strong dropping of the average residuals from positive to negative. Since we know from other data that there is a very strong negative correlation between age and expenditures on durable goods (here treated as a component of saving), it is quite possible that saving not put into durable goods is actually rather small for the early years and really increases up until retirement age. The group over 65 years old has a negative dollar residual but a positive homogenized residual, indicating that the negative saving by older people is done largely by the high-asset, high-income spending units; this is borne out by detailed analysis of those over 65 by income groups. Of course, there are some problems of definition here. An annuity is counted as income, as are social security payments. On the other hand, if instead of buying an annuity one lives off the earnings and occasional sale of stocks and other assets, then he appears as a dissaver. In a real economic sense, even social security payments are the using up of an "asset," the right to social security, and hence represent dissaving. Of course, the "asset" is not transferable.

Table 16 seems to indicate less saving by spending units with more than one earner. This may well indicate that, while the group is considered a single spending unit because the members pool their money for major items of expenditure, they are actually partially separate spending units with separate needs, and that saving is based on two separate and smaller incomes. Each earner may, for instance, keep his own car. It may also be, however, that people with expenditure patterns (or what seem to them to be absolute demands on their income) out of line with their incomes, can manage only by doubling up, i.e., that the same force which leads to low saving also leads to doubling up.

Table 17 indicates significantly lower saving for primary spending units and higher saving for secondaries. This may be partly the age

## TABLE 16

SAVING RESIDUALS BY PLACE AND NUMBER OF EARNERS IN THE SPENDING UNIT[a]

| Place | Number of Earners | $D/\sigma$ | $D$ (dollars) |
|---|---|---|---|
| Metropolitan area | 0 | 0.294[b] | 36[b] |
| | 1 | 0.089 | 33 |
| | 2 | 0.010 | 7 |
| | 3 | −0.286[c] | −132[c] |
| | 4 or more | −0.248[b] | −133[b] |
| Nonmetropolitan area | 0 | 0.119[b] | 250 |
| | 1 | −0.038 | −43 |
| | 2 | −0.192 | −107 |
| | 3 | −0.465[b] | −510[b] |
| | 4 or more | −0.828[b] | −2,600[b] |
| Both place Groups | 0 | 0.228[b] | 116[b] |
| | 1 | 0.043 | 6 |
| | 2 | −0.052 | −28 |
| | 3 | −0.346[c] | −258[c] |
| | 4 or more | −0.325[b] | −500[b] |

[a] 1948 only.    [b] Fewer than 10 cases.    [c] 10–49 cases.

## TABLE 17

SAVING RESIDUALS BY PLACE, LIQUID ASSETS, AND COMPOSITION OF SPENDING UNIT

| Place | Liquid Assets (dollars) | Composition of Spending Unit | $D/\sigma$ | $D$ (dollars) |
|---|---|---|---|---|
| Nonmetropolitan area | Less than 500 | Primary | 0.067 | 24 |
| | | Secondary, related | 0.133 | 57 |
| | | Secondary, unrelated | 0.002 | −1 |
| | 500 or more | Primary | 0.013 | 9 |
| | | Secondary, related | 0.501 | 237 |
| | | Secondary, unrelated | 0.267 | 116 |
| Metropolitan area | Less than 500 | Primary | −0.102 | −45 |
| | | Secondary, related | −0.036 | 4 |
| | | Secondary, unrelated | 0.081 | −21 |
| | 500 or more | Primary | −0.120 | −98 |
| | | Secondary, related | 0.216 | 128 |
| | | Secondary, unrelated | 0.029 | 66 |
| All places and assets | | Primary | −0.008 | −14 |
| | | Secondary, related | 0.189 | 89 |
| | | Secondary, unrelated | 0.098 | 34 |

## TABLE 18

### SAVING RESIDUALS BY OCCUPATION

| Occupation | $D/\sigma$ | D (dollars) |
|---|---|---|
| Professional | 0.063 | 46 |
| Self-employed or managerial (excluding business owners) | 0.065 | 78 |
| White collar | 0.047 | 16 |
| Skilled–semi-skilled | −0.012 | −22 |
| Unskilled | 0.104 | 38 |
| Retired | −0.080 | −92 |
| Other | −0.020 | −27 |

## TABLE 19

### SAVING RESIDUALS BY PLACE, LIQUID ASSETS, AND OCCUPATION

| Place | Liquid Assets (dollars) | Occupation | D (dollars) | $D/\sigma$ |
|---|---|---|---|---|
| Nonmetropolitan area | Less than 500 | Professional | 90 | 0.221 |
| | | Self-employed, Managerial | 84 | 0.118 |
| | | White collar | 59 | 0.114 |
| | | Skilled | 29 | 0.068 |
| | | Unskilled | 16 | 0.090 |
| | | Retired | −7 | −0.031 |
| | | Others | −12 | 0.007 |
| | 500 or more | Professional | 153 | 0.134 |
| | | Self-employed, Managerial | 68 | 0.076 |
| | | White collar | −12 | 0.040 |
| | | Skilled | 19 | 0.038 |
| | | Unskilled | 92 | 0.176 |
| | | Retired | −75 | −0.003 |
| | | Others | −11 | 0.033 |
| Metropolitan area | Less than 500 | Professional | 0[a] | 0.050[a] |
| | | Self-employed, Managerial | −180[a] | −0.233[a] |
| | | White Collar | −9 | −0.001 |
| | | Skilled | −72 | −0.118 |
| | | Unskilled | −9 | 0.007 |
| | | Retired | −54[a] | 0.116[a] |
| | | Others | 36 | −0.046 |
| | 500 or more | Professional | −77 | −0.082 |
| | | Self-employed, Managerial | 170 | 0.088 |
| | | White Collar | 21 | 0.018 |
| | | Skilled | −146 | −0.165 |
| | | Unskilled | 166 | 0.263 |
| | | Retired | −391[a] | −0.325[a] |
| | | Others | −158 | −0.163 |

[a] 10–49 cases.

(and durable good) effect again, but it also indicates some intra-family transfers of money or in kind, such as free room and/or board, gifts, etc. On the other hand, in spite of the possibility of these transfers, it would probably not be an improvement to lump the two spending units together and compute saving on a family basis, since it would then look as though multiple families were saving very little considering their (pooled) income.

Tables 18 and 19 show very little difference in average residuals between different occupation groups, the only residual significantly different from zero being, strangely enough, that for unskilled and service workers. It is possible, of course, that some more direct social-status variable, made up of a combination of occupation, education, income, and assets, might have some relation to saving behavior. However, it is also possible that occupation in particular and social status in general affect the forms of saving and not its total. It is possible, for instance, that moving into a wealthy district increases some forms of saving (mortgage payments) as much as it decreases other saving through more expenditures on luxury items.

A difficulty in defining income is the treatment of one-time payments such as gifts or inheritances. In the Surveys they are not treated as income. However, insofar as people do consider them as currently available resources, those with gifts would spend more. Two other considerations are involved, however. Inheritance may mean funeral expenses and legal expenses at the same time. Even apart from errors, if part of the money were kept in cash at home or in a safety deposit box, or if it were not reported for some other reason in the interview, or if it were received in kind but reported as though it were money, then it would not appear anywhere in the year-end balances, and it would look as though the spending unit had spent part or all of it. Table 20 indicates significantly lower saving for the group with gifts or inheritances. This could not, of course, be due to a tendency to spend such windfalls on durable goods, since such expenditures are not treated as consumption here.

In addition to variables indicating possible needs, or financial

TABLE 20

SAVING RESIDUALS FOR THOSE WITH GIFTS OR INHERITANCE
BY PLACE AND ASSETS

| Place and Assets (dollars) | Gifts or Inheritance (dollars) | $D/\sigma$ | D (dollars) | Number of Cases |
|---|---|---|---|---|
| Nonmetropolitan Area | | | | |
| Assets less than 500 | Less than 300 | −0.243 | 3 | 22 |
| | 300 or more | −0.505 | −90 | 21 |
| Assets 500 or more | Less than 300 | −0.298 | 89 | 8 |
| | 300 or more | −0.262 | −195 | 36 |
| All (those with gifts or inheritance) | | −0.265 | −93 | 87 |
| Metropolitan Area | | | | |
| All asset groups | Less than 300 | −0.359 | −382 | 26 |
| | 300 or more | −0.261 | −249 | 35 |
| All (those with gifts or inheritance) | | −0.303 | −306 | 61 |
| All places (those with gifts or inheritance) | | −0.280 | −181 | 148 |

means for satisfying them, we were also interested in general attitudes, particularly feelings of security or worry. However, since we have attitudinal material at the *end* of the period for which we have the financial information, we must view attitudes as possibly a result as well as a cause. In one year (early 1948) respondents were asked, "In general, when you think about the future, do you have many

TABLE 21

SAVING RESIDUALS BY PLACE, INCOME CHANGE,
AND FINANCIAL WORRIES[a]

| | | FINANCIAL WORRIES | | | |
|---|---|---|---|---|---|
| | | $D/\sigma$ | | D (dollars) | |
| PLACE | INCOME CHANGE | Yes | No | Yes | No |
| Metropolitan area | +25% or more | −0.135[b] | 0.195 | −58[b] | 220 |
| | −4% to +24% | −0.096 | −0.084 | −93 | −88 |
| | −5% or more | −0.088 | 0.020 | 58 | −70 |
| Nonmetropolitan area | +25% or more | 0.131 | 0.295 | 108 | 193 |
| | −4% to +24% | −0.084 | 0.107 | −66 | 51 |
| | −5% or more | −0.170 | 0.055 | −78 | −32 |

[a] 1947 only.          [b] Only 10–49 cases.

worries about how you, yourself, will get along financially? Do you have any special reason for feeling that way?" Table 21 indicates significantly lower past saving (after eliminating most of the effects of income, assets, home ownership, city size, and income change) for those who say they have financial worries. This would tend to lend some support to one of our original hypotheses, i.e., that people do have some vague conception of their overall net-worth position and its changes. It would be interesting to know whether these people saved more in the subsequent year.

TABLE 22

SAVINGS RESIDUALS BY PLACE, INCOME CHANGE,
AND CONTRIBUTION TO RETIREMENT FUNDS

| Place | Income Change | Contribution | $D/\sigma$ | $D$ (dollars) |
|-------|---------------|--------------|-----------|---------------|
| Metropolitan area | +25% or more | No | 0.114 | 89 |
|  |  | Yes | 0.134[a] | 281[a] |
|  | −4% to +24% | No | −0.110 | −132 |
|  |  | Yes | 0.099 | 6 |
|  | −5% or more | No | −0.278 | −104 |
|  |  | Yes | −0.137[a] | −165[a] |
| Nonmetropolitan area | +25% or more | No | 0.134 | 68 |
|  |  | Yes | 0.407[a] | 205[a] |
|  | −4% to +24% | No | 0.052 | 10 |
|  |  | Yes | 0.158 | 113 |
|  | −5% or more | No | −0.089 | −58 |
|  |  | Yes | 0.035[a] | 13[a] |
| All place groups | All income changes | No | 0.001 | −18 |
|  |  | Yes | 0.122 | 82 |

[a] 10–49 cases.

A question also arises whether or not the various elements in saving are really regarded as similar enough by the consumer, so that they compete with one another, i.e., are substitutes. For example: is coverage by social security or some other annuity scheme regarded as a substitute for other forms of saving? If we assume that those who make contributions to an annuity or retirement fund were so covered, Table 22 indicates that those who were covered had larger positive residuals than those who were not so covered, even when their incomes fell. It should be noted that Social Security payments are not included here.

A similar problem is whether or not contractual saving as a whole is a substitute for other forms of saving, i.e., whether the proportion of saving which is contractual can vary without any effect on total saving. Contractual saving consists of the annuity payments mentioned above, life insurance premiums, and repayment on mortgage principal. Table 23 indicates that there is a positive relation between contrac-

TABLE 23

SAVINGS RESIDUALS BY PLACE, ASSETS, AND CONTRACTUAL SAVING

| Place | Liquid Assets (dollars) | Contractual Saving (dollars) | $D/\sigma$ | $D$ (dollars) |
|---|---|---|---|---|
| Nonmetropolitan area | Less than 500 | None | −0.123 | −51 |
| | | 1–199 | 0.032 | −3 |
| | | 200 or more | 0.415 | 199 |
| | 500 or more | None | 0.115 | 4 |
| | | 1–199 | 0.028 | −5 |
| | | 200 or more | 0.096 | 102 |
| Metropolitan area | Less than 500 | None | −0.191 | −68 |
| | | 1–199 | −0.049 | −33 |
| | | 200 or more | 0.048 | 4 |
| | 500 or more | None | −0.218 | −215 |
| | | 1–199 | −0.079 | −93 |
| | | 200 or more | 0.000 | 27 |
| All place and asset groups | | None | −0.094 | −66 |
| | | 1–199 | −0.001 | −23 |
| | | 200 or more | 0.143 | 94 |

tual saving and total saving. We may conclude that when contractual saving is present, other saving is not reduced proportionately. These residuals, it should be remembered, have already "removed" the influence of home ownership by using different regressions for home owners and non-home-owners. This finding about imperfect substitutability of saving components may indicate that different forms of saving satisfy different needs, and that saturation—i.e., accumulation of enough saving so that future saving is reduced—is not as prevalent or plausible as we had thought. Also, a more detailed tabulation in Table 24 indicates that this positive correlation between

## Table 24

## Saving Residuals by Place, Assets, Contractual Saving, and Income Change

| PLACE | LIQUID ASSETS (dollars) | CONTRACTUAL SAVING (dollars) | INCOME CHANGE | | | | | |
|---|---|---|---|---|---|---|---|---|
| | | | Up 25% or More $D/\sigma$ | Up 5 to 24% $D/\sigma$ | $-4$ to $+4\%$ $D/\sigma$ | Down 5 to 24% $D/\sigma$ | Down 25% or More $D/\sigma$ | All Changes $D/\sigma$ |
| Nonmetropolitan area | 0–499 | 0 | −0.022 | −0.157 | −0.164 | −0.194[a] | 0.058[a] | −0.123 |
| | | 1–199 | 0.138 | 0.028 | 0.018 | −0.106 | −0.035 | 0.032 |
| | | 200 or more | 0.532 | 0.397 | 0.327 | 0.655[a] | −0.284 | 0.415 |
| | 500 or more | 0 | 0.314[a] | 0.002 | 0.258 | −0.161 | −0.332[a] | 0.115 |
| | | 1–199 | 0.159 | 0.121 | −0.083 | −0.020 | −0.305 | 0.028 |
| | | 200 or more | 0.262 | 0.096 | 0.114 | 0.039[a] | −0.572[a] | 0.096 |
| Metropolitan area | 0–499 | 0 | 0.009[a] | −0.252[a] | −0.111[a] | −0.343[a] | −0.901[a] | −0.191 |
| | | 1–199 | 0.094 | −0.030 | −0.106 | −0.255[a] | −0.024[a] | −0.049 |
| | | 200 or more | 0.235[a] | −0.101 | 0.105 | 0.252[a] | 0.139[a] | 0.048 |
| | 500 or more | 0 | −0.090[a] | −0.102[a] | −0.252[a] | −0.171[a] | −0.904[b] | −0.218 |
| | | 1–199 | 0.114 | −0.147 | −0.067 | −0.158 | −0.218[a] | −0.079 |
| | | 200 or more | 0.208 | −0.009 | −0.150 | 0.070[a] | 0.025 | 0.000 |

[a] 10 to 49 cases.    [b] Fewer than 10 cases.

contractual saving and total saving exists for all income-change, place, and asset groups except the high-asset, nonmetropolitan groups, where some people with no contractual commitments saved a good deal. This may be related to the known fact that there is far less life insurance carried by people who live outside the cities.[16]

*Some tabulations made for unhomogenized residuals only.* Some tabulations were made only for the dollar residuals. They are subject to possible distortion owing to the predominant effect of the high-income, high-asset spending units, but they are interesting in themselves and to some extent supplement the other material already

TABLE 25

SAVING RESIDUALS BY HOME OWNERSHIP, ASSETS,
AND INCOME CHANGE (DOLLARS)

| | | INCOME CHANGE | | | | |
|---|---|---|---|---|---|---|
| OWN HOME? | LIQUID ASSETS | *Up 25% or More* | *Up 5 to 24%* | −4 to +4% | *Down 5 to 24%* | *Down 25% or More* |
| No | 0 | 35 | 7 | −3 | −19 | 56 |
| No | 1–499 | 58 | 18 | −16 | −112 | −105[a] |
| No | 500 or more | 190 | 8 | −64 | −14 | −289 |
| Yes | 0–199 | 80 | 2 | −81 | 142 | −51[a] |
| Yes | 200–2,999 | 245 | −68 | −59 | −17 | 167[a] |
| Yes | 3,000 or more (1947) | 522 | 223 | −296 | −387 | −286 |
| Yes | 3,000 or more (1948) | 197 | 17 | 101 | −113 | −1,196[a] |

[a] 10–49 cases.

presented. In two cases they are supplemented by the computation of saving–income regressions.

Table 25 indicates not only the previously stated result that the effect of income change depends on assets, but also shows that home owners are less responsive to income changes at each asset level than non-owners, presumably because they have more contractual commitments.

It is often stated as a hypothesis that saving behavior will depend on the economic status and consumption patterns of those living near

[16] For an interesting analysis of the influence of contractual commitments, see Chapter II, pp. 72–73.

the spending unit, or those with whom the spending unit associates, or those who constitute the "reference group" of the spending unit. It is difficult to make such a hypothesis operational, because it is difficult to specify the group and the type of standards involved. One possibility existed with our data, however. We had available for the Census "block cities," cities of 50,000 and over, information on the rent level of the block, and an interviewers' rating, made previous to the interview, of the rent level of the dwelling.

Table 26 gives the results of the analysis by rent level of the block. There is clearly no relation to saving behavior as we define it. Neither the pattern of regressions nor the average residual from the seven regressions shows any relation. Table 27 gives equally negative results for rent level of the dwelling. If there is a reference group, it is apparently either not defined in terms of immediate neighborhood, or else the effect is not a simple one on saving but something far more complicated.

*Results of using variance analysis.* We have made some variance analyses on the original dollar-saving figures as well as on the dollar residuals from the regression lines and on the homogenized residuals. The first two types are of course illegitimate uses of variance analysis, since one of the basic assumptions of the statistical method is homogeneity of variances, and even the use of cell means instead of individual items does not remove the extreme heterogeneity. However, there are some reasons for presenting these results even though the *F*-test is deceptive: The homogenizing process involves weighting down the importance of the high-income, high-asset spending units, who tend to dominate aggregate saving. For statistical reasons we reshape the data (by homogenizing them) in such a way that they are more revealing of human behavior but perhaps less informative about the influences which tend to affect aggregate saving. If some variable is important only to upper income groups, and hence affects aggregate saving, then a method which homogenizes the data to make them fit the assumptions of the analytical methods may also make this variable look unimportant.

In order to save space, we shall give the results of the variance analyses of dollar saving and dollar residuals in terms only of the categories used and factors which appeared significant.

Using dollar saving, we ran a variance analysis with six income groups, five income-change categories, two home-ownership groups, and two years (1947 and 1948). This gave a basic table with 120 cells. If we treat the complex interaction variance between income, income change, home ownership and year as error, income and income change appear highly significant with $F$-ratios of 30.2 and 7.9. If we treat the two years as "replications" of an experiment, the error variance is reduced enough to make home ownership look significant at the 5-percent probability level and the income–home-ownership interaction nearly significant.

Using dollar residuals from the seven regression lines, we still do not have valid tests of significance because of the heterogeneity of variances, though the particular brackets used and the fact that the sample is "loaded" with more of the variable high-income people helps somewhat. The fact that we have "removed" most of the effect of income, assets, home ownership, and their interactions with one another means that we can include more other variables in the analysis. However, since there may still be important interactions between liquid assets and other variables, such as income change, we continue to use a rough liquid-asset grouping in some of the analysis.

One analysis of dollar residuals was confined to home owners with liquid assets of $200 to $2,999. Using three "expected-income" groups, four income-change groups, and two years, we found a significant $F$-ratio of 7.3 for expected income, and a highly significant ratio of 24.7 for income change. If year is treated as replication, we even find what appears to be a significant interaction effect between income change and expected income ($F$-ratio 3.6). However, examination of the tables shows that only two or three cells of the thirty in the basic table account for the result, two of these being cells for very large income increases with the expectation of a subsequent decrease. Particularly since the homogenized data do not

# TABLE 26

INCOME–SAVING REGRESSIONS BY YEAR, HOME OWNERSHIP, LIQUID ASSETS, AND RENT LEVEL OF BLOCK[a]

| Liquid Assets (dollars) | Rent Level of Block | Number of Interviews | $r^2$ | Regression Coefficient $b$ | Regression Saving at $3,000 Income (dollars) | Standard Error of $b$ | Standard Error of Mean Saving (dollars) |
|---|---|---|---|---|---|---|---|
| Home owners | | | | | | | |
| 1947–48 | | | | | | | |
| 0–199 | Low | 78 | 0.25 | 0.21 | 523 | 0.04 | 58 |
|  | Medium | 111 | 0.33 | 0.24 | 574 | 0.03 | 59 |
|  | High | 33 | 0.22 | 0.17 | 476 | 0.06 | 83 |
| 200–2,999 | Low | 106 | 0.40 | 0.37 | 507 | 0.04 | 92 |
|  | Medium | 207 | 0.31 | 0.35 | 489 | 0.04 | 66 |
|  | High | 148 | 0.48 | 0.33 | 495 | 0.09 | 100 |
| 1947 | | | | | | | |
| 3,000 or more | Low | 14 | 0.48 | 0.47 | 622 | 0.14 | 294 |
|  | Medium | 48 | 0.51 | 0.32 | 619 | 0.07 | 231 |
|  | High | 60 | 0.54 | 0.45 | 568 | 0.05 | 401 |
| 1948 | | | | | | | |
| 3,000 or more | Low | 18 | 0.03[b] | 0.15 | 303 | 0.28 | 267 |
|  | Medium | 44 | 0.15 | 0.20 | 436 | 0.08 | 173 |
|  | High | 47 | 0.50 | 0.24 | 668 | 0.11 | 250 |

Non-home-owners

| 1947–48 | | | | | | | |
|---|---|---|---|---|---|---|---|
| None | Low | 219 | 0.14 | 0.07 | 191 | 0.01 | 15 |
| | Medium | 113 | 0.14 | 0.11 | 287 | 0.03 | 33 |
| | High | 46 | 0.33 | 0.18 | 328 | 0.04 | 50 |
| 1–499 | Low | 171 | 0.17 | 0.20 | 313 | 0.03 | 37 |
| | Medium | 191 | 0.28 | 0.29 | 421 | 0.03 | 86 |
| | High | 76 | 0.21 | 0.17 | 395 | 0.04 | 54 |
| 500 or more | Low | 217 | 0.15 | 0.19 | 356 | 0.03 | 57 |
| | Medium | 345 | 0.54 | 0.42 | 198 | 0.02 | 67 |
| | High | 219 | 0.38 | 0.27 | 374 | 0.02 | 97 |

ALL SEVEN REGRESSION GROUPS

| Rent Level of Block | $D$ (dollars) |
|---|---|
| Low | −14 |
| Medium | −16 |
| High | +14 |

[a] Cities over 50,000 and the 12 large metropolitan areas only.　　[b] Not significant. All other correlations are significant.

## TABLE 27

### INCOME-SAVING REGRESSIONS BY HOME OWNERSHIP, ASSET LEVEL, AND RENT LEVEL OF DWELLING

| LIQUID ASSETS AT BEGINNING OF YEAR (DOLLARS) | HOME OWNERS | | | NON-HOME-OWNERS | | |
|---|---|---|---|---|---|---|
| | High-Rent Dwelling | Medium and Not Specified | Low-Rent Dwelling | High-Rent Dwelling | Medium and Not Specified | Low-Rent Dwelling |
| **SAVING AT INCOME OF $3,000, FROM REGRESSION LINES (DOLLARS)** | | | | | | |
| 0 | | 601 | 542 | 363[a] | 282 | 244 |
| 1–499 | 560[a] | 532 | 625 | 174[a] | 399 | 339 |
| 500–1,999 | 483 | 506 | 498 | 290 | 315 | 300 |
| 2,000–4,999 | 556 | 432 | 495 | 331 | 313 | 392 |
| 5,000 or more | 646 | 621 | 420 | 246 | 426 | 807[a] |
| **SLOPE OF REGRESSION LINES** | | | | | | |
| 0 | | 0.27 | 0.20 | 0.25[a] | 0.11 | 0.09 |
| 1–499 | 0.14[a] | 0.34 | 0.31 | 0.10[a] | 0.21 | 0.19 |
| 500–1,999 | 0.28 | 0.31 | 0.30 | 0.33 | 0.27 | 0.26 |
| 2,000–4,999 | 0.41 | 0.32 | 0.34 | 0.35 | 0.35 | 0.32 |
| 5,000 or more | 0.34 | 0.37 | 0.45 | 0.27 | 0.44 | 0.08[a] |
| **NUMBER OF INTERVIEWS** | | | | | | |
| 0 | 2 | 153 | 204 | 15 | 333 | 486 |
| 1–499 | 18 | 309 | 210 | 32 | 427 | 338 |
| 500–1,999 | 57 | 377 | 152 | 61 | 437 | 230 |
| 2,000–4,999 | 39 | 241 | 75 | 32 | 207 | 93 |
| 5,000 or more | 68 | 149 | 40 | 33 | 80 | 32 |

[a] Correlation is not significant.

show any significant expected income or expected-income–income-change effects, this would indicate that the effect is concentrated among a few rich or high-income spending units with substantial changes in income.

A second analysis of these residuals used two age groups, metropolitan and nonmetropolitan locations, four income-change groups (combining small and large decreases), and four expected-income groups (with a separate group for those who are uncertain), but it combined the two years. Using the interaction between age, place, income change and expected income as "error," income change again appeared highly significant (15.3) and place of residence appeared significant (8.9). In addition, two interaction terms appeared significant at the 5-percent level: age with expected income, and age with expected income with place of residence ($F$-ratios 6.3 and 6.1 for three and nine degrees of freedom). Expected income is not significant, perhaps because of the inclusion of many people with little or no liquid assets. Examination of the tables which produced the significant interactions indicates that the effect of expected declines in income was pronounced only for people over 44 years old and outside the metropolitan areas.

Finally, as a partial solution to the problem of heterogeneous variances, one variance analysis was run using as the variable the proportion of each group which saved more than the expected (regression) value, i.e., had a positive residual. The analysis used two age groups, two place categories, four income-change groups, and four expected-income groups. Only "place" appeared significant, and only at the 5-percent level ($F$-ratio of 5.9). Income change was not significant, indicating, we feel, that it is the drastic effect of income changes on a few people which tends to dominate averages, rather than the behavior of the majority.

We also used the homogenized residuals for a series of variance analyses. The results are given in Tables 28–32. In general, place (city size), income change, number in the unit, and contractual saving were significant; expected income, assets, and age were not.

Where effects were significant, we have generally tried to present in the tables not only the $F$-ratios but also the averages, in order to indicate the linearity and direction of the effects. It is necessary to remember that these are averages of mean residuals, for subgroups matched on all the other variables in the analysis. They are thus less representative of the population, but they are the numbers upon which the variance analysis is based.

TABLE 28

VARIANCE ANALYSIS OF $D/\sigma$[a]

| | Degrees of Freedom | Mean Square | F-ratio Using Error |
|---|---|---|---|
| P = Place | 1 | 1.71 | 17.1[b] |
| L = Liquid assets | 1 | 0.01 | |
| C = Contractual saving | 2 | 1.96 | 19.6[b] |
| E = Expected income | 3 | 0.07 | |
| I = Income change | 4 | 1.12 | 11.2[b] |
| P × L | 1 | 0.15 | |
| P × C | 2 | 0.22 | 2.2 |
| P × E | 3 | 0.12 | |
| P × I | 4 | 0.01 | |
| L × C | 2 | 0.80 | 8.0[b] |
| L × E | 3 | 0.30 | 3.0 |
| L × I | 4 | 0.08 | |
| C × E | 6 | 0.12 | |
| C × I | 8 | 0.15 | |
| E × I | 12 | 0.15 | |
| P × L × C | 2 | 0.02 | |
| P × L × E | 3 | 0.08 | |
| P × L × I | 4 | 0.22 | |
| P × C × E | 6 | 0.37 | 3.7[b] |
| P × C × I | 8 | 0.40 | 4.0[b] |
| P × E × I | 12 | 0.12 | |
| L × C × E | 6 | 0.46 | 4.6[b] |
| L × C × I | 8 | 0.04 | |
| L × E × I | 12 | 0.10 | |
| C × E × I | 24 | 0.19 | 1.9 |
| P × L × C × E | 6 | 0.11 | |
| P × L × C × I | 8 | 0.26 | 2.6[c] |
| P × C × E × I | 24 | 0.24 | |
| P × L × E × I | 12 | 0.16 | |
| L × C × E × I | 24 | 0.11 | |
| P × L × C × E × I = Error | 24 | 0.10 | |

[a] 1947–1948.     [b] Significant at 1-percent level.     [c] Significant at 5-percent level.

# TABLE 29

## AVERAGES OF AVERAGES OF $D/\sigma$[a]

### MAIN EFFECTS

| | *Averages of Averages of $D/\sigma$* |
|---|---|
| *Place* | |
| Metropolitan area | −0.14 |
| Nonmetropolitan area | 0.03 |
| *Contractual Saving* | |
| None | −0.22 |
| $1–199 | −0.03 |
| $200 or more | 0.10 |
| *Income Change* | |
| +25% or more | 0.11 |
| +5 to +24% | −0.02 |
| −4% to +4% | −0.02 |
| −5% to −24% | −0.03 |
| −25% or more | −0.30 |

### INTERACTIONS

#### LIQUID ASSETS[b]

| CONTRACTUAL SAVING (DOLLARS) | *Less Than $500* | *$500 or More* |
|---|---|---|
| None | −0.32 | −0.12 |
| 1–199 | −0.02 | −0.05 |
| 200 or more | 0.20 | 0.00 |

#### EXPECTED INCOME—METROPOLITAN AREA

| | *Up* | *Same* | *Down* | *Don't Know* |
|---|---|---|---|---|
| None | −0.33 | −0.42 | −0.10 | −0.56 |
| 1–199 | −0.09 | 0.02 | −0.10 | −0.12 |
| 200 or more | 0.02 | 0.27 | −0.30 | 0.09 |

#### EXPECTED INCOME—NONMETROPOLITAN AREA

| | *Up* | *Same* | *Down* | *Don't Know* |
|---|---|---|---|---|
| None | −0.11 | 0.02 | −0.21 | 0.00 |
| 1–199 | 0.00 | −0.03 | −0.01 | 0.05 |
| 200 or more | 0.26 | 0.07 | 0.16 | 0.20 |

## TABLE 29 (Continued)
### AVERAGES OF AVERAGES OF $D/\sigma^a$

| CONTRACTUAL SAVING (DOLLARS) | INCOME CHANGE—METROPOLITAN AREA | | | | | INCOME CHANGE—NONMETROPOLITAN AREA | | | | |
|---|---|---|---|---|---|---|---|---|---|---|
| | +25% or More | +5% to +24% | -4% to +4% | -5% to -24% | -25% or More | +25% or More | +5% to +24% | -4% to +4% | -5% to -24% | -25% or More |
| None | -0.05 | -0.21 | -0.20 | -0.26 | -1.05 | 0.02 | -0.10 | -0.07 | -0.07 | -0.16 |
| 1–199 | 0.04 | -0.10 | -0.07 | -0.18 | -0.06 | 0.16 | 0.09 | -0.01 | -0.07 | -0.18 |
| 200 or more | 0.13 | -0.07 | 0.00 | 0.08 | -0.03 | 0.39 | 0.26 | 0.22 | 0.32 | -0.34 |

| INCOME CHANGE | EXPECTED INCOME—LESS THAN $500 IN LIQUID ASSETS | | | | EXPECTED INCOME—$500 OR MORE IN LIQUID ASSETS | | | |
|---|---|---|---|---|---|---|---|---|
| | Up | Same | Down | Don't Know | Up | Same | Down | Don't Know |
| +25% or more | 0.22 | 0.14 | -0.05 | 0.03 | 0.22 | 0.09 | 0.10 | 0.16 |
| +5% to +24% | 0.02 | -0.05 | -0.23 | 0.03 | -0.15 | -0.01 | 0.10 | 0.13 |
| -4% to +4% | 0.11 | 0.03 | -0.28 | 0.16 | -0.10 | 0.03 | 0.02 | -0.10 |
| -5% to -24% | -0.07 | 0.02 | -0.18 | 0.15 | -0.10 | -0.04 | -0.01 | 0.00 |
| -25% or more | -0.02 | -0.16 | -0.11 | -0.67 | -0.55 | -0.18 | -0.28 | -0.46 |

a Supplement to Table 28.
b Contractual saving has its greatest effect on low asset people.

Tables 28–29, based on a five-way variance analysis, indicate important relations between place, change in income, and contractual saving on the one hand, and the homogenized residuals on the other. They also indicate some significant interaction effects, most important of which is one between assets and contractual saving, indicat-

TABLE 30

VARIANCE ANALYSIS OF $D/\sigma$ [a]

| | Degrees of Freedom | Mean Square or Variance | F-ratio |
|---|---|---|---|
| P = Place | 1 | 1.45 | 14.5[b] |
| I = Income change | 3 | 0.54 | 5.4[b] |
| E = Expected income | 3 | 0.02 | |
| N = Number in the unit | 5 | 0.31 | 3.1[c] |
| | | | |
| P × I | 3 | 0.02 | |
| P × E | 3 | 0.00 | |
| P × N | 5 | 0.22 | |
| I × E | 9 | 0.08 | |
| I × N | 15 | 0.09 | |
| E × N | 15 | 0.07 | |
| | | | |
| P × I × E | 9 | 0.08 | |
| P × I × N | 15 | 0.07 | |
| P × E × N | 15 | 0.11 | |
| I × E × N | 45 | 0.12 | |
| | | | |
| P × I × E × N = Error | 45 | 0.10 | |

| Number in Unit | Means of Means of 32 Matched Subcells |
|---|---|
| 1 | 0.12 |
| 2 | −0.02 |
| 3 | −0.03 |
| 4 | −0.01 |
| 5 | −0.17 |
| 6 or more | −0.08 |

[a] 1947–1948.    [b] Significant at 1-percent level.    [c] Significant at 5-percent level.

ing that contractual saving commitments have their greatest effect on low-asset people. This has the obvious interpretation that these people, already constrained not to dissave by their low asset holdings, are also constrained to save by their contractual commitments. There are other interaction effects which are not easy to interpret even with the use of Table 29. The interaction between contractual saving and

## TABLE 31

### VARIANCE ANALYSIS OF $D/\sigma$[a]

|  | Degrees of Freedom | Mean Square or Variance | F-ratio |
|---|---|---|---|
| P = Place | 1 | 0.58 | 6.5[b] |
| A = Age | 5 | 0.17 | 1.9 |
| I = Income change | 3 | 0.36 | 4.0[b] |
| E = Expected income | 3 | 0.02 | |
| P × A | 5 | 0.04 | |
| P × I | 3 | 0.02 | |
| P × E | 3 | 0.01 | |
| A × I | 15 | 0.10 | |
| A × E | 15 | 0.09 | |
| I × E | 9 | 0.15 | |
| P × A × I | 15 | 0.12 | |
| P × A × E | 15 | 0.13 | |
| P × I × E | 9 | 0.05 | |
| A × I × E | 45 | 0.12 | |
| P × A × I × E | 45 | 0.09 | |

| AGE | AVERAGE OF AVERAGES FOR 32 MATCHED SUBGROUPS | STRAIGHT AVERAGE OF $D/\sigma$ | AVERAGE $D/\sigma$ Metropolitan Assets Less than 500 | Metropolitan Assets Over 500 | Nonmetropolitan Assets Less than 500 | Nonmetropolitan Assets Over 500 |
|---|---|---|---|---|---|---|
| Under 25 | 0.127 | 0.169 | 0.082 | 0.014 | 0.198 | 0.334 |
| 25 34 | 0.051 | 0.088 | 0.017 | 0.023 | 0.173 | 0.058 |
| 35–44 | −0.047 | −0.027 | −0.125 | −0.105 | 0.020 | −0.011 |
| 45–54 | −0.075 | −0.064 | −0.205 | −0.056 | −0.068 | −0.016 |
| 55–64 | −0.010 | −0.003 | −0.199 | −0.065 | −0.008 | 0.093 |
| 65 or over | 0.005 | 0.024 | 0.009 | −0.256 | 0.020 | 0.182 |

[a] 1947–1948.    [b] Significant at 5-percent level.

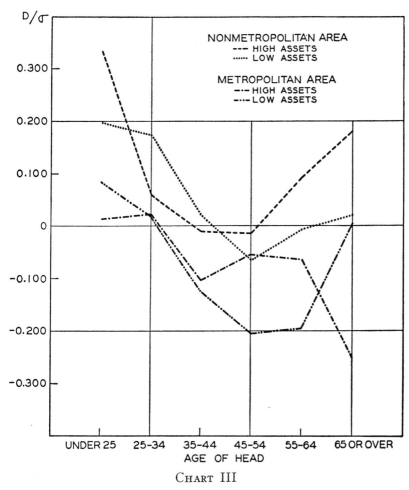

CHART III

*D/σ* by Age, Assets, and Place

expected income in their effects on saving seems to be stronger in the metropolitan areas. We must be careful in interpretations here, because contractual saving is part of total saving and hence is bound to be correlated with it, which means that it is also correlated indirectly with the relations of other variables to total saving.

If we combine the two asset groups, we lose information. The

TABLE 32

VARIANCE ANALYSIS OF $D/\sigma$

|  | Degrees of Freedom | Mean Square or Variance | F-ratio |
|---|---|---|---|
| P = Place (5 categories; see Table 11) | 4 | 1.12 | 4.0[a] |
| I = Income change (up versus same or down) | 1 | 1.54 | 5.5[b] |
| L = Liquid assets | 1 | 0.10 | 0.4 |
| D = Demographic structure | 6 | 1.41 | 5.0[a] |
| P × I | 4 | 0.13 | |
| P × L | 4 | 0.07 | |
| P × D | 24 | 0.13 | |
| I × L[c] | 1 | 0.02 | |
| I × D | 6 | 0.19 | |
| L × D | 6 | 1.42 | 5.1[a] |
| P × I × L | 4 | 0.62 | 2.2 |
| P × I × D | 24 | 0.26 | |
| P × L × D | 24 | 0.26 | |
| I × L × D | 6 | 0.62 | 2.2[b] |
| P × I × L × D | 24 | 0.34 | |
| Error (years treated as replications) | 140 | 0.28 | |

[a] Significant at 1-percent level.
[b] Significant at 5-percent level.
[c] Insufficiently fine groupings to show effect.

error variance becomes three and a half times as large because of the asset interactions embodied in it, and only the main effects of city size, income change, and contractual saving remain statistically significant.

Table 30 introduces the number of people in the spending unit as a new additional variable, and it turns out significant. One cell was empty and had to be assigned a value, hence the number of degrees of freedom for the error term should be one less. This would not alter any conclusions we might draw from the table. Somewhat surprisingly, expected income seems to have no relation to these residuals, even by way of an interaction with actual past income change.

In Table 31 we introduce age as a variable, and find no significant effect. However, the averages do seem to show a pattern, and a plotting of the straight average residuals indicates that perhaps there exists an interaction between age and assets (see Chart III).

Table 32 introduces the "demographic structure" (see p. 97 above), made up of a combination of age, number in the unit, and number of children, which attempts to put spending units into a rough "life cycle" ordering. The categories are these:

| Number in Unit | Age of Head | Number of Children (under 18) |
|---|---|---|
| 1 | Under 45 | None |
| 2 or more | Under 45 | None |
| 2 or more | Under 45 | 1–2 |
| 2 or more | Under 45 | 3 or more |
| 2 or more | 45 or over | 1 or more |
| 2 or more | 45 or over | None |
| 1 | 45 or over | None |

As a variable, it is clearly significant and even has significant interaction effects with assets and income-change-asset combinations. The direction and magnitude of these interaction effects can be appreciated by examining Table 33. The low-asset people show a wave-like pattern, saving more (larger positive residuals) as they go from the first stage to the second and third, then less for two stages, then slightly more for the last two; whereas the high asset spending units show a U-shaped or even V-shaped pattern, with its bottom at the fourth stage. The difference between those whose income had gone up and those whose income had stayed the same or gone down seems to have been systematic in the early stages of the life cycle for low-asset people and in the later stages for high-asset people: those whose income had increased saved more. The same pattern is evident if we use unhomogenized residuals; hence, it is not a result of the homogenizing procedure. On the other hand, the income-change-asset inter-

TABLE 33

AVERAGES OF AVERAGES OF $D/\sigma$ FOR NEWLY SIGNIFICANT EFFECTS OF TABLE 32

DEMOGRAPHIC STRUCTURE

|  | UNDER 45 YEARS OLD | | | | 45 YEARS OR OVER | | |
|---|---|---|---|---|---|---|---|
|  | 1 Adult in Unit, No Children | 2 or More Adults in Unit, No Children | 2 or More Adults in Unit, 1–2 Children | 2 or More Adults in Unit, 3 or More Children | 2 or More Adults in Unit, 1 or More Children | 2 or More Adults in Unit, No Children | 1 Adult in Unit, No Children |
| Averages of averages over place, year, income change, and assets | 0.240 | 0.090 | 0.053 | −0.155 | −0.060 | −0.040 | 0.156 |
| Averages of averages over place, year, and income change groups |  |  |  |  |  |  |  |
| Liquid assets less than $500 | 0.019 | 0.134 | 0.174 | −0.022 | −0.071 | −0.079 | −0.015 |
| Liquid assets $500 or more | 0.436 | 0.046 | −0.068 | −0.289 | −0.050 | −0.002 | 0.328 |
| Averages of place and year groups Liquid assets less than $500 |  |  |  |  |  |  |  |
| Income up | 0.250 | 0.402 | 0.180 | 0.084 | −0.020 | −0.112 | −0.084 |
| Income same or down | −0.111 | −0.135 | 0.166 | −0.127 | −0.122 | −0.046 | 0.051 |
| Liquid assets $500 or more |  |  |  |  |  |  |  |
| Income up | 0.498 | 0.008 | 0.072 | −0.233 | 0.017 | 0.015 | 0.502 |
| Income same or down | 0.374 | 0.083 | −0.207 | −0.344 | −0.116 | −0.019 | 0.154 |

action is not significant here, presumably because we used only two income-change groups and only two asset groups. Furthermore, as we shall see below, with a different type of residual and with more detailed asset and income-change groups, none of the interactions with demographic structure are significant.

Ordinarily in variance analysis, finer groupings are assumed to lead to smaller error variance. However, where averages are used as the basic items, finer groupings mean that the primary cells of the basic table are smaller and that their means have a greater variance. Consequently, there are limits to the effectiveness of finer classifications of factors.

*Reconsideration of the method of obtaining residuals.* The fact that income change and assets did not have a significant interaction in the variance analysis raised once more the question whether, by using income–saving regressions for groups including all income changes, we removed some of the income-change effect along with the income effect. There is, in any one year, a positive correlation between income and past change in income, those with high incomes containing a larger proportion of people who have had increases, and vice versa. Our original plottings of mean saving within income brackets, by income-change groups, seemed to show little difference in slope over the central region (Chart IV). We had also computed separate regression coefficients for each income-change group for each of the seven asset–home-ownership groups. The results are given in Table 34. There seemed to be some differences, but when we weighted the regression coefficients and averaged them, they came out very close to the regression coefficients for the pooled data as given in Table 35.

However, an examination of Table 34 shows that the low regression coefficients were generally for the groups with little income change—indicating perhaps an average "propensity to save" lower than the marginal one. Therefore, use of these pooled regressions could give us a saving function which was partly an average and partly marginal—taking out some of the income-change effect. We

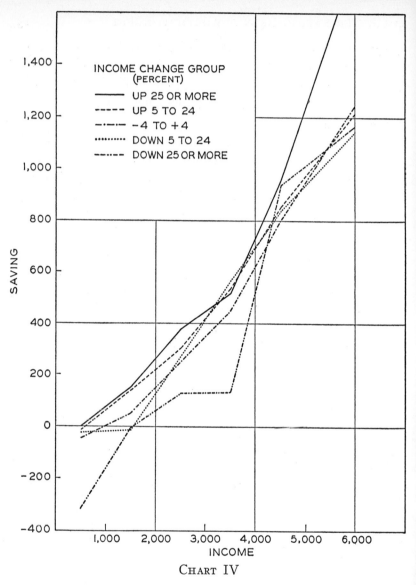

CHART IV

Saving by Income by Income-Change Groups

MEAN SAVING FOR 1948 FOR THE INCOME GROUP $7,500–9,999

| Income Change | Saving | Income Change | Saving |
|---|---|---|---|
| Up 25% or more | $4,610 | Down 5% to 24% | $3,249 |
| Up 5% to 24% | 3,477 | Down 25% or more | 2,465 |
| —4% to +4% | 3,027 | | (2 cases) |

TABLE 34

INCOME-SAVING REGRESSIONS BY YEAR, HOME-OWNERSHIP,
ASSET LEVEL, AND INCOME CHANGE[a]

| | Liquid Assets (dollars) | Income Change (percent of previous year) | Number of Cases N | Square of Correlation Coefficient $r^2$ | Slope of Regression Line b | Regression Saving at $3,000 Income (dollars) |
|---|---|---|---|---|---|---|
| Non-home-owners | | | | | | |
| 1947–1948 | None | 125 or more | 178 | 0.23 | 0.14 | 340 |
| | | 105–124 | 237 | 0.17 | 0.10 | 269 |
| | | 96–104 | 247 | 0.13 | 0.09 | 216 |
| | | 76–95 | 81 | 0.17 | 0.08 | 227 |
| | | 0–75 | 57 | 0.29 | 0.22 | 504 |
| | 1–499 | 125 or more | 194 | 0.21 | 0.24 | 470 |
| | | 105–124 | 287 | 0.19 | 0.19 | 378 |
| | | 96–104 | 177 | 0.26 | 0.17 | 338 |
| | | 76–95 | 78 | 0.14 | 0.19 | 247 |
| | | 0–75 | 43 | 0.12[b] | 0.17 | 245 |
| | 500 or more | 125 or more | 233 | 0.55 | 0.43 | 444 |
| | | 105–124 | 443 | 0.35 | 0.29 | 364 |
| | | 96–104 | 300 | 0.18 | 0.20 | 292 |
| | | 76–95 | 134 | 0.37 | 0.25 | 370 |
| | | 0–75 | 78 | 0.21 | 0.28 | 33 |
| Home owners | | | | | | |
| 1947–48 | 0–199 | 125 or more | 105 | 0.29 | 0.27 | 649 |
| | | 105–124 | 200 | 0.31 | 0.25 | 567 |
| | | 96–104 | 183 | 0.23 | 0.16 | 402 |
| | | 76–95 | 70 | 0.42 | 0.30 | 760 |
| | | 0–75 | 35 | 0.17[b] | 0.18 | 425 |
| | 200–2,999 | 125 or more | 148 | 0.61 | 0.46 | 591 |
| | | 105–124 | 406 | 0.30 | 0.26 | 486 |
| | | 96–104 | 311 | 0.24 | 0.21 | 466 |
| | | 76–95 | 109 | 0.31 | 0.29 | 506 |
| | | 0–75 | 42 | 0.58 | 0.58 | 856 |
| 1947 | 3,000 or more | 125 or more | 35 | 0.67 | 0.42 | 1065 |
| | | 105–124 | 76 | 0.66 | 0.50 | 507 |
| | | 96–104 | 78 | 0.64 | 0.34 | 399 |
| | | 76–95 | 23 | 0.37 | 0.24 | 601 |
| | | 0–75 | 16 | 0.26[b] | 0.38 | 281 |
| 1948 | 3,000 or more | 125 or more | 34 | 0.50 | 0.32 | 588 |
| | | 105–124 | 62 | 0.16 | 0.17 | 730 |
| | | 96–104 | 65 | 0.44 | 0.25 | 660 |
| | | 76–95 | 28 | 0.50 | 0.39 | 215 |
| | | 0–75 | 14 | 0.17[c] | 0.20 | −738 |

[a] $S = a + b(I)$.
[b] Correlation significant only at 5-percent level.
[c] Not a significant correlation.

TABLE 35

REGRESSION COEFFICIENTS FROM POOLED DATA VERSUS AVERAGE
OF INDIVIDUAL REGRESSION COEFFICIENTS

|  | Liquid Assets (dollars) | Weighted Average of b for 6 Groups (5 income-change groups and the NA's)[a] | Regression Coefficient (b) from Pooled Data |
|---|---|---|---|
| Non-home owners | None | 0.11 | 0.11 |
|  | 1–499 | 0.20 | 0.20 |
|  | 500 or more | 0.29 | 0.31 |
| Home owners | 0–199 | 0.23 | 0.24 |
|  | 200–2,999 | 0.29 | 0.31 |
| 1947 | 3,000 or more | 0.40 | 0.41 |
| 1948 | 3,000 or more | 0.26 | 0.29 |

[a] Not ascertained cases.

therefore decided to repeat the calculation of residuals, this time using a more restricted set of groups to estimate the basic income–saving regressions. The results of this new analysis are reported in the next chapter.

# IV: ANALYSIS OF RESIDUALS FROM "NORMAL" REGRESSIONS

## by James N. Morgan

### COMPUTATION OF A NEW SET OF RESIDUALS

*Selection of groups for "normal" regressions.* In choosing groups for a new set of saving–income regressions, we decided to do more than eliminate the spending units with income changes. What we wanted was groups of people in reasonably "normal" circumstances, and groups small enough to be quite homogeneous. We included a third year, 1949, in this analysis, and this allowed us to use more groups.

From the groups used in computing these regressions, the following were excluded: those with decreases in income of more than 4 percent, those with increases in income of more than 24 percent, the unemployed, the retired, those where the head of the spending unit was 65 years old or more, and those who had received large gifts or inheritances ($500 or more). We also made a more detailed distinction between housing status groups, dividing them into home owners with mortgages, home owners without mortgages, renters, and those who neither owned nor rented. We classified the home owners into those with and those without mortgage payments because the degree of hidden capital consumption is different for those with mortgage payments, and perhaps also the motivation to save is greater. We divided the non-owners into renters and nonrenters because the latter generally receive income in kind, being largely related secondary spending units, household servants who live in the house and receive free room and board, and older people who might be considered dependents except for the fact that they have some income and keep their expenses separate.

We then found ourselves with sixteen groups—four asset groups times four home-ownership groups—for which we wanted saving–income regressions. Before doing this, we computed mean saving within income brackets for each group for each of the three years 1947, 1948, 1949, and also computed the regressions for each year separately. As far as we could tell from these, there were no systematic differences between the years, except perhaps a slight tendency for 1949 saving to be a little lower generally. Of course, the number of cases also became rather small, so that the regression coefficients were somewhat erratic. Even lumping the three years gave somewhat smaller frequencies because of the exclusions and because of the use of sixteen regression groups instead of seven. Table 1 gives the regression coefficients, the number of cases, and the number of excluded cases for which that same regression was used in later computation of residuals. Table 2 gives similar data for the excluded groups. These data are of interest in themselves, even though they are only one step in the analysis. The regression lines are consistently steeper for the higher asset groups, and for the home owners, particularly those with mortgages. The most unusual thing about Table 1 is the very steep line for people with a home and a mortgage but no liquid assets. The slopes are not very different when we compare renters with those who neither own nor rent, but the level is generally higher for the latter, presumably representing gifts, income in kind, and perhaps also the youth of these people.

*Excluded groups.* As for the excluded groups, aside from the low saving of the receivers of large gifts or inheritances, the most striking thing is the different saving–income slopes within income-change groups according to the level of liquid asset holdings. In both tables, levels of liquid assets have very little relation to levels of saving, as can be seen most clearly by computing the regression values for some reasonable income figure, say $3,000, as in Table 1. But liquid assets have a powerful and consistent relation to the slope of the line,

## Table 1

### Saving–Income Regressions for "Normal" Groups—1947, 1948, and 1949 Combined[a]

| Housing Status | Liquid Assets (dollars) | Number Excluded | Number Included | $b$ | $S_b$ | $a$ (dollars) | $r^2$ | $S_s$ (dollars) | $S_e$ (dollars) |
|---|---|---|---|---|---|---|---|---|---|
| Rent | None | 427 | 396 | 0.1090 | 0.013 | −64 | 0.16 | 292 | 268 |
| | 1–499 | 315 | 389 | 0.1851 | 0.018 | −234 | 0.21 | 460 | 409 |
| | 500–1,999 | 314 | 363 | 0.1995 | 0.023 | −333 | 0.18 | 686 | 623 |
| | 2,000 or more | 230 | 281 | 0.3310 | 0.025 | −655 | 0.39 | 1,289 | 1,012 |
| Neither own nor rent | None | 293 | 167 | 0.1128 | 0.026 | −47 | 0.10 | 315 | 301 |
| | 1–499 | 209 | 207 | 0.2286 | 0.027 | −216 | 0.26 | 442 | 382 |
| | 500–1,999 | 145 | 170 | 0.1927 | 0.049 | −180 | 0.08 | 562 | 539 |
| | 2,000 or more | 80 | 93 | 0.3343 | 0.071 | −394 | 0.20 | 966 | 870 |
| Home with mortgage | None | 110 | 131 | 0.2530 | 0.035 | −125 | 0.29 | 566 | 471 |
| | 1–499 | 195 | 250 | 0.1899 | 0.031 | −1 | 0.13 | 670 | 626 |
| | 500–1,999 | 159 | 257 | 0.2853 | 0.024 | −323 | 0.35 | 1,027 | 829 |
| | 2,000 or more | 90 | 163 | 0.3832 | 0.038 | −679 | 0.39 | 2,002 | 1,569 |
| Home without mortgage | None | 175 | 119 | 0.1415 | 0.030 | −54 | 0.16 | 440 | 404 |
| | 1–499 | 169 | 153 | 0.1870 | 0.032 | −129 | 0.18 | 517 | 468 |
| | 500–1,999 | 182 | 214 | 0.2596 | 0.023 | −349 | 0.38 | 797 | 627 |
| | 2,000 or more | 332 | 276 | 0.3416 | 0.019 | −497 | 0.55 | 1,518 | 1,018 |
| | | 3425 | 3629 | | | | | | |

[a] $S = a + b\,(I)$.
$S_s$ = Estimate of standard deviation of saving.
$S_e$ = Estimate of standard deviation of residuals.
$S_b$ = Standard error of b.
$b$ = Slope of regression line.
$r^2$ = Square of correlation coefficient.

| Reasons for Exclusion | Number of Cases |
|---|---|
| Over 65 years old | 758 |
| Unemployed or retired | 375 |
| Gifts or inheritance | 92 |
| Large increase in income | 1,188 |
| Small (5%–24%) decrease in income | 706 |
| Large (25% or more) decrease in income | 306 |

All correlations are statistically significant.

## TABLE 2

### REGRESSION COEFFICIENTS FOR GROUPS EXCLUDED IN COMPUTING NORMAL REGRESSION

| | b | a (dollars) | Average Income I (dollars) | N |
|---|---|---|---|---|
| Over 65 years old | 0.25 | −270 | 2,508 | 292 |
| Large gifts | 0.33 | −779 | 4,268 | 95 |
| Retired, unemployed[a] | | | | |
| 1947 | 0.19 | −254 | 1,688 | 268 |
| 1948 | 0.11 | −138 | 1,776 | 231 |
| 1949 | 0.36 | −670 | 2,015 | 550 |
| Open country, nonfarm[b] | 0.27 | −205 | 2,142 | 541 |

| Housing Status | Assets (dollars) | Income Change | b | a (dollars) | Saving at $3,000 Regression (dollars) | N |
|---|---|---|---|---|---|---|
| Rents | 0–499 | +25% or more | 0.29 | −459 | 421 | 105 |
| | 500 or more | +25% or more | 0.42 | −941 | 313 | 94 |
| | 0–499 | −5% or more | 0.14 | −190 | 226 | 96 |
| | 500 or more | −5% or more | 0.26 | −611 | 156 | 81 |
| Neither owns nor rents | 0–499 | +25% or more | 0.20 | −129 | 478 | 49 |
| | 500 or more | +25% or more | 0.43 | −639 | 638 | 70 |
| | 0–499 | −5% or more | 0.23 | −220 | 459 | 68 |
| | 500 or more | −5% or more | 0.30 | −441 | 450 | 103 |
| Home with mortgage | 0–499 | +25% or more | 0.19 | −158 | 722 | 202 |
| | 500 or more | +25% or more | 0.49 | −1,005 | 456 | 165 |
| | 0–499 | −5% or more | 0.35 | −393 | 670 | 205 |
| | 500 or more | −5% or more | 0.61 | −1,594 | 237 | 181 |
| Home, no mortgage | 0–499 | +25% or more | 0.31 | −379 | 566 | 228 |
| | 500 or more | +25% or more | 0.31 | −322 | 614 | 89 |
| | 0–499 | −5% or more | 0.19 | −118 | 466 | 84 |
| | 500 or more | −5% or more | 0.30 | −436 | 478 | 49 |
| All home-ownership groups | 0–499 | +25% or more | 0.26 | 261 | 526 | 584 |
| | 500 or more | +25% or more | 0.40 | 700 | 501 | 429 |
| | 0–499 | −5% or more | 0.25 | 322 | 439 | 453 |
| | 500 or more | −5% or more | 0.33 | 650 | 326 | 414 |

[a] Includes also students, housewives, and, for 1949, protective service workers. These were put back into the deck of IBM cards before final "normal regressions were computed.

[b] Later put back for normal regressions.

indicating that perhaps they are related to saving in its dynamic aspects (marginal propensities) rather than to levels of saving under stable conditions.

*Computation of residuals.* The next step was to compute, and punch into the cards, the residuals from these regressions for each of the sixteen regression groups. This step is simple and rapid on IBM machinery, and it leaves us with a new dependent variable—residuals from the pattern of "normal" saving–income regressions or, in other words, residuals with the effects of income, home ownership, liquid asset holdings, and their interactions with one another (though not necessarily with other variables) "removed." For those not in "normal" circumstances, the expected saving for that income level of the most nearly similar "normal" group was used. We shall call these residuals $ND$.

*Transforming the residuals for homogeneity.* Again, however, the problem of heterogeneous variances of these residuals arose, and it was necessary to examine the pattern of variances of the residuals in order to develop a method for transforming them to approximate the homogeneity assumed in the analysis of variance. Table 3 presents standard deviations of these dollar residuals for subgroups according to income, liquid assets, and change in income. It is clear from this table that, again, income and assets account for most of the variability in the standard deviations. Income change had some effect, particularly for those whose income had changed by more than 25 percent, but it was not great. Furthermore, any attempt to use income change in transforming the residuals would make it impossible to analyze it later as an explanatory variable. The more variable people who had large income changes will also be large savers or dissavers, and if we attempted to reduce their residuals to make the variability of these groups comparable with the rest of the population, we would in the process reduce the size of these interesting residuals.

Taking income and asset groupings, then, and using the midpoints of the asset brackets, we can develop a relation between the variabil-

# TABLE 3

## STANDARD DEVIATIONS OF POOLED RESIDUALS FROM 16 REGRESSIONS BY INCOME, ASSETS, AND INCOME-CHANGE GROUPS

| INCOME (DOLLARS) | INCOME CHANGE | ASSETS (DOLLARS) | | | | | | | |
|---|---|---|---|---|---|---|---|---|---|
| | | 0 | 1–199 | 200–499 | 500–999 | 1,000–1,999 | 2,000–4,999 | 5,000–9,999 | 10,000 or More |
| 1–999 | +25% or more | 181 | 179 | 156 | 364 | 352[a] | 241[a] | | |
| | +5% to +24% | 76 | 107 | 206[a] | 171 | 477[a] | 1,026[a] | | |
| | −4% to +4% | 69 | 323 | 236 | 345 | 516 | 766 | | |
| | −5% to −24% | 209 | 134 | 157[a] | 469[a] | 518[a] | 455[a] | | |
| | −25% or more | 69 | 222 | 930[a] | 318 | 566 | 852 | 562 | 966[a] |
| | All groups | 124 | 228 | 370 | 347 | 562 | 754 | | |
| 1,000–1,999 | +25% or more | 211 | 306 | 290 | 349 | 499 | 421[a] | | |
| | +5% to +24% | 218 | 199 | 218 | 329 | 591 | 380 | | |
| | −4% to +4% | 295 | 189 | 233 | 369 | 443 | 471 | | |
| | −5% to −24% | 178 | 222 | 214 | 279 | 461 | 694 | | |
| | −25% or more | 331 | 1,276 | 255 | 362[a] | 800 | 633 | 516 | 1,064 |
| | All groups | 252 | 449 | 249 | 347 | 568 | 546 | | |
| 2,000–2,999 | +25% or more | 405 | 396 | 451 | 628 | 559 | 562 | | |
| | +5% to +24% | 297 | 379 | 394 | 492 | 544 | 623 | | |
| | −4% to +4% | 350 | 329 | 414 | 400 | 473 | 594 | | |
| | −5% to −24% | 383 | 436 | 600 | 549 | 458 | 519 | | |
| | −25% or more | 456 | 365 | 637 | 653[a] | 562 | 580[a] | 876 | 1,182 |
| | All groups | 356 | 379 | 466 | 513 | 511 | 591 | | |
| 3,000–3,999 | +25% or more | 439 | 613 | 505 | 580 | 730 | 847 | | |
| | +5% to +24% | 461 | 489 | 549 | 539 | 656 | 833 | | |
| | −4% to +4% | 369 | 619 | 555 | 535 | 686 | 906 | | |
| | −5% to −24% | 389 | 522 | 498 | 720 | 755 | 690 | | |
| | −25% or more | 572[a] | 990 | 640[a] | 951[a] | 648 | 1,188 | 1,259 | 1,073 |
| | All groups | 429 | 559 | 538 | 586 | 697 | 862 | | |

177 of 288

| Income (dollars) | Income change | | | | | | | | |
|---|---|---|---|---|---|---|---|---|---|
| 4,000–4,999 | +25% or more | 863 | 706 | 746 | 989 | 1,084 | 1,100 | | |
| | +5% to +24% | 602 | 699 | 625 | 668 | 721 | 916 | | |
| | −4% to +4% | 844 | 288 | 706 | 649 | 778 | 962 | | |
| | −5% to −24% | 584ª | 622 | 904 | 592 | 765 | 882ª | | |
| | −25% or more | 1,245ª | | 1,980ª | 1,094ª | | 682ª | | |
| | All groups | 726 | 663 | 739 | 744 | 807 | 964 | 1,041 | |
| 5,000–7,499 | +25% or more | 822 | 1,068 | 1,809 | 1,113 | 1,059 | 1,479 | | |
| | +5% to +24% | 503 | 737 | 1,155 | 977 | 1,072 | 961 | | |
| | −4% to +4% | 812 | 565ª | 553 | 947 | 908 | 1,359 | | |
| | −5% to −24% | 245 | | 837ª | 1,307ª | 1,140 | 1,131 | | |
| | −25% or more | | | | | 106ª | 1,311ª | | |
| | All groups | | | | | 1,036 | 1,154 | 1,007 | |
| 7,500 or more | All groups | 658 | 862 | 1,212 | 1,083 | | | 1,473 | 1,355 |
| All groups | All groups | 1,212ª | 2,012ª | 2,108 | 1,918 | 1,966 | 2,141 | 2,754 | |

STANDARD DEVIATIONS OF RESIDUALS FROM 16 REGRESSIONS BY INCOME, ASSETS, AND INCOME-CHANGE GROUPS—CONSOLIDATED INCOME GROUPS FOR HIGH ASSET GROUPS

| Income (dollars) | Income change | Liquid assets (dollars) | |
|---|---|---|---|
| | | 5,000–9,999 | 10,000 or More |
| 1–3,999 | +25% or more | 759 | 376ª |
| | +5% to +24% | 910 | 1,330 |
| | −4% to +4% | 786 | 862 |
| | −5% to −24% | 584 | 1,066 |
| | −25% or more | 1,660 | 1,542ª |

ª Based on fewer than 10 cases.

# TABLE 3 (*Continued*)

|  | LIQUID ASSETS (DOLLARS) | |
|---|---|---|
| INCOME CHANGE | 5,000–9,999 | 10,000 or More |
| +25% or more | 1,799 | 2,015 |
| +5% to +24% | 1,553 | 2,083 |
| −4% to +4% | 1,212 | 1,900 |
| −5% to −24% | 1,657 | 2,286 |
| −25% or more | 1,930[a] | 1,353[a] |

INCOME (DOLLARS) 4,000 or more

## STANDARD DEVIATIONS OF POOLED RESIDUALS FROM 16 REGRESSIONS BY INCOME AND ASSET GROUPS

| DISPOSABLE INCOME (DOLLARS) | 0 | 1–199 | 200–499 | 500–999 | 1,000–1,999 | 2,000–4,999 | 5,000–9,999 | 10,000 or More |
|---|---|---|---|---|---|---|---|---|
| | | | | | LIQUID ASSETS (DOLLARS) | | | |
| 1–999 | 124 | 228 | 370 | 347 | 562 | 754 | 562 | 966[a] |
| 1,000–1,999 | 252 | 449 | 249 | 347 | 568 | 546 | 516 | 1,064 |
| 2,000–2,999 | 356 | 379 | 466 | 513 | 511 | 591 | 876 | 1,182 |
| 3,000–3,999 | 429 | 559 | 538 | 586 | 697 | 862 | 1,259 | 1,073 |
| 4,000–4,999 | 726 | 663 | 739 | 744 | 807 | 964 | 1,007 | 1,041 |
| 5,000–7,499 | 658 | 862 | 1,212 | 1,083 | 1,036 | 1,154 | 1,473 | 1,355 |
| 7,500 or more | | 1,212[a] | 2,012[a] | 2,108 | 1,918 | 1,966 | 2,141 | 2,754 |

[a] Based on fewer than 10 cases.

ity of saving residuals within the group on the one hand and income
and assets on the other. Using the same combination we used before
—income plus assets up to $2,500—we find the following relation:

$$\sigma_{ND} = 0.20 + 0.16 \,(I + A \text{ up to } \$2,500)$$

where $\sigma_{ND}$ is the standard deviation of the residuals from the "normal" regressions, $I$ is income, and $A$ is liquid asset holdings.

The square of the correlation coefficient is 0.86. Graphical investigation of the relation indicates that an even closer approximation
would have been to use income plus assets up to $2,500, plus one-
fifth of assets above $2,500. Here the square of the correlation co-
efficient is 0.89.

It is interesting to note that the regression coefficient we find here
for "income plus assets up to $2,500" is extremely close to the one
we found before, using residuals for two years instead of three, from
seven regressions instead of sixteen, computed from the whole sample and not just from units in reasonably normal circumstances. The
coefficient in that case was 0.1640, and here it is 0.1638. The constant term is lower in absolute value for the present case, being $0.20
instead of — $24.

Rather than divide all the residuals by 0.16 times "income-plus-
assets-up-to-$2,500," as we did before, we chose to take the simpler
course of dividing by "income-plus-assets-up-to-$2,500." This means
that the standard errors of means of these homogenized residuals, or
of differences between them, will be smaller, just as the residuals are
smaller. Since these residuals are not divided by their standard deviations but by numbers 6¼ times as large, we shall multiply the
residuals by 10,000 and call the resulting variable $NDH$. Chart I
presents estimated standard errors for use in interpreting subsequent
tables. The reader should understand that the use of clustering in
the original sample design means that these are not strictly legitimate,
since the number of degrees of freedom is not equal to the number of
cases. Further, some degrees of freedom should be deducted for the
computations involved in the sixteen regressions. These regressions

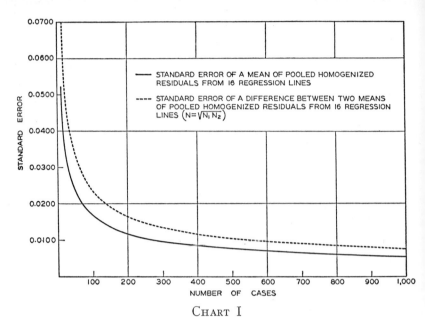

CHART I

Standard Errors of Mean Homogenized Residuals from 16 "Normal"
Regressions and of Differences between Such Means

*The standard errors are not strictly valid because the data are unweighted and
from a clustered sample with varying sampling rates. They are conservative because
the removal of 9 additional extreme cases after the computation of variances reduced
the standard deviation by 2½ percent (not conservative because of the overestima-
tion of the number of degrees of freedom). In subsequent tables, the symbol NDH
is used to denote residuals and is multiplied by $10^4$ to eliminate decimal points in
tables.*

could be considered as computation of a slope and constant term sixteen times, or 32 degrees of freedom, or they could be considered as equivalent to computing one multiple regression with the following variables:

Income

Assets

Home ownership

Income times Assets

Income times Home ownership

Assets times Home ownership

Income times Assets times Home ownership

These plus a constant term involve 8 degrees of freedom. The loss of degrees of freedom in clustering is much more difficult to analyze. The Sampling Section of Survey Research Center has made some computations for the whole sample, for such variables as income and assets, but the within-cluster intraclass correlation might be quite high for income or assets, and quite low for such behavior indicators as the residuals with which we are now dealing. On the other hand, if there were an extremely powerful "reference group" effect, the residuals might be more highly intercorrelated within clusters than incomes. Also, our estimates of the variances are made larger by using unweighted data and by the fact that we excluded a few extreme cases *after* the computation of the variances but before the computations of the tables and the variance analyses. Our general conclusion is that a highly conservative procedure would be to halve the number of cases in using the chart.

*Test of the homogenizing process.* As we did before, on the other set of residuals, we have computed the standard deviation, skewness, and kurtosis of the "homogenized" residuals. Nine cases were omitted even before this was done, because they were extreme, with income plus assets less than $100 for eight of them, with a problem of an annual room and board payment of $2,080 from a relative not treated as income in the ninth case. Since we divided the residuals by income plus assets up to $2,500, instead of 0.16 times this figure, we should expect the standard deviation of these homogenized residuals to be approximately 0.16, as is the case.

Partially as an experiment in statistics, we removed the three largest remaining negative residuals, then the next six. The effect on the skewness and kurtosis was quite striking, the removal of nine cases out of 7,045 reducing kurtosis from 28 to 8 and skewness from −3 to −0.001. The standard deviation fell only from 0.168 to 0.156.

It seemed worthwhile to remove these cases and treat them separately, not only because of their possible adverse effects on tests of significance, but also because of their tendency to dominate means of cells with small frequencies. Insofar as we use means of very small cells in variance analysis, the distribution of these might not be sufficiently normal and the $F$-tests might have been affected in a nonconservative direction.

Again, while even these eliminations did not bring the distribution to exact normality, the means we use in our variance analyses can be presumed to be roughly normally distributed, and the tables of means are not likely to be dominated by a few cases.

### ANALYSIS OF RESIDUALS FROM "NORMAL" INCOME–SAVING RELATIONS

*Tabular analysis.* We have not repeated with these residuals all the tables which we computed with the earlier set, because of the time and effort involved, and because at crucial points the results were largely similar. Table 4 shows much the same pattern as Table 13 did in the previous chapter, even though the former is in terms of residuals from a pattern of sixteen "normal" regressions, and the latter was from seven regressions using the whole nonentrepreneurial sample. Further, Table 4 and all those which present $ND$ and $NDH$, are for the three years 1947, 1948, and 1949, instead of the first two only. In addition to the comments made on Table 13, we should also point out that the people with less than 5 percent change in income are in many cases lower savers than those with a slight decrease in income. Our interpretation is that more of the former are fixed-income people, who have perhaps not had so many increases since World War II as others, and are consequently in a relatively bad economic situation.

Table 5 again shows no particular relation between occupation and

TABLE 4

HOMOGENIZED SAVING RESIDUALS $(NDH)$[a] BY PLACE, EXPECTED INCOME, AND INCOME CHANGE

EXPECTED INCOME

| PAST INCOME CHANGE | Up | Same | Down | Do Not Know | All Expected- Income Groups |
|---|---|---|---|---|---|
| Metropolitan Area | | | | | |
| +25% or more | 307 | 176 | 152 | −198 | 199 |
| +5% to +24% | −156 | −134 | −205 | −102 | −106 |
| −4% to +4% | −223 | −258 | −138 | −130 | −220 |
| −5% to −24% | −226 | −204 | −331 | −339 | −259 |
| −25% or more | −623 | 2[b] | −1,597[b] | −894[b] | −676 |
| All income-change groups | −81 | −138 | −247 | −240 | −144 |
| | | | | | |
| Cities, Towns, and Villages | | | | | |
| +25% or more | 333 | 269 | 428 | 343 | 320 |
| +5% to +24% | 247 | 108 | 134 | 3 | 95 |
| −4% to +4% | 88 | −4 | −23 | −304 | −28 |
| −5% to −24% | −211 | 12 | 410 | −67 | 10 |
| −25% or more | −318 | −602 | −330 | −382[b] | −420 |
| All income-change groups | 140 | 51 | 144 | −80 | 68 |
| | | | | | |
| Open Country (Nonfarm) | | | | | |
| +25% or more | 1,000[b] | 606[b] | 1,558[b] | 278[b] | 779 |
| +5% to +24% | 441[b] | 215 | 172[b] | 437[b] | 313 |
| −4% to +4% | −95[b] | 346 | 239[b] | 457[b] | 292 |
| −5% to −24% | −195[b] | 126[b] | 1,661[c] | 17[c] | 236 |
| −25% or more | 174[b] | −167[b] | −385[b] | 166[b] | −28 |
| All income-change groups | 407 | 302 | 490 | 353 | 360 |

[a] Residuals from the 16 normal regressions divided by income-plus-assets-up-to-$2,500 to homogenize, then multiplied by 10,000 to eliminate the decimal points.
[b] Only 10–49 cases.     [c] Fewer than 10 cases.

saving behavior, but a persistent effect of "place" or population density. Actually, there is no very good reason why there should be a relation with occupation, particularly in view of the heterogeneous nature of the concept of occupation. Occupation is a mélange of the following, at least: skill level, background training and experience, income prospects if not achievement, degree of supervision over other men, managerial functions, entrepreneurial functions, steadiness of income, security of income.

Table 6 indicates a pronounced relation between age and saving, with differences between different population densities and different levels of liquid assets at the beginning of the year. The "usual" relation between assets and saving, which is posited on the grounds that assets facilitate dissaving, seems to exist only among the very young or the very old and then more strikingly in the metropolitan areas. Why should age be related to saving, and particularly in the fashion shown here? It must be remembered that we are treating purchase of

TABLE 5

SAVING RESIDUALS (*NDH*) BY PLACE AND OCCUPATION

|  | PLACE | | |
|---|---|---|---|
| OCCUPATION | *Metropolitan Areas* | *Cities, Towns, and Villages* | *Open Country (Nonfarm)* |
| Professional | −173 | 150 | 685[a] |
| Managerial, self-employed | 36 | −29 | 286[a] |
| Other white collar | 140 | −79 | 581[a] |
| Skilled–semi-skilled | −184 | 83 | 375 |
| Unskilled | 75 | 87 | 398 |
| Other | −411 | −164 | 139 |

[a] 10–49 cases.

durable goods as an investment and not as a consumption expenditure. On the other hand, we are not treating depreciation on houses or durable goods as consumption. Durable goods are purchased largely by younger people, so our definition gives them the benefit of larger saving than other definitions. However, our failure to subtract depreciation from saving also gives older people larger saving, not by so much per person as for young durable goods purchasers, but by about as much perhaps, as the whole younger group including the nonpurchasers. Implicitly, age is used because it is related to the idealized concept of the "life cycle" of the family. The life cycle is a useful theoretical construct, but how should it be related to saving? Presumably in the early stages saving should be heavy, particularly

## TABLE 6
## SAVING RESIDUALS (*NDH*) BY PLACE, LIQUID ASSETS, AND AGE

| AGE OF HEAD OF SPENDING UNIT | METROPOLITAN AREAS LIQUID ASSETS (DOLLARS) | | | | CITIES, TOWNS, AND VILLAGES LIQUID ASSETS (DOLLARS) | | | | OPEN COUNTRY, NONFARM AREAS LIQUID ASSETS (DOLLARS) | | | |
|---|---|---|---|---|---|---|---|---|---|---|---|---|
| | *None* | *1–499* | *500 or More* | *All Asset Groups* | *None* | *1–499* | *500 or More* | *All Asset Groups* | *None* | *1–499* | *500 or More* | *All Asset Groups* |
| 18–24 | 102 | 241 | −224 | 69 | 318 | 276 | −7 | 220 | 702[a] | 1314[a] | 457[a] | 817 |
| 25–34 | 147 | −16 | −144 | −48 | 210 | 279 | 194 | 227 | 506 | 645[a] | 13[a] | 457 |
| 35–44 | −290 | −78 | −159 | −158 | −30 | 0 | 51 | 16 | 383[a] | 769[a] | 103[a] | 371 |
| 45–54 | −255 | −342 | −213 | −248 | −142 | −203 | −35 | −100 | −5[a] | −3[a] | 204[a] | 62 |
| 55–64 | −489 | −298 | −173 | −250 | 166 | 158 | 86 | 118 | 384[a] | −9[a] | 429[a] | 320 |
| 65 or over | 127[a] | 150[a] | −563 | −330 | −86 | 85 | −96 | −63 | 298[a] | −184[a] | −617[a] | −32 |

[a] 10–49 cases.

if we treat durables as an investment. When the children are being reared, needs are likely to be at their peak, affected of course by the people's own aspirations and standards. After the children leave home, needs should diminish if we interpret them in a mechanistic

TABLE 7

SAVING RESIDUALS (*NDH*) BY PLACE, ASSETS, AND DEMOGRAPHIC STRUCTURE

DEMOGRAPHIC STRUCTURE

| PLACE AND LIQUID ASSETS, BEGINNING OF YEAR (DOLLARS) | Under 45 Single | Under 45 No Children | Under 45 Children | 45 or Older Children | 45 or Older No Children | 45 or Older Single |
|---|---|---|---|---|---|---|
| Metropolitan Areas | | | | | | |
| None | 68 | 2[a] | −59 | −345[a] | −425 | 98[a] |
| 1–499 | 163 | 177 | −100 | −463 | −200 | −23[a] |
| 500 or more | −19 | −159 | −238 | −322 | −211 | −426[b] |
| All asset groups | 65 | −55 | −161 | −362 | −235 | −218 |
| Cities, Towns, and Villages | | | | | | |
| None | 77 | 307 | 148 | −25 | −154 | 80 |
| 1–499 | 337 | 222 | 102 | −44 | −95 | 146 |
| 500 or more | 212 | 133 | 48 | −146 | 3 | 64 |
| All asset groups | 210 | 199 | 95 | −77 | −47 | 83 |
| Open Country, Non-farm | | | | | | |
| None | 853[a] | 383[a] | 467 | 419[a] | −114[a] | 39[a] |
| 1–499 | 1,664[a] | 895[a] | 544 | −102[a] | −107[a] | 100[a] |
| 500 or more | 527[a] | 312[a] | −111[a] | 398[a] | 64[a] | 202[a] |
| All asset groups | 973 | 474 | 369 | 298 | −42 | 127 |

[a] 10–49 cases.
[b] There is a powerful age effect beyond 45:

| Age | NDH |
|---|---|
| 45–54 | −85 |
| 55–64 | −300 |
| 65 or more | −951 |

way. And, of course, after the wage earner retires, he is likely to dissave in the strict economic sense—living on an annuity, pension, etc. Since annuity payments are treated as income, these people are likely to show up as zero savers in the survey, except the very wealthy people who have other ways of dissaving. Of course, the high income

SAVING RESIDUALS (*NDH*) BY PLACE, INCOME CHANGE, AND DEMOGRAPHIC STRUCTURE

| | | | INCOME CHANGE | | | |
|---|---|---|---|---|---|---|
| PLACE AND DEMOGRAPHIC STRUCTURE OF SPENDING UNITS | Up 25% or More | Up 5-24% | Changed Less Than 5% | Down 5-24% | Down 25% or More | All Income Changes |
| Metropolitan Areas | | | | | | |
| Under 45 years old | | | | | | |
| 1 adult; no children | 298 | 88 | 62 | -438 | -678[a] | 65 |
| 2 or more; no children | 264 | -109 | -247 | -145[a] | -257[a] | -55 |
| 2 or more; 1-2 children | 248 | -176 | -234 | -188 | -271[a] | -108 |
| 2 or more; 3 or more children | -294[a] | -290 | -551[a] | -430[a] | -240[a] | -385 |
| 45 years and over | | | | | | |
| 2 or more; 1 or more children | 119[a] | -342 | -338 | -427[a] | -1,142[a] | -362 |
| 2 or more; no children | -102 | -290 | -209 | 18 | -820[a] | -235 |
| 1 adult; no children | 101[a] | 172 | -215 | -735[a] | -1,071[a] | -218 |
| Cities, Towns and Villages | | | | | | |
| Under 45 years old | | | | | | |
| 1 adult; no children | 597 | 63 | 3 | -230[a] | 233[a] | 210 |
| 2 or more; no children | 199 | 254 | 24 | 358 | 344[a] | 199 |
| 2 or more; 1-2 children | 388 | 122 | 24 | 38 | -113 | 127 |
| 2 or more; 3 or more children | 349 | 82 | -181 | -113 | -439[a] | 7 |
| 45 years and over | | | | | | |
| 2 or more; 1 or more children | 178 | 17 | -216 | 38 | -864[a] | -77 |
| 2 or more; no children | -79 | -53 | -61 | 82 | -896 | -47 |
| 1 adult; no children | 331 | 507 | 88 | -571[a] | -726[a] | 83 |
| Open Country | | | | | | |
| Under 45 years old | | | | | | |
| 1 adult; no children | 1,194[a] | 924[a] | 710[a] | 482[a] | 290[b] | 973 |
| 2 or more; no children | 1,041[a] | 747[a] | 442[b] | -820[b] | -1,198[a] | 474 |
| 2 or more; 1-2 children | 763[a] | 701[a] | 275[b] | 80[a] | 810[b] | 484 |
| 2 or more; 3 or more children | 1,408[a] | -483[a] | 427[a] | 671[a] | -752[b] | 223 |
| 45 years and over | | | | | | |
| 2 or more; 1 or more children | 68[a] | 612[a] | 482[a] | 254[a] | -100[a] | 298 |
| 2 or more; no children | 115[a] | -115[a] | 80[a] | 218[b] | -659[b] | -42 |
| 1 adult; no children | -416[b] | -74[a] | 90[a] | 959[b] | 1,235[b] | 127 |

[a] 10-49 cases.    [b] Less than 10 cases.

## TABLE 9

### Original Saving Residuals (from 7 Regressions) by Demographic Structure and Place

| AGE | NUMBER OF ADULTS | CHILDREN | METROPOLITAN AREAS | | CITIES | | TOWNS[a] | | VILLAGES | | OPEN COUNTRY | |
|---|---|---|---|---|---|---|---|---|---|---|---|---|
| | | | D (dollars) | $D/\sigma$ | D (dollars) | $D/\sigma$ | D (dollars) | $D/\sigma$ | D (dollars) | $D/\sigma$ | D (dollars) | $D/\sigma$ |
| Under 45 | 1 | None | 58 | 0.099 | 67 | 0.129 | 68 | 0.144 | 159 | 0.368 | 243 | 0.465 |
| Under 45 | 2 or more | None | 0 | −0.033 | 81 | 0.038 | 5 | 0.034 | 122 | 0.273 | 151 | 0.408 |
| Under 45 | 2 or more | 1–2 | 14 | −0.053 | 45 | 0.002 | 13 | 0.050 | 26 | 0.102 | 198 | 0.418 |
| Under 45 | 2 or more | 3 or more | −279 | −0.353 | −96 | 0.017 | −13 | −0.091 | 62 | 0.023 | 41 | 0.083 |
| 45 or over | 2 or more | 1 or more | −148 | −0.195 | −96 | −0.155 | −97 | −0.093 | −92 | −0.046 | 80 | 0.149 |
| 45 or over | 2 or more | None | −150 | −0.137 | 17 | −0.036 | 20 | 0.052 | −21 | −0.064 | −19 | 0.054 |
| 45 or over | 1 | None | −14 | 0.046 | −12 | 0.105 | 96 | 0.174 | 6 | 0.027 | 90 | 0.320 |

a 2,500 to 50,000 population.

people who consume most of their income will have negative residuals in our tables—see the high-asset, over-sixty-five groups in Table 6.

Table 7 approaches the life cycle concept more directly, and the relation is somewhat more striking and persistent. Table 8, in addition to introducing income change, divides the spending units where the head is under forty-five into three groups instead of two: no children, one to two children, and three or more children. Income change was introduced to see whether it had different effects at dif-

TABLE 10

VARIANCE ANALYSIS OF *ND* AND OF *NDH*, USING YEARS FIRST
AS A FACTOR, THEN AS REPLICATION

|  | Degrees of Freedom | F-RATIOS YEAR AS FACTOR | | F-RATIOS YEAR AS REPLICATION | |
|---|---|---|---|---|---|
|  |  | *ND* | *NDH* | *ND* | *NDH* |
| Place (metropolitan area, open country, other) | 2 | 25.3[a] | 44.1[a] | 26.9[a] | 34.6[a] |
| Demographic structure | 6 | 5.7[a] | 9.1[a] | 5.1[a] | 7.2[a] |
| Place × Demographic structure | 12 | 0.9 | 1.9 | 0.9 | 1.5 |
| Year (1947, 1948, 1949) | 2 | 0.5 | 1.5 |  |  |
| Place × Year | 4 | 1.8 | 1.3 |  |  |
| Demographic structure × Year | 12 | 0.6 | 1.8 |  |  |
| Place × Demographic structure × Year | 24 |  |  |  |  |

[a] Significant at 1-percent level.

ferent stages in the life cycle. It does not seem to have. Table 9 is a recomputation using the first set of residuals to make sure that the same general results appear. They do. The table also furnishes additional evidence for the similarity among cities, towns, and villages, as opposed to metropolitan areas on the one hand and open country on the other.

*Analysis of NDH—Variance analysis.* We turn now to some variance analyses, since we are interested in interactions as well as direct effects. Table 10 shows that treating year as a factor rather than as a replication of an experiment produces almost identical results; hence in the more complicated analyses year is treated as replication or ignored entirely by combining years. Place and demographic structure are both highly significant (1-percent level), but none of the interactions are. In Table 11 we have added income change and assets. There should not be any main asset effect, since we used different asset groups in the original regressions, residuals from which we are now analyzing, and further used them in the "homogenizing" process. However, there is a significant interaction effect

### TABLE 11

### VARIANCE ANALYSIS OF *NDH*

| | Degrees of Freedom | Mean Square or Variance ($\times 10^{-4}$) | F-ratio |
|---|---|---|---|
| I  = Income change | 3 | 482 | 9.3[a] |
| L  = Liquid Assets (0, 1–499, 500–1,999, 2,000 or over) | 2 | 7 | 0.1 |
| P  = Place (metropolitan, nonmetropolitan-excluding open country) | 1 | 613 | 11.8[a] |
| D  = Demographic Structure | 6 | 256 | 4.9[a] |
| I $\times$ L | 6 | 167 | 3.2[a] |
| I $\times$ P | 3 | 10 | |
| I $\times$ D | 18 | 70 | 1.3 |
| L $\times$ P | 2 | 62 | |
| L $\times$ D | 12 | 36 | |
| P $\times$ D | 6 | 17 | |
| I $\times$ L $\times$ P | 6 | 60 | |
| I $\times$ L $\times$ D | 36 | 66 | 1.3 |
| I $\times$ P $\times$ D | 18 | 44 | |
| L $\times$ P $\times$ D | 12 | 44 | |
| I $\times$ L $\times$ P $\times$ D | 36 | 37 | |
| Error (year treated as replication)[b]    336 − 8 = 328 | | 52 | |
| Total variance (0.00587 in original units) | 503 | | |

### AVERAGES OF AVERAGES FOR THE ABOVE SIGNIFICANT INTERACTION

| INCOME CHANGE (PERCENT) | LIQUID ASSETS (DOLLARS) | | |
|---|---|---|---|
| | 0 | 1–499 | 500 or more |
| +25% or more | 16 | 301 | 246 |
| +5% to +24% | −44 | 35 | −19 |
| −4% to +4% | −290 | −250 | −124 |
| −5% or more | 115 | −311 | −459 |

[a] Significant at 1-percent level.
[b] Eight empty cells were assigned mean values for identical cells in other years. At a minimum, subtract 8 from degrees of freedom for replication.

between income change and assets, as we have pointed out before in the simple tables. The averages of averages involved are given at the bottom of the table. In this analysis, 8 of the 504 cells in the basic table were empty. In each case there was at least one other year for which the matching cell (matched on income change, assets, place, and demographic structure) was not empty, and we assigned these values of the matched cells to the empty cells. This particular "missing-plot" technique does not seem to be discussed in the litera-

### TABLE 12

#### VARIANCE ANALYSIS OF *NDH*

|  | Degrees of Freedom | Mean Square or Variance ($\times 10^{-4}$) | F-ratio |
|---|---|---|---|
| A = Age of head | 4 | 702 | 2.8 |
| L = Liquid assets | 2 | 383 | |
| C = Single, multiple without children, multiple with children | 2 | 308 | |
| P = Place (excepting open country) | 1 | 4053 | 16.4[a] |
| A × L | 8 | 327 | |
| A × C | 8 | 207 | |
| A × P | 4 | 601 | |
| L × C | 4 | 238 | |
| L × P | 2 | 316 | |
| C × P | 2 | 156 | |
| A × L × C | 16 | 152 | |
| A × L × P | 8 | 354 | |
| A × C × P | 8 | 350 | |
| L × C × P | 4 | 374 | |
| A × L × C × P (treated as error) | 16 | 248 | |

[a] Significant at 5-percent level.

ture, but it seems clear that at a minimum we must subtract eight degrees of freedom from the error (replication) term.

Table 12 indicates that taking two components of the demographic structure separately—(a) age and (b) whether the spending unit is a single person, several people without children, or several people with children—tends to mask the real life-cycle effect, nothing being significant except place of residence. The comparison is not perfect, however, because we did not take the three years separately as replications.

## TABLE 13

### ANALYSIS OF DEMOGRAPHIC STRUCTURE BY VARIOUS MEASURES

| DEMOGRAPHIC STRUCTURE | MEAN SAVING (DOLLARS) | $D/\sigma$—1947-1948 | | | $D$—1947-1948 (DOLLARS) | | |
|---|---|---|---|---|---|---|---|
| | | SIMPLE MEANS | MEANS OF MEANS | | SIMPLE MEANS | MEANS OF MEANS | |
| | | | Place | Place, Income Change, Assets, and Year | | Place | Place, Income Change, Assets, and Year |
| Under 45 Years Old | | | | | | | |
| 1 adult; no children | 221 | 0.156 | 0.241 | 0.240 | 80 | 119 | 125 |
| 2 or more; no children | 600 | 0.055 | 0.144 | 0.090 | 38 | 72 | 74 |
| 2 or more; 1–2 children | 740 | 0.043 | 0.104 | 0.053 | 35 | 59 | 27 |
| 2 or more; 3 or more children | 515 | −0.081 | −0.064 | −0.155 | −63 | −59 | −113 |
| 45 Years and Over | | | | | | | |
| 2 or more; 1 or more children | 710 | −0.100 | −0.068 | −0.060 | −92 | −71 | −60 |
| 2 or more; no children | 640 | −0.044 | −0.026 | −0.040 | −45 | −31 | 27 |
| 1 adult; no children | 108 | 0.113 | 0.134 | 0.156 | 29 | 33 | 62 |

|  | NDH—1947–1949 | | | ND—1947–1949 (DOLLARS) | | |
|  | MEANS OF MEANS | | | MEANS OF MEANS | | |
| DEMOGRAPHIC STRUCTURE | SIMPLE MEANS | Year and Place | Year, Place, Assets, and Income Change[a] | SIMPLE MEANS | Year and Place | Year, Place, Assets, and Income Change[a] |
|---|---|---|---|---|---|---|
| Under 45 Years Old |  |  |  |  |  |  |
| 1 adult; no children | 197 | 415 | 70 | 43 | 81 | 25 |
| 2 or more; no children | 118 | 213 | 134 | 63 | 97 | 59 |
| 2 or more; 1–2 children | 70 | 166 | 76 | 40 | 63 | 4 |
| 2 or more; 3 or more children | −52 | −53 | −190 | −22 | −36 | −61 |
| 45 Years and Over |  |  |  |  |  |  |
| 2 or more; 1 or more children | −131 | −46 | −226 | −67 | −52 | −88 |
| 2 or more; no children | −110 | −10 | −353 | −42 | −51 | −215 |
| 1 adult; no children | −2 | −20 | 36 | −12 | 26 | 3 |

[a] Excluding open country (nonfarm).

*The life cycle—a case study in the effects of statistical method.* In general, then, the results seem to be about the same as with the first set of residuals. The life cycle-variable seemed important enough to suggest the possibility of using it for a case study of the effect of the methods we used for "removing" the income, home ownership, and asset effects, and for homogenizing the residuals (see Tables 8, 10, 11 in this chapter and Table 32 in Chapter III). Furthermore, the variance analyses actually use averages of averages without regard to the differential numbers of cases involved, and it is interesting to see whether these averages of averages, which tend to isolate the effect of the variables tested from side effects through correlations with the other variables used, differ from simple mean residuals. Table 13 presents the main results, some of which are plotted on Charts II and III. Apparently the only important effect of the homogenizing procedure is to reverse the positions of the single people under 45 and the multiple childless spending units where the head is under 45, and this only for the first set of residuals.

The use of the sixteen "normal" regressions with the finer classifications of home-ownership status and the addition of a third year seems to have no effect other than a slight decrease in the level of the residuals for spending units where the head is over forty-five years old. Chart II shows this quite clearly. Chart III shows a rather marked difference depending on whether we use simple mean residuals from the sixteen regression lines, or averages of averages for matched subgroups. The high level of the year–place averages at the left is probably the result of the very large positive residuals for young people in the open-country nonfarm group, a small group numerically. This group is excluded from the means for the 72 group average of averages. The low level of these averages for the later stages in the life cycle results largely from this exclusion and the consequent domination of the averages by the large negative residuals for the metropolitan groups.

The apparent instability of the averages of averages used in the variance analyses is partly due to their treating each subgroup, how-

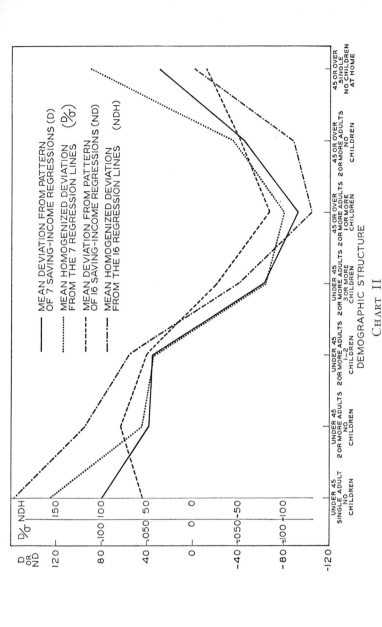

CHART II

Demographic Structure with Different Dependent Variables

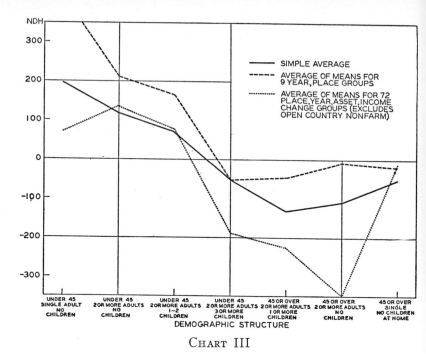

CHART III

*NDH* Demographic Structure with Various Averaging Procedures

ever small, as a unit. More basically, it results from the fact that, for all our transformation of the data and exclusion of wild cases, it remains true that large deviations from usual behavior exist and that they are more likely when the spending unit is in unusual circumstances. In other words, the smaller the number of cases in a particular subcell, the more likely their behavior is to show large deviations from "normal." This means that heterogeneity is a basic characteristic of people and really cannot be eliminated by statistical means. Variances are not only greater as frequencies are smaller, they are disproportionately greater.

The result of this is that, although we are always trying to find results which apply to large groups in the population or to the whole population, behavior, and even the aggregates, tends to be dominated by the unusual cases. Our analysis has involved a compromise between isolation of subgroups and the preservation of a large group of the population for analysis. Our feeling is that further progress in the analysis of behavior will come most fruitfully through further isolation of subgroups.

### GENERAL SUMMARY AND INTERPRETATION

Throughout our analysis we have kept theoretical comment and analysis at a minimum simply because of the magnitude of the task of explaining the procedure and the main significance of the results. The variables we have found to be important seem to be concentrated among those which indicate the needs of and the pressures upon the spending units, but this does not mean that their perceptions, motivations, and aspirations are not important. It means largely that it is easier to secure information and design variables to measure the physical situation than it is to measure the psychological variables, which may well be more important. Certainly, detailed analysis of the data indicates a tremendous variety of behavior, some people with very high incomes saving almost nothing, and some people managing to save several hundred dollars out of an income of $2,000.

What are the variables which proved to be important as well as measurable? It was clear from the beginning that income and income change were important variables, and the reason is clear: the first indicates the ability to save (or spend), and the second the dynamic changes in that ability, plus, presumably, changes in long-run expectations and aspirations. Farmers and business owners behave quite differently from ordinary consuming spending units. The whole motivation for saving is clearly different, and the alternative is to borrow funds (if possible) at the cost not only of interest payments but partial loss of control over the operation of the business. Further, the necessity for reinvesting profits in business or farm, particularly at a time of rising prices, may well seem absolute, and business or farm losses are involuntary dissaving. It is tempting to think that perhaps we should isolate a businessman's personal finances from his business affairs and see whether, apart from profits he reinvests in his business, he saves about as much as other people. The difficulty with this procedure is that there is no neat conceptual solution to the problem of separation, for profits reinvested in business are an increase in personal net worth. Two possibilities exist. One is to subtract from the businessman's saving the amount which nonentrepreneurs in that income class save and to derive a business-saving function. The other is to find out whether business owners actually regard profits left in a business as income or as a sort of capital gain. Detailed analysis of interviews with businessmen now being carried on by Lawrence Klein and Julius Margolis indicates that many of them treat debt repayment as a business expense in thinking about business profits.

The interpretation of home ownership and asset level, both of which were important, was more difficult. We have indicated our hypotheses regarding them and will summarize them briefly here: Home ownership involves income and consumption in real terms which do not enter the accounts except as consumption in the forms of interest on mortgage, taxes, upkeep, etc. Those who neither own nor rent are receiving an important amount of income in real terms, without the contractual saving commitments of those who have mortgage payments to make.

The level of liquid asset holdings at the beginning of the year is related to saving, but differentially at different income levels, and with an important interaction with income change. For those with income decreases or other pressures to spend, the assets are clearly a facilitating circumstance. On the other hand, they may have been accumulated for the purposes for which they are now being used, such as children's education. At high income levels, spending units with large amounts of liquid assets tend to save more than those with fewer assets. We have interpreted this as follows: given a certain degree of continuity of income and of behavior through time, those with large amounts of liquid assets now are likely to have been saving more in the past than those with few liquid assets. Given continuity of behavior, they will save more in the future as well.[1] By splitting the sample according to their liquid assets, we have also classified them according to their basic psychology, or at least their past saving behavior. Indeed, insofar as people can become motivated to save, for whatever purposes, we can assume that the psychologists' theories and experiments with "aspiration level" apply here too. We could then state the hypothesis that the more savings a person has accumulated in the past, the more likely he is to accumulate savings out of current income. Assets then become an indicator of the level of aspiration to save. It is not only true that high-income people save more if they have more assets; it is also true that the effect of an *increase* in income is a larger amount of saving if the spending unit has more assets. This may be further indication of high saving aspirations. It may also indicate something still more important— the possibility that people with fluctuating incomes have greater reason to have high marginal propensities to save, in order to maintain a large liquid asset balance for the "lean years," and to be willing to dissave when income is low.

In general, then, assets can be looked at in several ways: as allowing added consumption when pressures exist; as resulting from

[1] Compare similar remarks by Klein in Chapter V and G. Katona, *Psychological Analysis of Economic Behavior* (New York: McGraw-Hill Book Co., 1951), pp. 167–70.

conscious planning to take care of pressures (e.g., one expects a fluctuating income); as indicating intentions to make large expenditures (e.g., for a house) for which the assets were accumulated; or
as indicating a high aspiration level for the accumulation of saving,
and hence a high average and marginal propensity to save. Only a
series of studies which followed identical spending units through
long periods of time would allow us to weight the relative importance of these interpretations, and even here it would not be easy,
for many things happen to spending units through time even if they
remain a single identifiable spending unit.

In addition to these variables, we found two other variables which
were extremely important. One was size of city, and more particularly the differences between metropolitan areas, open country, and
everything else. Again interpretation is not easy: population density
not only provides more opportunities for spending and more illus-
trations of the joys of, say, owning a television set, but it also means
a way of life which involves more "necessary" expenditures, for
transportation, taxes, etc. It also means that the "cost of living," the
prices of the same commodities and services, is higher. Hence we
cannot say whether it is differences in costs or in standards of life
which make people save less when they live closer together.

The other important variable was demographic structure, a loose
analogue to the sociological concept of "life cycle." As an indicator
of pressures to spend money, it is presumably better than age, number of people in the spending unit, etc. The rather surprising thing
is that our data do not show more of an increase in saving in later
stages of the cycle. It is a common belief that when children leave
home and are on their own, parents can then begin to save for their
old age. It is possible that this is true except in times of rising prices
and wages, when older people do not share proportionately in the
increased incomes. It is also possible that our statistical methods are
inadequate, estimating "normal" saving for high incomes including
single people, etc., and not just for those in the normal stage in the
life cycle to be receiving such incomes. If we take any one income

group, the life cycle effect does not show up so clearly. Further research is needed here but is beyond the scope of this project.

In addition to the differences between subgroups in the population and to the effects of certain variables, there remains the question of the relevance of our definition of saving to an analysis of motivation, and indeed the relevance of any definition of saving to motivation. We rejected at the outset the idea that people make current decisions without any regard to their effect on the net worth of the spending unit. However, it became clear during the analysis that saving in the form of investment in durable goods or houses behaves differently from other forms. It also has a different impact on the economy, since it is not deflationary (it is automatically offset). Particularly in the short run, it may well be that our most important next task is the analysis of these consumer investment decisions.

### A FINAL NOTE ON THE RELATION BETWEEN
### THE STATISTICAL METHODS USED AND
### THE RESULTS REPORTED HERE

A natural question in view of the elaborate qualifications as to the applicability of the statistical methods, and the complicated methods used to overcome objections, is whether the results are based on valid statistical inference. In general the author thinks it is true that any relations we have reported as statistically significant are validly so, but that, in view of the very conservative nature of our statistical treatment, there may be some relations which exist even though we have not found them significant.

Are these results in the nature of hypotheses or of findings? This raises a difficult philosophical question, which occurs in its simplest form when someone runs 100 tests of significance and finds five of them significant at the 5-percent probability level. The purist would suggest that we use one set of data to develop specific hypotheses and another set to test them. To some extent this has been done, in that data for additional years have been added as they became available and showed the same general patterns. Even the more elaborate variance analyses have been checked by running them first with two years for the first set of residuals, and then with three years and a different set of residuals. In general, moreover, our results are not statements of exact relations but inferences that such relations exist in the population.

Then, too, the variety of methods used, all providing similar results, leaves us with some confidence that our findings are not the results of the particular statistical method used. Insofar as ours differ from those of Klein elsewhere in this book, the reason is in the definition of saving rather than in the statistical method.

If we had to select a single finding which seems to us most important, it would be this: While there is basic variability in behavior and motivation among people, there are groups which are reasonably homogeneous as to their spending–saving behavior within the population and distinctively different from the other groups. These groups are important for several reasons: differences between them can be interpreted in terms of differences in motivation or of forces impinging on them; similarities within groups make it possible to analyze them for further variables affecting their behavior; and, finally, the existence of such disparate groups has significance for the problems of aggregation in economics and the building, use, and interpretation of aggregate statistics.

# V: STATISTICAL ESTIMATION OF ECONOMIC RELATIONS FROM SURVEY DATA

## by *Lawrence R. Klein*

### PRINCIPLES OF ESTIMATION FROM SURVEY DATA

*Engel curves and their interpretation.* The attempt to make quantitative estimates of patterns of consumer behavior from data collected in surveys goes back at least as far as the work of Engel in the development of the celebrated "Engel's laws." The subsequent calculation of Engel curves from numerous family-budget inquiries has become commonplace. Such curves are designed to show the relation between a variety of expenditures and income. They serve as a convenient starting point for demonstrating the general problems involved in estimating economic relations from survey data.

Within a short time span, data, such as those on expenditures and income, are collected from a number of households. The data are customarily arrayed by income size, from the smallest to the largest, and, within income classes, mean expenditures and mean incomes are calculated. The lines joining the successive means or smooth curves fitted to the scatter of means for each type of expenditure and total income are the Engel curves. Examples of such curves are the savings–income regressions used by Morgan in Chapter III.

To obtain an economic interpretation of the Engel curves, let us denote two points $(X_1, Y_1)$ and $(X_2, Y_2)$ on some particular curve. $X_1 =$ expenditure estimated by the curve at income level $Y_1$; $X_2 =$ expenditure estimated by the curve at income level $Y_2$. The basic assumption underlying the entire analysis is that a household spending $X_1$ out of income $Y_1$ would behave like another household spend-ing $X_2$ out of income $Y_2$ if the former's income were $Y_2$ instead of $Y_1$. Since the curves are seldom exact—in that all observations of income–expenditure couplets, for individual households or even for means by income classes, do not lie precisely on the curves—the interpretation is one of average or statistical behavior subject to error.

Many qualifications and refinements must be added, however, be-fore this interpretation of Engel curves is acceptable. The classical theory of consumer behavior tells us that demand for a particular commodity by an individual depends on the income of the individual and on relative prices such as the ratio of prices of other commodities to the price of the good in question. Can we interpret the expression

$$\frac{\text{percentage change in expenditure}}{\text{percentage change in income}}$$

calculated at points along the Engel curve, as estimates of income elasticity of demand as it would be calculated from the demand curves of economic theory? The neglect of prices in the determination of Engel curves is probably not important and does not, in itself, mean that income elasticity cannot be determined from the curves. Survey data are usually gathered during a short period of time so that each household is confronted with the same price structure when it reports its income and its expenditure. In some situations this will not be exactly true because of geographical price differentials, but data reported in a single survey of households can for most practical pur-poses be analyzed apart from price variations.[1] The absence of sepa-rate price variables does not invalidate the use of Engel curves for

[1] Duesenberry and Kistin report a recent attempt to estimate price elasticities from regional price variations in budget studies, but their results are unsatisfactory in a number of respects, important among which is the fact that regional price variation is not great enough to lend reliability to their estimates. See J. Duesen-berry and H. Kistin, "The Role of Demand in the Economic Structure," in *Studies in the Structure of the American Economy* (New York: Oxford University Press, 1953). For an earlier analysis of interlocal price variations and saving patterns, see H. Mendershausen, "Differences in Family Savings between Cities of Different Size and Location, Whites and Negroes," *Review of Economic Statistics,* XXII (1940), 122–37.

studying properties of consumer-demand relations; moreover, the expenditure–income relation embodied in Engel curves represents associated fluctuations in real income and real expenditures, since the price components of money expenditures and incomes are the same for all observations.

These remarks do not apply to the problems of studying Engel curves derived from each of several successive surveys or to the problem of pooling data from several surveys to obtain a single expenditure–income relation.

*The multivariate nature of behavior.* Although we may not be confronted with any complications due to the neglect of price variables in our interpretation of Engel curves, we cannot dispose as easily of complications due to the neglect of other variables. Does the expenditure $X_1$ of a household having income $Y_1$ differ, apart from random error, from the expenditure $X_2$ of another household in the survey sample only because the latter's income is $Y_2(\neq Y_1)$? Perhaps the first household is young while the second is not. This fact will account for differences in spending aside from that which can be explained by income differences. Similarly differences in size of household, liquid asset holding, income change, economic outlook, and a large list of other variables are of potential importance in explaining interindividual variations in expenditure.

In theoretical economics we often assume that other variables besides income, expenditures, and prices are given, or we construct abstract hypothetical models that refer to behavior in a social setting from which these other variables are absent. However, if we are to infer theoretical income elasticities or some other parameters of economic behavior from data reported on a real-life process, we cannot neglect many of these other variables. One of the primary requirements for the estimation of economic relations from survey material is that the analysis must be highly multivariate.

One way of proceeding would be to divide a sample into several small groups, so that each group contains only households with the same age of head, size, asset level, income change, etc. According to such characteristics, the households within a group are homogeneous. Then estimate Engel curves for each group. Income elasticities calculated from such detailed Engel curves would be more reliable, provided the groups are not chosen so finely that there are too few observations in each group for purposes of statistical estimation. The common sense of this method is evident in terms of theoretical analysis, although it is often ignored. A subjective utility function, in the theoretical analysis, is associated with each household, but obviously this function will vary according as household tastes vary. Tastes, in turn, will vary with age, household size, wealth, income change, and like variables. The demand equations of microeconomics depend on the parameters of the utility functions; therefore it is necessary to choose a homogeneous group of households in order to estimate income elasticities of demand from interindividual variation in a survey sample.

Multiple cross classifications grow rapidly as the number of classifying variables grows. Unless samples are very large—20,000 or more observations—it is extremely likely that there will be too few observations per homogeneous group for statistical reliability. The investigator is usually forced to compromise by using fewer variables than desirable for the cross classification or by making broad groupings for each classifying variable, so that some homogeneity is lost. An alternative approach, adopted in this paper, is to perform no grouping of observations and to study the joint effect of several variables simultaneously. The advantage of this method is that it allows a large number of degrees of freedom for the study of several variables. A disadvantage is that it leaves wide variability in the data. Variance among individual households in a given sample is far greater than variance among averages of variables referring to the same sample of households. The former variance is so large that it is often hard to single out the systematic effects for which we are searching. On the other hand, wide variance permits us to find effects of more than one or two variables. In dealing with aggregative economic data, statisticians have often found so much of the variance accounted for by one or two major variables that it has been impossible to discover more subtle effects of other variables. When expenditure–income relations are estimated for subgroups which have been cross-classified by a number of variables, the mathematical form of the relation connecting all the variables simultaneously is not necessarily specified. This adds generality to the first approach. In the second approach of simultaneous estimation of the effects of several variables, the form of the equation must be specified in advance; however, a screening process making a rough preliminary study by the previous method can contribute measurably toward an accurate specification of the form of the underlying equation. By the second method, it is simpler to get a quantitative measure of partial effects of each of several variables. In samples of several hundreds or thousands of individual observations, the computational effort is obviously much greater by the second method, which involves no grouping; however, we feel that the added information justifies the extra work.

Another advantage of using ungrouped data is that it permits us to introduce semiqualitative variables in the analysis. Consumer attitudes can be readily studied in relation to economic variables if there is no grouping, since each household may be assigned a single attitudinal measure. An average attitudinal measure of groups of households is not usually a meaningful concept. Prior classification of households into separate groups—each having the same attitudinal measure—followed by a study of averages of other variables within each group can be used, but a large number of observations is necessary in order to perform such groupings.

Variance analysis, as described in chapters III and IV is another useful technique of screening relations which are planned to be estimated eventually in multivariate equations. Variance analysis tests for existence of significant relationship without specifying linearity or any other particular mathematical form of the underlying equation connecting the variables being studied. Variance analysis is more helpful in showing *directions* of significant influence and does not directly give quantitative estimates of the several partial effects of variables on each other. The interaction terms in variance analysis are, however, extremely important in finding other than purely additive effects of the primary variables treated. The basic interaction effect between liquid assets and income (or income change) on savings, estimated in the next section, shows up prominently in variance analyses of savings, income, income change, and liquid assets. It would be found as an essential component of a straightforward variance analysis but would have to be introduced explicitly in a regression equation. In fact, Morgan's variance analyses bringing out this interaction effect figured importantly in its introduction into savings equations given in the next section.

*Comparisons of estimates from time series and from survey data.* It is instructive to compare the analysis of survey samples with the more conventional statistical analysis of time-series aggregates. We might designate the two cases as spatial *vs.* temporal variation. It has often been questioned whether we actually estimate the same relations from the two types of samples. Our contention is that both kinds of information are valuable in estimating economic relations and should be used jointly to supplement each other in reaching a final result that is as statistically significant as possible.

As a matter of practical applications, cross-section analysis of survey data has usually dealt with microeconomic behavior, while time-series analysis has usually dealt with macroeconomic behavior. This difference is not a necessary consequence of the two approaches but is likely to occur frequently as long as the collecting of data continues in its present patterns. From data of a single cross-section sample, we attempt to estimate economic relationships describing the behavior of individual units. In order to compare the findings from such a sample with estimates of the same relation inferred from time-series aggregates, we must try to solve the problem of aggregation, i.e., develop a method of passing from microeconomic behavior equations to macroeconomic behavior equations. In most cases the underlying distributions of explanatory variables will influence the macroeconomic relationship, depending on the mathematical form of the equations being aggregated. For example, the dispersion of the income distribution may influence the relation between aggregate savings or expenditures and aggregate income. Time-series data provide little information on characteristics of the income distribution; hence, a comparison of time-series and cross-section estimates of saving or spending equations must allow for the fact that the appropriate distributional variables are not included in the former estimates. Obviously, a procedure superior to pure time-series or pure cross-section analysis would be a statistically efficient pooling of the two types of information. A simple pooling method in the present example would be to use estimates of the dispersion of the income distribution from successive surveys as a variable in the equation involving time-series aggregates. Other pooling methods will be discussed below.

Some variables change widely from one household to another at an instant of time and yet change little, on the average, from one time point to the next. Age and family size are examples of variables that show a wide range within cross-section samples but change only gradually, as averages, over time. The same was true of liquid asset holdings in the interwar period. It is for this reason that the stress on multivariate relations in the analysis of survey data is much more important than in time-series analysis, where smooth trends or constants supplant the explicit use of many variables. On the other hand, prices are held constant in a single survey but vary in time-series samples. A widely used technique of pooling cross-section and time-series information in past studies of consumer demand has been the estimation of income elasticities from family-budget studies (from Engel curves essentially) and the subsequent combination of this estimate in a time-series sample together with other data to estimate price elasticities. The estimates of the two different elasticities are combined to give the coefficients of a single equation.

One of the most important steps in the development of estimates of economic relations is a clear formulation of the probability model describing the aspects of human behavior being studied. The probability model makes assumptions about the nature of the random elements of behavior, and it is upon these assumptions that the logic of any particular method of statistical estimation rests. The small samples of time-series aggregates are, in practice, always too small to make adequate tests of these assumptions from an analysis of residuals, the divergences between observed values of variables studied, and the values calculated from statistical equations. The empirical distribution of residuals is the counterpart of the theoretical probability distribution of random disturbances. A remarkable contribution of survey analysis is that it provides us with large samples of residuals from which we can test the underlying probability assumptions. For example, it is interesting to test the hypothesis that the "disturbing" elements of saving behavior are drawings from a normal distribution. Other examples of tests of probability assumptions will be given in the empirical results below.

An interpretation frequently advanced is that equations estimated from cross-section samples are long-run relationships, while those estimated from time-series samples are short-run relationships. The argument states that in estimating an equation from interindividual variation of a cross-section sample we assume that when an individual arrives at some level of explanatory variables he will behave like individuals already at that level. It is then pointed out that the first individual will adopt the behavior of the second individual only after an adjustment period, a period as long as that which the second individual required to adopt the behavior actually observed. In periods of wide economic fluctuation, few individuals in the sample have had time to adjust themselves to their observed situations. In addition, explicit dynamic variables can be used in cross-section studies to take account of the adjustment period of the various individuals; therefore it is not generally valid to interpret equations estimated from cross-section data as purely long-run relationships. Conversely, equations estimated from time-series data are not purely short-run relationships. Both methods include short- and long-run aspects of behavior.

Cross-section analysis does not purport to estimate the behavior of each individual microeconomic unit. It attempts to derive average patterns of relationships, patterns in which the parameters can be considered as averages, in some sense, of each individual's parameters. In a similar way, it is possible to interpret macroeconomic equations estimated in time-series analysis as averages of individual behavior, the parameters of the equations being some general averages of individual parameters. Except by accident, the two types of averages—those of cross-section analysis and those of time-series analysis—will not be *identical*. This fact must be kept in mind in making comparisons between the two methods of analysis.

Ultimately, there should be no competition between time-series and cross-section analysis. We can expect to pool the two types of information in the most general way to obtain a time series of survey and aggregative data. In constructing a model to serve as a framework of the analysis of the pooled material we must distinguish between micro- and macroeconomic equations, between variables which the individual takes as given and those which the entire economy takes as given. The formal structure of pooled models is merely indicated here but is studied more completely elsewhere.[2]

### A MODEL OF SAVING BEHAVIOR

*Savings in economic theory.* In the Surveys of Consumer Finances we have a fund of cross-section data to be used for the estimation of equations of household saving and spending behavior. As will be explained below, only certain types of household expenditures are included in this material; therefore we shall not proceed like other investigators in the past, who have estimated Engel curves for a variety of durable and nondurable expenditures. We shall concentrate attention on savings and expenditures for durables. We shall treat these two variables separately, defining savings according to the concept used in the Surveys of Consumer Finances, and not add them as Morgan has done in his analysis.

[2] L. R. Klein, *A Textbook of Econometrics* (Evanston: Row, Peterson and Co., 1953), Chap. V.

Let us first turn to saving behavior. What are the hypotheses in both the economic and the probability model? If classical economic theory states that the demand by a household for any item of current consumption depends on relative prices of all commodities and the household income, a savings–demand equation can be derived as the difference between money income and money expenditure, with the demand equations for commodities substituted into the latter term. "Real" savings, according to classical theory, should depend on "real" income and relative prices. If the classical model is constructed with savings explicitly represented by the consumption of future commodities, the prices of the future commodities will be relevant variables, which in turn call for the use of interest rates in order to discount future items to the present.

Within the classical framework, we can generalize the formulation of household behavior by developing a multiperiod analysis and allowing borrowing and asset holding to influence individual decisions. Then demand for commodities, present or future, depends on relative prices, income, and initial asset–debt holdings. Saving is interpreted as the demand for future commodities. The implications of this model for survey analysis are that savings in a single cross-section sample vary from household to household because incomes, initial asset, and initial debt positions vary. These, as we shall see, are not the only explanatory variables, but they are candidates for use in empirical work and should account for a good part of the observed variation in saving behavior. Prices and interest rates will, as usual, be assumed constant in our sample. An assumption often made in classical theory is that income has a positive effect on demand—the larger the income (*cet. par.*), the larger the demand. The same assumption is made about the effect of income on savings. The extended theory shows definitely that initial wealth variables influence demand and savings, but it does not tell us about the direction of effect. In many instances it is assumed that net wealth is inversely correlated with savings (*cet. par.*), assets showing an inverse effect and liabilities the opposite. Initial assets are regarded as an enabling factor permitting one to spend more and save less than would be possible in their absence. Another way of putting the matter is that one assumes that the more a person has accumulated through past saving, the less he wants to accumulate further. A psychological theory of habit formation may run counter to this hypothesis, so that we cannot be certain about the direction of effect to look for on a priori grounds.[3] In the case of initial debts, there is a pressure for subsequent repayment giving rise to positive saving. This is especially true for mortgage and installment debt, which require periodic repayment. These two types account for the bulk of consumer debt.

A narrow account of static economic theory suggests equations of saving behavior including only economic variables, and those may not even be complete within economics. Income change is a dynamic type of economic variable that is probably important for the interpretation of consumer behavior. Several hypotheses about the impact of income change seem plausible, but the most common one is that savings are positively related to income change. The underlying argument states that consumers tend to persist in maintaining their recent consumption patterns when income changes; thus, if a household's income falls and it consumes the amount it previously consumed at the higher income status, a reduced amount will be left for savings, and there will tend to be low savings associated with income decreases. The converse argument attempts to establish an association between high saving and income increase; therefore the overall relation is assumed to be positive. The arguments about the relation between saving and income change are not conclusive, and other hypotheses seem reasonable. Income increase and income decrease may show different types of effect. If so, a simple linear relation between income change and saving is not justified. Another important qualification is that individuals' perceptions of income change may have a bearing on the direction and magnitude of effect. Changes regarded

---

[3] A fuller discussion of saturation and habit formation in relation to the effect of liquid asset holdings on saving behavior is given in G. Katona, *Psychological Analysis of Economic Behavior* (New York: McGraw-Hill Book Co., 1951), pp. 167–70.

as temporary may well influence saving the way income change in general is assumed to influence saving in the habit-persistence argument. Households experiencing an income change which they regard as temporary are likely to maintain their previous consumption levels and allow savings to fluctuate in the same direction as the income change. Under the impact of permanent change it is not at all likely that households will simply tend to retain their past levels of consumption. These different possibilities are studied empirically below.

*Noneconomic variables in saving behavior.* A more serious deficiency of classical economic theory is its failure to treat explicitly the influence of noneconomic variables on economic behavior. We shall divide our variables into three categories—economic; demographic or sociological; attitudinal or psychological. Our economic variables in equations of saving behavior are savings, income, assets, debt, and income change. Demographic variables are age of household head, size of household, race of household head, education of household head, and marital status. Occupation and home-ownership status are mixed variables that are partly demographic and partly economic. The distributions among occupational or home ownership categories are very stable over time; hence we treat them like purely demographic variables. Attitudinal variables are expected income change, perception of past income change, general economic outlook, expected price change, and feeling of economic security.

*The mathematical form of savings functions.* The argument of parsimony and simplicity would use theoretical and other a priori information to obtain a list of relevant variables affecting saving behavior and would then estimate linear relations among these variables. However, we shall try to push the analysis further in specifying the mathematical form of the savings equations that we shall study empirically. It has frequently been suggested that savings are not linearly related to income (*cet. par.*). The marginal propensity to save is assumed to increase as income increases. This property of the savings function is critical in appraising the arguments about the effect of income redistribution on saving and spending. If the marginal propensity to save is the same for people at all income levels—the case of a linear savings function—income redistribution has a zero effect. If the marginal propensity to save grows with growing income, redistribution toward income equality stimulates spending and depresses saving. There is slight empirical evidence of the suspected curvature in the savings function on the basis of previous studies, but these investigations suffer from the paucity of high-income observations. Linearity seems to be a tolerable approximation over much of the income range, and curvature appears mainly at higher income levels, say $5,000 and over in the studies before World War II. We shall use empirical equations that are nonlinear in the savings–income relation.

Previous remarks brought out the point that theory is not unambiguous on the direction of effect of assets on savings. Assets as an enabling factor are positively associated with spending and negatively with saving; assets as an indicator of past saving habits are negatively associated with spending and positively with saving. The enabling aspect of assets would seem to be more important for poor or low income people who are not habitually large savers and who have many urgent uses for spending accumulated assets; thus we look for an inverse relation between savings and assets in low income groups. Contrariwise, asset holding by rich or high-income people is more a representation of their past saving habits, and they do not have urgent uses for spending their wealth. We look for a weaker inverse relation between saving and assets in high income groups or even a positive relation among very high income groups. This type of relation implies that the marginal propensity to save increases with increasing assets. There is thus an interaction effect on saving between assets and income, this interaction being another form of nonlinearity in the savings equation. As mentioned previously, the asset–income interaction is quite prominent in various regressions studied by Morgan. Evidence found in his analysis is, in this way, helpful in the problem of constructing a more general savings function.

Liquid assets appear to interact with income not only in affecting the slope of the savings–income relation but also the curvature. The normally assumed curvature of the savings–income relation is stronger in low-asset groups and becomes less evident as we move up the asset scale. For high-asset holders, we can probably achieve no better smooth approximation to the savings–income relation than that of a straight line.

The diverse assumptions about the possible effects of income change have already been mentioned. They, too, imply departures from a simple linear scheme. The effect of age on saving is another phenomenon that is suspected to be nonlinear. Young households, trying to build up supplies of equipment and other items, can save relatively little. As they grow older, savings can grow; but in old age, after retirement from active occupation, they tend to live on capital to some extent. These arguments imply rising and then falling savings as a function of age. It must be pointed out, though, that income similarly goes through a rising and then falling life cycle; therefore a savings equation involving both income and age may not show low savings among the oldest people if one takes into account the fact that these people have low incomes.

The possible properties of a savings equation that we have mentioned so far come from considerations about economic behavior. In addition, the probability model may suggest other properties. A basic assumption in the probability model usually adopted is that we are trying to estimate parameters of behavior equations subject to additive random impulses, these random elements arising from the large list of small and rare factors that influence behavior in addition to those explicitly covered by the variables of the model. We assume that the random impulses are distributed according to some probability law with particular characteristics. In some methods of statistical estimation it is assumed that the variance of the random terms is independent of the explanatory variables.[4] It is both well-known

---

[4] In other methods it may be assumed that proportions among the variances are known. The known proportionality factors are then used as weights in the estimation equations. Our approach accomplishes the same thing by transforming the variables as explained in the text below.

and reasonable that the variability of savings is not uniform in all income or asset classes. A good approximation states that the standard deviation of savings within each of several income classes is proportional to the average income of each class. The variability of savings is perhaps more closely approximated as a function of both income and assets, although income appears to be the dominant variable.[5] Since saving in our equations is expressed as a function of several variables plus a disturbance term, the remarks about saving variability apply directly to the variance of the probability elements, and we find a contradiction of the basic assumption of the probability model, namely that the variance of the disturbance is independent of explanatory variables (income and assets). In many cases, models that do not conform to certain maintained probability assumptions can be made to do so by transforming the variables and equations of the model. In the present case, we find that the savings–income ratio does show approximate uniformity of variance by income and asset levels; therefore, by making the savings–income ratio rather than savings the principal variable of analysis, we obtain an equation that does meet a major assumption of the probability model.

In terms of the simple mathematics involved, we set out with a savings equation of the form

$$(2.1) \qquad S = S(Y, Y_{-1}, L_{-1}, N, A, \cdots) + u, \text{ in which}$$

$$S = \text{savings}$$
$$Y = \text{income}$$
$$Y_{-1} = \text{last year's income}$$
$$L_{-1} = \text{beginning-of-year liquid assets}$$
$$N = \text{size of household}$$
$$A = \text{age of head of household}$$
$$u = \text{random disturbance}$$

If the savings function in (2.1) is linear in its parameters, though not necessarily in the variables, statistically efficient estimates of the parameters can be obtained by the familiar methods of (unweighted)

---

[5] See Morgan's analysis of this problem in Chapter III above.

least-squares, provided our sample consists of a set of independent values of $u$, drawn from some probability distribution with variance

$$\sigma_u^2 < \infty,$$

$\sigma_u^2$ independent of $Y$, $Y_{-1}$, $L_{-1}$, $N$, $A$

If we further specify the probability distribution of $u$ to be normal, we assume that $\sigma_u^2$ is some unknown constant, a population parameter. These assumptions are not fulfilled. Instead we have

$$\sigma_u^2 = \sigma_v^2 Y^2,$$

where $\sigma_v^2$ is a constant. The transformed variable, $u/Y = v$, does, however, have constant variance

$$\sigma_{u/Y}^2 = \frac{1}{Y^2}\,\sigma_u^2 = \sigma_v^2;$$

thus we rewrite (2.1) as

(2.2)          $S/Y = 1/Y\,[S(Y, Y_{-1}, L_{-1}, N, A, \cdots)] + v$

and apply the standard least-squares methods to (2.2) instead of (2.1).[6]

   Implicit, in our use of the method of least-squares, is the assumption that saving behavior is affected by income, beginning-of-year liquid assets, size of household, age, and other explanatory variables but that saving behavior does not simultaneously affect the explanatory variables. At the level of the aggregative economy this unique line of causation would not necessarily exist, but it does seem to give a reasonable representation of individual behavior. Most individuals take whatever income they can get and adjust their saving and spending patterns to it. The amount of income earned through saving during the current year is negligible. In the case of lagged liquid assets and age, there is no question of the cause–effect relation. Household size is probably not significantly affected by the savings of one year.

   In all our calculations for this paper we proceed as though savings

---

[6] For an empirical study of the different results obtained before and after this type of transformation, the reader is referred to L. R. Klein and J. N. Morgan, "Results of Alternative Statistical Treatments of Sample Survey Data," *Journal of the American Statistical Association*, XLVI (1951), 442–60.

represented an endogenous variable and as though all the explanatory variables were predetermined for an individual.

*A particular savings function.* The problem now is to develop a mathematical expression for the right-hand side of (2.2), taking into account the criteria already considered for the shape of the savings equation. A basic equation for our analysis is

$$(2.3) \quad S/Y = \alpha_0 + \alpha_1 \log Y + \alpha_2 \log N + \alpha_3 L_{-1}/Y + \alpha_4 L_{-1}$$
$$+ \alpha_5 \frac{Y - Y_{-1}}{Y_{-1}} + \alpha_6 A + v$$

Equation (2.3) has the property of possessing the principal characteristics we require for our savings equation and is, in addition, linear in the unknown parameters, $\alpha_i$.

The marginal propensity to save in (2.3) is given by the expression

$$\alpha_0 + \alpha_1 \log Y + \alpha_1 + \alpha_2 \log N + \alpha_4 L_{-1} + 2 \alpha_5 \frac{Y}{Y_{-1}} - \alpha_5 + \alpha_6 A + v$$

The proposed savings function has curvature in the $(S,Y)$-plane since the marginal propensity to save depends on income, the principal dependence coming from the term $\alpha_1 \log Y$. The magnitude and direction of the variation of the marginal propensity with respect to income depends upon $\alpha_1$, an unknown parameter. From a statistical point of view, the equation (2.3) allows us the freedom of testing whether there is any curvature in the savings–income relation by determining the significance of estimates of $\alpha_1$. If the estimate is significantly positive, we find consistency between the data and our a priori hypothesis.

The marginal effect of liquid assets on saving is $\alpha_3 + \alpha_4 Y$. The hypothesis that the marginal asset effect is greater (negatively) for lower than for upper income groups assumes that $\alpha_3 < 0$ and $\alpha_4 > 0$. Our equation permits a test of this hypothesis by examining the significance of the signs of estimates of $\alpha_3$ and $\alpha_4$. In case this marginal effect changes from a negative to a positive direction, estimates of equation (2.3) enable us to say approximately at what income level the change takes place. The curvature of (2.3) is independent of the level of liquid assets; thus we have not built into this equation a property evident in some empirical data cited above, namely that curvature of the savings–income relation is more pronounced in low-asset groups and dwindles to linearity for high-asset groups.

The reason for using log $N$ instead of $N$ as a separate variable in (2.3) is primarily to enable us to test simultaneously the significance of household size in saving behavior and the relative advantages of per capita or aggregate household variables. In formulations which omit $L_{-1}$, the variable accounting for the interaction between income and liquid assets, and impose the restriction, $a_2 = -a_1$, the equation can be considered as one relating per capita variables of the several households in the sample. We thus find (2.3) a convenient form in which to test this hypothesis. Moreover, Morgan finds some evidence in his analysis that household size does not affect saving linearly. By using log $N$ we impart decreasing quantitative significance to additional persons at higher levels of household size.

Percentage change in income is a variable in (2.3). This measure was conveniently available to us on punched cards but is not particularly preferable to (log $Y$ — log $Y_{-1}$). In our empirical studies we have used both types. As we have written (2.3), no distinction is made between income increase and income decrease, a distinction which may prove to be of some importance. In some calculations, (2.3) is used in the form written above; in others, separate estimates are made for households receiving income increases and those receiving decreases.

Age is ordinarily thought to be nonlinearly related to saving in such a way that very young and very old people save less than middle age groups. On the other hand, the savings–income ratio does not exhibit the same pattern, because income shows a similar nonlinear movement. Our equation does permit the age effect on savings to vary by income level, a relationship found elsewhere.[7]

[7] See Janet Fisher, "Income, Spending, and Saving Patterns of Consumer Units in Different Age Groups," *Studies in Income and Wealth,* Vol. XV (New York: National Bureau of Economic Research, 1952), pp. 75–102.

It is not essential that curvature in the $(S, Y)$-plane take the particular form suggested in (2.3). Another way of getting a similar relationship would be to relate $S$ to $Y$ and $Y^2$ (or $S/Y$ to $1/Y$ and $Y$) in a parabolic form. This method uses an additional parameter. Extensive calculations have been made with both forms.[8]

Qualitative variables such as home-ownership status, business-ownership status, income expectations, general economic outlook, etc., which are coded either yes–no, or high–low, or in some other broad categories, are incorporated into a study of equation (2.3) in a number of ways. In some instances the sample is sorted into separate groups associated with each broad category, and then (2.3) is estimated for each group. In other instances dummy variables taking on the values 0 or 1 are used to indicate nonnumerical classifications. Finally, we have studied the distribution of residual variation, estimates of $v$, within several qualitative classifications.

Equation (2.3) takes us a good part of the distance toward the goal of estimating autonomous patterns of saving behavior, patterns that get at underlying motivations in a form that will remain valid under the widest possible set of circumstances. However, there are numerous deficiencies remaining. We shall reserve a discussion of these to the next section, where they can best be dealt with in terms of a thorough discussion of the empirical results.

### THE ESTIMATION OF SAVINGS EQUATIONS

*The samples and variables used.* The reader must have a clear idea about the sample and the definitions of variables used in order to gain a full understanding of the empirical findings. Some of this information is included in other chapters of this volume, but, at the risk of being repetitious, we want to leave as little doubt as possible about the interpretation of our results.

Two basic types of samples are used. In some cases we use data from the full samples in the Surveys of Consumer Finances. These

---

[8] See L. R. Klein and J. N. Morgan, "Results of Alternative Statistical Treatments of Sample Survey Data."

data refer to one-time interviews. Extensive analysis will be made, however, from a special subsample of the 1949 Survey containing spending units who were also interviewed in 1948. Particular importance attaches to the analysis of the reinterview sample because income change and beginning-of-year variables (assets and attitudes) are best estimated from repeated rather than one-time interviews. In order to approximate the theoretical formulations as closely as possible, we must use beginning-of-year variables in several cases—hence the importance of the reinterview sample. This sample covers only urban areas and gives us a representative picture of a part of the nation specifically excluding farmers. This relative homogeneity of respondents is an attractive feature of the sample.

The variables of the savings analysis are

$S$ = savings as defined in the Surveys of Consumer Finances
$Y$ = disposable income—total income minus estimated federal income taxes
$Y_{-1}$ = disposable income of the preceding year
$L_{-1}$ = beginning-of-year holdings of liquid assets—bank deposits plus U.S. government bonds
$N$ = number of persons in the spending unit
$A$ = age of head of spending unit
$H$ = 1 if spending unit owns home, and 0 if spending unit rents

All variables are defined in terms of spending units, the basic household concept of the Surveys of Consumer Finances.[9] Calculations are made in most cases on spending units who actually report on all variables used in the analysis. Missing values of components of savings, income, or liquid assets are assigned to spending units by the Survey Research Center by a method approximating missing plot techniques of agricultural field experiments, but the assigned values are usually excluded from our work. Parallel calculations for nonassigned and assigned-plus-nonassigned cases show nearly identical results.

*Preliminary estimates from the reinterview sample.* The first set of calculations is made from the reinterview sample and is done sepa-

[9] See Lansing's discussion in Chapter I.

rately for home owners and renters. There are several reasons for drawing a distinction between these two groups. In the first place our material does not impute rental income to owner-occupiers of residences or subtract home depreciation from savings. Secondly, home owners have, to a large extent, a significant contractual commitment to save, namely, to repay mortgage debt. Nearly one-half the home owners have mortgages. Finally, liquid assets give a better indication of the wealth position of renters than of home owners, who have a relatively large share of their total wealth in the form of real estate.

Table 1 summarizes a collection of savings equations previously published by the author. They all involve per capita variables and neglect the possibility of an interaction effect between liquid assets and income. These and other equations determined from the reinterview sample are weighted estimates in which the weights are chosen so as to represent differential sampling and response rates in the several strata of the population covered. In practice, the weights do not make a great deal of difference in estimated parameters of the equations studied. At a later stage we shall present some unweighted estimates. Elsewhere, alternative calculations of weighted and unweighted data are given for comparison.[10]

In the seven equations of this table, $S/Y$ is expressed as a linear function of the variables heading each of the columns. The numbers in parentheses below coefficients are standard errors. The algebraic signs attached to coefficients indicate direction of relationship. Thus a negative coefficient of $L_{-1}/Y$ means that larger ratios of liquid assets to income tend to be associated with smaller values of ratios of savings to income, *cet. par.* Savings can be positive or negative, and relative sizes of this variable are ordered algebraically.

The principal difference between (3.1) and (3.2) is in the constant term; therefore we pool the home owners and renters to estimate a single relation in (3.3) with the added variable $H$. Income

---

[10] See L. R. Klein and J. N. Morgan, "Results of Alternative Statistical Treatments of Sample Survey Data."

# TABLE 1

## COEFFICIENTS AND RELATED STATISTICS OF EMPIRICAL SAVINGS EQUATIONS

| | Constant | Log $Y/N$[a] | $L_{-1}/Y$ | $\dfrac{Y - Y_{-1}}{Y_{-1}}$ | $A$ | $H$ | Correlation Coefficient | Standard Error of Estimate | Description |
|---|---|---|---|---|---|---|---|---|---|
| (3.1) | −0.93 | 0.35 (0.08) | −0.21 (0.02) | 0.03 (0.05) | 0.0013 (0.0022) | | 0.57 | 0.42 | 288 home owners |
| (3.2) | −1.61 | 0.48 (0.11) | −0.25 (0.03) | 0.07 (0.06) | 0.0054 (0.0024) | | 0.49 | 0.56 | 318 renters |
| (3.3) | −1.36 | 0.41 (0.07) | −0.23 (0.02) | 0.06 (0.04) | 0.0038 (0.0017) | 0.13 (0.05) | 0.52 | 0.50 | 606 home owners and renters |
| (3.4) | −1.15 | 0.47 (0.14) | −0.31 (0.03) | −0.54 (0.38) | | | 0.78 | 0.50 | 89 home owners $Y - Y_{-1} < 0$ |
| (3.5) | −0.93 | 0.45 (0.30) | −0.25 (0.06) | 1.61 (0.49) | | | 0.59 | 0.83 | 111 renters $Y - Y_{-1} < 0$ |
| (3.6) | −0.68 | 0.26 (0.08) | −0.06 (0.03) | 0.02 (0.05) | | | 0.26 | 0.34 | 199 home owners $Y - Y_{-1} > 0$ |
| (3.7) | −0.31 | 0.11 (0.05) | 0.00 (0.02) | 0.01 (0.02) | | | 0.16 | 0.20 | 207 renters $Y - Y_{-1} > 0$ |

[a] In all calculations, logarithms are to the base 10.

and initial liquid assets are the dominant variables in (3.1)–(3.3). The age variable is correlated to some extent with assets but shows a consistent pattern in all equations. A possible reason for finding a more significant age effect among renters than among home owners is that in the latter group many older persons will have retired their mortgage debt and will, on this account alone, have a smaller contractual savings obligation than younger home owners.

Income change shows a consistent but nonsignificant effect on savings. The usual assumption is that income change is negatively related to consumer expenditures and positively related to savings, as our equations indicate in a rough way. Further probing into the effect of income change is carried out in (3.4)–(3.7) through examination of the hypothesis that income decreases and income increases have different directions of effect on savings. The main finding in (3.4)–(3.7) appears to be that the strength of the asset effect is most marked among those receiving income decreases. The argument is that when people have an income decrease which would ordinarily make it difficult for them to maintain past levels of living, those who simultaneously possess liquid assets will use them to maintain expenditures and thus impede savings. The equations present evidence, in this way, of an interaction effect between liquid assets and income change; however, there is some correlation between current income level and income change over the past year; therefore we cannot rule out the possibility that the true interaction effect is that which was discussed earlier between assets and income level.

*Analysis of residuals—reinterview sample.* A virtue in the estimation of economic relations from survey data is that we can study the distribution properties of a large sample of residuals, the estimates of the disturbance terms in the equations. For (3.1) and (3.2) we have calculated the difference between each spending unit's saving–income ratio and that which would be given by the equations. We shall denote by $u_1$ the residuals from (3.1) and by $u_2$ the residuals from (3.2). The savings equations were transformed into the types used in (3.1) and (3.2) in order to obtain equations with uniform variability in the disturbances, the main assumption being that untransformed equations connecting $S$, $Y$, $Y_{-1}$, $L_{-1}$, $N$, $A$, etc., would have disturbances with increasing variability as income grows. Table 2 gives the standard deviation of $u_1$ and $u_2$ within income deciles. Except for the larger variability in the bottom income decile, we have uniformity in an empirical sense. By assuming that the variability depends on assets as well as income, we could perhaps eliminate the discrepancy observed in the first decile. A small number of extreme cases, however, accounts for the greater variability in the lowest decile. For example, in the sample of renters there is one extreme

### TABLE 2

#### STANDARD DEVIATIONS OF RESIDUALS OF (3.1) AND (3.2) BY INCOME DECILES

| Decile | Standard Deviation of $u_1$ | Standard Deviation of $u_2$ |
|---|---|---|
| lowest   1 | 1.00 | 1.44 |
| 2 | 0.23 | 0.16 |
| 3 | 0.39 | 0.19 |
| 4 | 0.24 | 0.52 |
| 5 | 0.27 | 0.34 |
| 6 | 0.25 | 0.25 |
| 7 | 0.20 | 0.36 |
| 8 | 0.32 | 0.41 |
| 9 | 0.31 | 0.23 |
| highest 10 | 0.36 | 0.33 |

item, and the standard deviation of the remaining values of $u_2$ is only 0.36, in line with the other values in Table 2. These extreme items have less effect on the estimation of the coefficients in the savings equations than on the estimated variance of the disturbances.

For many statistical purposes we need not specify the parametric form of the probability distribution of the disturbances; we assume merely that our sample consists of independent drawings from some probability distribution. In order to apply certain significance tests, though, the assumption of normality of disturbances is required. Moreover, the nature of the origin of the disturbances—assumed to be due to the neglect of numerous minute variables affecting behavior

—indicates asymptotic normality. On finding evidence of normally distributed residuals from our equations, we should feel safer about drawing the inference that systematic relationships have been extracted, leaving only chance variation to be accounted for. It is not necessary to have normality in order to make this inference, but normality is patently desirable.

On fitting a normal distribution to our residuals, we find a particular type of divergence between the fitted curve and observations, namely, that our samples of residuals show a considerably more peaked distribution than the normal curve.

## TABLE 3

### RELATIVE FREQUENCIES OF RESIDUALS OF (3.1) AND (3.2) BY DECILES OF FITTED NORMAL DISTRIBUTIONS

| Decile | Observed Relative Frequency, $u_1$ | Observed Relative Frequency, $u_2$ |
|---|---|---|
| lowest 1 | 0.02 | 0.03 |
| 2 | 0.05 | 0.02 |
| 3 | 0.07 | 0.03 |
| 4 | 0.16 | 0.14 |
| 5 | 0.18 | 0.24 |
| 6 | 0.15 | 0.31 |
| 7 | 0.15 | 0.12 |
| 8 | 0.10 | 0.06 |
| 9 | 0.07 | 0.02 |
| highest 10 | 0.05 | 0.03 |

A perfect fit to a normal distribution would be indicated by observed relative frequencies of 0.10 in each decile. We note, in Table 3, one particular type of departure from normality—excessive peakedness of our empirical distribution. This is known technically as *leptokurtosis,* a property not uncommon in the type of data we are using. Peaked distributions imply that we have a few extreme cases and a large number of cases with small deviation from average behavior. As extreme cases are eliminated from the sample, *leptokurtosis* tends to disappear. As Morgan has already pointed out, the main effect of this kind of nonnormality is to lead us to accept, as statistically significant, findings which really are not significant at the probability levels chosen. We attempt to guard against incorrect decisions of this type by repeating analyses in independent samples or within subgroups of a single sample.

A possible contribution to the explanation of the nonnormality of residuals is that our equations may be defective in not allowing an interaction effect between liquid assets and income on saving. If the variable $L_{-1}$ were included among the list of explanatory factors in equations (3.1)–(3.3) involving the savings–income ratio, an interaction effect on savings would be implicit in the equation; thus we study the mean residuals within liquid asset groups.

TABLE 4

MEAN RESIDUALS OF (3.1) AND (3.2) BY LIQUID ASSET GROUPS

| Liquid Assets (dollars) | Frequency | $\bar{u}_1$ | Frequency | $\bar{u}_2$ |
|---|---|---|---|---|
| 0–499 | 108 | −0.042 | 156 | −0.021 |
| 500–1,999 | 79 | −0.059 | 91 | 0.006 |
| 2,000–4,999 | 55 | 0.109 | 44 | −0.144 |
| 5,000 or more | 46 | 0.191 | 27 | 0.508 |

Standard errors of these means can be determined by considering them as sample drawings from populations with standard deviations 0.42 and 0.56, respectively. Approximate formulas are

$$S_{ui} = \frac{S_{u_i}}{\sqrt{n}}, \; i = 1, 2, \text{ in which}$$

$$S_{u_1} = 0.42$$

$$S_{u_2} = 0.56$$

$$n = \text{frequency}$$

Since the $u_i$ are weighted means, this formula is not strictly correct but is actually a very close approximation. The data in Table 4 show strong evidence of the supposed interaction effect.

In early 1949, the respondents of our sample were asked to indicate their expected income for the coming calendar year in comparison with realized income in 1948. Following a device introduced by Katona,[11] we group respondents simultaneously by realized past

[11] G. Katona, "Effect of Income Changes on the Rate of Saving," *Review of Economics and Statistics,* XXXI (May 1949), 95–103.

and expected future income change. Those who expect their incomes to change in the same direction as their past change or to remain stable are classed as those with permanent change. Others are classed as having nonpermanent or temporary change. They expect a reversal of past change or are undecided what to expect.

A small number of observations with zero income change are excluded. The principal result here is that income increase of either sort, temporary or permanent, shows little relation to the residuals, while income decrease shows significant relations which are different for those in the permanent and the temporary categories. Both home owners and renters show an association between low residuals and temporary decline, between high residuals and permanent decline.

TABLE 5

MEAN RESIDUALS OF (3.1) AND (3.2) BY INCOME CHANGE AND EXPECTED INCOME CHANGE GROUPS

| Income Change 1947–1948 | Expected Income Change 1948–1949 | Frequency | $\bar{u}_1$ | Frequency | $\bar{u}_2$ |
|---|---|---|---|---|---|
| + | + or 0 | 144 | −0.026 | 152 | −0.005 |
| − | − or 0 | 52 | 0.157 | 49 | 0.196 |
| + | − or ? | 47 | −0.028 | 50 | −0.028 |
| − | + or ? | 27 | −0.132 | 51 | −0.152 |

These findings seem to be quite reasonable on a priori grounds and agree in principle with those of Katona in other survey samples. Our tabulations differ in that they take account of income, assets, size of spending unit, age of head, and home-ownership status as well as type of income change. Katona's calculations consist of distributions of the savings–income ratio within income-change, expected-income-change classes. Although income change does not appear to be a strong variable in (3.1) and (3.2), our sample reveals interesting findings about the effect of income change on saving behavior. Decreases affect saving differently from increases, while permanent decreases affect saving differently from temporary decreases.

A major advantage of the reinterview sample is that variables determined at a prior time point can be taken from the first survey and related to variables determined at a later time point, taken from the second survey. Expectations are customarily used in economics as predetermined variables influencing subsequent behavior. Beginning-of-year expectations and calendar-year behavior are not ideal from this point of view, because decisions made during the latter part of the year will often be related to changed expectations; but this pair of variables comes closer to measurement of the concepts of theoretical economics than data from one-time surveys relating, say, calendar-year behavior to end-of-year expectations.

Prior income expectations are studied in relation to the residuals of our equations in Table 6.

TABLE 6

MEAN RESIDUALS OF (3.1) AND (3.2) BY EXPECTED INCOME CHANGE GROUPS

| Expected Income Change 1947–1948 | Frequency | $\bar{u}_1$ | Frequency | $\bar{u}_2$ |
|---|---|---|---|---|
| + | 60 | −0.012 | 92 | 0.031 |
| 0 | 151 | 0.017 | 151 | −0.025 |
| − | 47 | 0.068 | 40 | 0.110 |
| ? | 30 | −0.075 | 35 | −0.054 |

The most interesting findings here are the positive residuals for those expecting income decreases, indicating a tendency to save in anticipation of economic difficulties ahead. The interpretation of the category with unknown expectations is dubious, and the other entries in the table do not differ significantly from zero. Among those who expected a decline, those who actually received declines show even larger average residuals, 0.074 and 0.133 for the two groups respectively. Other combinations of expected income change and subsequent realized change show no systematic or significant patterns.

The reinterview sample can be similarly used to study the relation between respondents' beginning-of-the-year expectations for the economy as a whole and the residuals from the savings equations. This tabulation contrasts with the previous one in replacing personal by general expectations.

An important pattern seen from the inspection of these results is that the optimists (good times ahead) have lower residuals than the pessimists (bad times ahead).

Other variables have been studied in relation to the residuals but no significant conclusions can be drawn. Among the other groupings are beginning-of-year price expectations, occupation, change in number of children under eighteen years of age, change in number of adults, education, and race. Prior price expectations form an interesting variable, especially since actual prices are assumed constant over the sample during a single survey. Unfortunately, a sharp break in the commodity price markets during the middle of the interviewing period, February, 1948, caused a marked change in the frequency distribution of expected price movements after the event occurred.

TABLE 7

MEAN RESIDUALS OF (3.1) AND (3.2) BY GENERAL ECONOMIC OUTLOOK GROUPS

| General Economic Outlook | Frequency | $\bar{u}_1$ | Frequency | $\bar{u}_2$ |
|---|---|---|---|---|
| Good times ahead | 150 | −0.034 | 149 | −0.036 |
| Neither good nor bad | 13 | 0.142 | 21 | −0.032 |
| Bad times ahead | 76 | 0.082 | 87 | 0.044 |
| Undecided | 22 | −0.069 | 40 | 0.081 |
| Not ascertained | 27 | −0.013 | 21 | 0.004 |

In this sample, price expectations pertain to different reference situations depending on the day of interview. Methodologically, however, our methods of survey analysis do provide techniques for the study of such interesting phenomena as price expectations in future samples, when it is hoped that more usable data may become available.

There are no striking or consistent occupational differences in our analysis of residuals, but the major difference to be expected, between farmers and nonfarmers, is excluded by the nature of the sample. The change in the number of children does not have unambiguous meaning, but for both renters and homeowners an increase in the number of children under eighteen is associated with positive residuals, while a decrease is associated with negative residuals. The frequencies are small except in the zero-change group, so that any conclusions drawn from these calculations are dubious. In a similar way, the change in the number of adults presents no reliable patterns. The mean residual for units having a decrease in the number of adults is consistently negative. Insofar as this decrease is due to death, especially of a breadwinner, it is reasonable to expect low savings. Educational differences in mean residuals are inconsistent between home owners and renters as well as nonsignificant. Nonwhites are so rare in the small sample at hand that little can be said about racial differences; however, we do find small positive residuals among Negro spending units.[12]

The method used here of first calculating residuals from a multivariate savings equation and then studying these residuals in relation to other variables, mainly attitudinal and demographic, one at a time, is not optimal. The supplementary variables studied against residuals may not be independent among themselves nor independent of the variables used in calculating the residuals. Liquid assets show in Table 4 a positive correlation with the residuals, yet intercorrelation between $\log Y$ and $L_{-1}$ would change the estimated coefficient of $\log Y$ in an equation incorporating $L_{-1}$ as compared with the value used in calculating the residuals of Table 4. This will be seen below. While we do recognize deficiencies in our own approach, we nevertheless submit our results as an advance over previous work in the study of consumer behavior in that we do try to assess the full multivariate structure of household saving decisions and try to bring in demographic and attitudinal variables as well as the familiar economic variables.

*Further estimates from the reinterview sample.* The results of Table 4 suggest a revision of our estimated equations by the addition of $L_{-1}$ as a separate variable. Simultaneously with this revision we

---

[12] The suggestive though statistically nonsignificant results showing greater providence among Negroes have been extensively studied from a pooled sample of four successive Surveys of Consumer Finances by H. W. Mooney, "Some Factors Associated with Negro–White Savings Differentials," unpublished Ph.D. thesis, University of Michigan, 1953. Racial differences are found to be significant in Mooney's study. For a summary presentation of his findings and an analysis of their economic importance, see L. R. Klein and H. W. Mooney, "Negro–White Savings Differentials and the Consumption Function Problem," *Econometrica*, XXI (1953), 425–56. See also H. Mendershausen, "Differences in Family Savings."

drop the per capita form of the equation by letting $\log N$ have a freely determined coefficient. The result is

*606 home owners and renters*

$$(3.8) \quad S/Y = -0.65 + 0.21 \log Y/N - 0.12 \log N - 0.29\, L_{-1}/Y$$
$$\phantom{(3.8) \quad S/Y =} (0.09) \qquad\qquad (0.11) \qquad\qquad (0.02)$$

$$+ 0.000039 L_{-1} + 0.06\, \frac{Y - Y_{-1}}{Y_{-1}} + 0.0026A + 0.11H$$
$$(0.000006) \qquad (0.04) \qquad\qquad (0.0017) \qquad (0.05)$$

$$R = 0.55 \qquad S_u = 0.49$$

In most respects, equation (3.8) seems to be an improvement over (3.3) and does agree with the hypothesis that the marginal asset effect varies according to income level. A prominent result of permitting an income–asset interaction effect on savings is to decrease the curvature of the savings function in the $(S, Y)$-plane. This can be seen from the drop in the coefficient of $\log Y$ between (3.3) and (3.8), since this term is primarily responsible for the curvature. The coefficient of $\log N$ in (3.8) is $-(0.21 + 0.12) = -0.33$, with a standard error in the neighborhood of 0.1; thus the size of the spending unit is significantly related to saving behavior, but the term accounting for divergence from a per capita income concept is not statistically significant.[13]

The reinterview sample has been used further to examine two other hypotheses about savings behavior. One case is the use of debts as well as assets to estimate the relation between savings and wealth. The other is the adoption of a longer accounting period, two years instead of one, on the assumption that savings decisions are not made with reference to the events of a single year. Beginning-of-year debt data for our sample are more satisfactory for renters than for home owners because of the ambiguity of mortgage payment data on the separation between interest and principal payments. The debt variable, D, covers consumer installment, personal loan, bank loan, and other types of nonmortgage debt. On the whole, only short-term debt is included. For a group of 316 renters reporting debt information in the reinterview sample, we get

[13] This remark is only approximate since $L_{-1}$ is not in per capita terms in (3.8).

(3.9) $S/Y = -1.64 + 0.49 \log Y/N - 0.25 L_{-1}/Y + 0.07 \dfrac{Y - Y_{-1}}{Y_{-1}}$
$\quad\quad\quad\quad\quad (0.11) \quad\quad\quad\quad\quad (0.03) \quad\quad\quad (0.06)$
$\quad\quad + 0.0054A - 0.09 D_{-1}/Y$
$\quad\quad\quad (0.0024) \quad\ (0.13)$

$$R = 0.49 \quad\quad S_u = 0.55$$

This equation compared with (3.2) shows practically no change in the coefficients of variables common to the two equations and a small insignificant coefficient associated with debt. Even the direction of effect is not that which we expect, but since the sign of the estimate is not significant, positive values are admissible on the basis of the observed sample.

Perhaps a year is too short a period in which to arrive at savings decisions; therefore we consider the use of the reinterview sample to study the relation between twenty-four months' saving, twenty-four months' income, and liquid assets. It has been noted before in cross-section studies of investment behavior of business firms that two-to-five-year statistical relationships show more stability than one-year relationships. Our sample is slightly changed in that some assigned values for savings and income are used, but these are known to have an unimportant influence on the results. Liquid assets and size of spending unit are dated as of the middle of the twenty-four months' period. The calculations show

*319 home owners*

(3.10)     $S'/Y' = -0.92 + 0.31 \log Y'/N' - 0.20 L'/Y'$
$$R = 0.37 \quad\quad S_{u'} = 0.38$$

*311 renters*

(3.11)     $S'/Y' = -0.45 + 0.14 \log Y'/N' + 0.02 L'/Y'$
$$R = 0.24 \quad\quad S_{u'} = 0.18$$

Equation (3.10) is similar to (3.1), but (3.11) seems to give a poorer estimate of consumer behavior than (3.2). Other variables, such as age, income change, asset–income interaction, etc., will not account for the differences obtained. Standard errors of the weighted regressions in (3.10)–(3.11) have not been exactly computed, but approximations show that they are of the same order of magnitude as those of corresponding coefficients in (3.1)–(3.2). It is worth noting that the estimates of the variance of the disturbances decreases in the twenty-four months' data, while the correlations also fall. On the whole, we do not accept the hypothesis that data on a two-year accounting period are superior to those on a single-year accounting period for the analysis of saving behavior.[14]

As an alternative to the use of two-year data, we have considered using a lagged value of the savings–income ratio as a separate variable in the previous equations obtained from one year's data. There is some evidence in time-series material to the effect that an aggregate consumption function, with lagged consumption as a separate variable, used together with current income gives a much more satisfactory interpretation of prewar and postwar data than other variants that have been suggested. The use of the lagged consumption–income ratio in a *microeconomic* consumption equation implies the use of the lagged savings–income ratio in a *microeconomic* savings equation. These formulations, under some aggregation restrictions, approximate the time-series formulation. The reinterview data show low correlation between $(S/Y)$ and $(S/Y)_{-1}$. If $(S/Y)_{-1}$ is introduced in our empirical savings equations in place of $Y - Y_{-1}/Y_{-1}$, we find little change in other coefficients and small positive coefficients of $(S/Y)_{-1}$, which are not statistically significant in either the homeowner or renter groups.

*Estimates from the 1950 Survey of Consumer Finances.* A stringent test recommended for empirical estimates of economic relationships from some particular sample is confrontation of the estimates with an independent sample. We have used the 1950 Survey of Con-

---

[14] An hypothesis held by M. Friedman is that the "permanent" as opposed to the "temporary" components of a person's savings and income are proportional to each other. By computing savings and income over a twenty-four-month period we approach closer to measures of the "permanent" concept. If Friedman's hypothesis is correct, the savings–income ratio of twenty-four months should be less sensitive to income classifications. The low correlations in (3.10) and (3.11) are consistent with the hypothesis of greater constancy of the ratio between "permanent" savings and "permanent" income.

sumer Finances with data referring to 1949 to estimate an equation such as (3.8), with the exception that income change is not included as a separate variable. The 1950 Survey does not contain reinterviews, i.e., spending units visited on two separate occasions. Income change, therefore, cannot be calculated as the difference between two current income estimates but must be determined on the basis of respondents' memory. The memory estimates of past income change lack numerical precision and are given only in broad classifications such as increases, decreases, or no change. The full sample in the 1950 Survey gives many more observations than the small reinterview group considered previously. We shall first exclude farm spending units, to be in conformity with the reinterview sample and because we feel that farm saving behavior is different from urban. Rural, nonfarm spending units are not excluded; therefore the present sample differs from the reinterview sample above. The latter covered urban areas alone. The number of businessmen in the reinterview group is small, and we have found that their inclusion or exclusion has no appreciable effect on the results. However, we do recognize the possibility that businessmen also have different savings patterns from the bulk of the sample. Morgan reports on this matter in Chapter III. There is a sufficient number of businessmen in the 1950 Survey to make a separate estimate of their savings equation; therefore, we first study the nonfarm, nonbusiness sector of the economy. The remaining cases amount to more than 2,500 observations, and for computational facility we have excluded 25 cases for which the absolute values of the ratios $S/Y$ and $L_{-1}/Y$ exceed 9.99. Positive savings cannot be larger than income, but negative savings are not necessarily restricted by income size. Likewise holdings of liquid assets do not bear any necessary relationship to income. In all cases the excluded observations are extreme and have little effect on the coefficients of the equations. Mainly they increase the estimate of the variance of the disturbances and alter the estimate of the overall correlation. Experience shows that we get nearly the same equations from weighted and unweighted data ;[15] hence, we ease our computational burden by estimating unweighted equations.

*2,521 home owners and renters*

$$(3.12) \quad S/Y = -0.82 + 0.24 \log Y/N + 0.16 \log N - 0.19\, L_{-1}/Y$$
$$\phantom{(3.12) \quad S/Y =} (0.03) \qquad\qquad (0.04) \qquad\quad (0.01)$$
$$+ 0.000029\, L_{-1} + 0.0010A + 0.05H$$
$$(0.000003) \qquad (0.0006) \qquad (0.02)$$
$$R = 0.41 \qquad S_u = 0.42$$

The coefficient of log $N$, combining $-0.24$ and $+0.16$ to get $-0.08$, has a standard error of 0.04. There is a remarkable similarity between this equation, estimated from the 1950 Survey, and (3.8), estimated from the reinterview sample of the 1949 Survey. Liquid assets have a sharper effect in (3.8), as do age and home-ownership status. Apart from minor divergences such as these, we draw the principal conclusion that an independent sample confirms our estimate in (3.8).

*Analysis of residuals—1950 Survey of Consumer Finances.* The residuals determined from (3.12) can be examined by much the same methods as were used in the analysis of the reinterview data with the exception that beginning-of-year expectations and attitudes are not available in the one-time sample of the 1950 Survey.

The assumption that $u$ has uniform variance by income classes is largely validated by a study of the variance of residuals in income classes, but as in the reinterview sample we find a larger variance in the lowest decile. As before, we find the frequency distribution of residuals to be excessively peaked compared with a best-fitting normal curve.

In Table 5 we presented mean residuals of savings equations by income-change, expected-income-change groups, where the expectations referred to an end-of-year date. A similar tabulation with the present data can be made, since respondents were asked in early 1950

[15] See L. R. Klein and J. N. Morgan, "Results of Alternative Statistical Treatments of Sample Survey Data."

### TABLE 8

STANDARD DEVIATIONS OF RESIDUALS OF (3.12) BY INCOME DECILES

| Decile | Standard Deviation of $u$ |
|---|---|
| lowest 1 | 0.96 |
| 2 | 0.25 |
| 3 | 0.30 |
| 4 | 0.32 |
| 5 | 0.24 |
| 6 | 0.45 |
| 7 | 0.24 |
| 8 | 0.32 |
| 9 | 0.24 |
| highest 10 | 0.31 |

their realized income change from 1948–1949 and their expected change from 1949–1950. The reader is reminded however that income change is not a variable in (3.12), while it is in (3.1) and (3.2). We first calculate the mean residuals by realized income change groups alone and then subdivide some of these groupings by expected-income-change categories.

Table 10 shows the relation between $S/Y$ and $(Y - Y_{-1})/Y_{-1}$ if the latter had been included as a variable in (3.12). On balance, there is some positive net correlation between these two variables with the main effect coming from the low saving in the group experiencing extreme income decrease. Table 11, however, shows a lack of consistency with previous results in that the direction of effect of income decrease does not differ between those expecting a further

### TABLE 9

RELATIVE FREQUENCIES OF RESIDUALS OF (3.12) BY DECILES OF A FITTED NORMAL DISTRIBUTION

| Decile | Observed Relative Frequency, $u$ |
|---|---|
| lowest 1 | 0.033 |
| 2 | 0.034 |
| 3 | 0.054 |
| 4 | 0.077 |
| 5 | 0.232 |
| 6 | 0.275 |
| 7 | 0.144 |
| 8 | 0.083 |
| 9 | 0.041 |
| highest 10 | 0.027 |

TABLE 10

MEAN RESIDUALS OF (3.12) BY INCOME CHANGE GROUPS

| Income Change, 1948–1949 | Frequency | $\bar{u}$ |
|---|---|---|
| +25% or more | 416 | 0.022 |
| +5% to +24% | 661 | 0.009 |
| +4% to −4% | 738 | 0.041 |
| −5% to −24% | 369 | 0.002 |
| −25% or more | 185 | −0.175 |
| Change unknown | 12 | 0.022 |
| Not ascertained | 140 | −0.035 |

decrease or leveling of change and those expecting an upward movement—the permanent and temporary income declines. The mean residual is significantly negative in both groups. We are obliged to consider whether the previous findings were very special, whether there has been a change of behavior, or whether the differences between the equations and samples account for the changed results. The fact that temporary income decline was associated with lower savings than permanent income decline was found in two independent samples by Katona[16] and subsequently by our methods in the reinterview sample (independent of Katona's samples); therefore, we may place a measure of reliability in the plausible general hypothesis implied. We lack information to judge whether there has been a real change in behavior, but we can point out some differences between the data underlying our own calculations in Tables 5 and 11. The reinterview data used in Table 5 are classified by change in two

TABLE 11

MEAN RESIDUALS OF (3.12) BY INCOME CHANGE AND
EXPECTED INCOME CHANGE GROUPS

| Income Change 1948–1949 | Expected Income Change 1949–1950 | Frequency | $\bar{u}$ |
|---|---|---|---|
| + | + or 0 | 875 | 0.017 |
| − | − or 0 | 293 | −0.063 |
| + | − | 127 | 0.000 |
| − | + | 184 | −0.061 |
| 0 | + | 129 | −0.048 |
| 0 | 0 | 440 | 0.062 |
| 0 | − | 110 | 0.034 |

[16] G. Katona, "Effect of Income Changes on the Rate of Saving."

reported incomes with imputed federal income taxes subtracted; whereas the data used in Table 11 are classified by a single figure on remembered change in total income. A consequence of these differences is that nearly all spending units in the reinterview sample are classified into some income-increase or decrease group, while a very large number of spending units in the one-time survey are classified in the group with no change, i.e., −4 percent to +4 percent. A large number of respondents report no change when there really was substantial change; they are coded in the ±4 percent class.[17] There are 550 spending units with average positive residuals in the groups with no income change and no expected change or expected decrease. Some of these should legitimately be in the group with permanent decrease. Any counterbalancing omission from the group with temporary decrease would have to come from the category "zero change, expected increase" where the average residual is negative. Thus the difference between reinterview and one-time survey data *could* account for some of the discrepancy. The failure to use income change as a variable in (3.12) could also be partly responsible for the discrepancy, since the residuals would not appear as low as they do throughout the entire range of the decreased-income group of 25 percent or more if income change were used as a variable, as in (3.1)–(3.2). Equation (3.12) is different from (3.1)–(3.2) in that it contains $L_1$ and log $N$ as separate free variables while the latter do not; however, this difference is not likely to account for the changed pattern of residuals. Two main respects in which the computations of Tables 5 and 11 differ are in the use of weights and unascertained expected-income-change observations in the former case but not in the latter. It is quite certain, however, that neither of these differences cause any appreciable alteration in the figures. The unascertained cases are omitted in Table 11 because we have ample observations without using them.

None of the above reasons, though, reconcile the findings from

[17] It is generally true of one-time surveys that an excessive number of respondents are in the no-change group.

the 1950 Survey with the earlier findings of Katona, since he did not employ reinterview data or residuals from savings equations. Further tabulations from the 1951 Survey of Consumer Finances, prepared in the same manner as Katona's earlier studies, support the original findings; thus we do not accept the results of Table 11 as disproof of the proposition that temporary and permanent perceptions of income change have different effects on saving behavior.

With the reinterview sample we were able to study variations in residuals by change in the number of children or adults between two surveys. In the 1950 Survey a question was included for the first time on the occurrence of births during the past calendar year or during the current year prior to the interview date. Spending units having a child born during 1949 or early 1950 show a small but nonsignificant negative residual, the opposite of the indications from the reinterview sample by change in the number of children under eighteen years of age.

A more interesting tabulation of the residuals in the present study is by size of gift or inheritance.

TABLE 12

MEAN RESIDUALS OF (3.12) BY SIZE OF GIFTS AND INHERITANCES

| Gifts and Inheritances (dollars) | Frequency | $\bar{u}$ |
|---|---|---|
| 0 | 2,452 | 0.010 |
| 1–499 | 28 | −0.111 |
| 500–999 | 9 | −0.078 |
| 1,000–1,999 | 14 | −0.121 |
| 2,000–4,999 | 12 | −0.431 |
| 5,000 or over | 4 | −1.440 |
| Not ascertained | 2 | 0.085 |

Not many spending units are affected by this classification, yet there is a marked influence on saving behavior in these few cases and a strong association with the size of the asset transfer. We cannot be altogether satisfied with the treatment of gifts and inheritances in the survey analysis, because they are entered automatically as negative components of savings, and in complicated situations some additional transactions are left obscure. This type of variable, however, does seem to account for some of the few extreme dissavers in the sample.

*Saving behavior of businessmen and farmers.* Although we are not satisfied with the comprehensiveness or accuracy of the data for farmers and businessmen, we have used the available material to estimate separate equations of savings behavior for these two groups. The form of the equation is the same as that in (3.12) with the minor exception that we do not use an indicator of home ownership, this variable being less important among businessmen and farmers, especially the latter. We expect to obtain quite different coefficients because of the complicated mixture of production and household accounts and the presence of substantial income in kind on the farm. Nevertheless, we also feel that these two groups actually behave differently from the rest of the population and attribute some of the expected differences in coefficients to this fact.

*353 businessmen*

$$(3.12b) \quad S/Y = -1.19 + 0.39 \log Y/N + 0.33 \log N - 0.064 \, L_{-1}/Y$$
$$\quad\quad\quad (0.27) \quad (0.07) \quad\quad\quad\quad (0.37) \quad\quad\quad (0.026)$$
$$+ 0.0000038 L_{-1} - 0.00092 A$$
$$(0.0000034) \quad\quad (0.00183)$$
$$R = 0.36 \quad\quad S_u = 0.38$$

*381 farmers*

$$(3.12f) \quad S/Y = 1.91 + 0.69 \log Y/N + 0.10 \log N - 0.33 \, L_{-1}/Y$$
$$\quad\quad\quad (0.45) \quad (0.13) \quad\quad\quad\quad (0.23) \quad\quad\quad (0.05)$$
$$+ 0.000055 L_{-1} + 0.0016 A$$
$$(0.000022) \quad\quad (0.0034)$$
$$R = 0.52 \quad\quad S_u = 0.91$$

Directions of effect of the several variables on saving are the same as in (3.12). The coefficient of $A$ in (3.12b) changes sign but not significantly. The age effect is not significant in any of the equations computed from this sample. In (3.12), the coefficient of $\log N$ shows a significant departure from a per capita formulation but not in (3.12b) or (3.12f). If we combine the two separate coefficients of log $N$, we get $-0.06$ with a standard error of $0.11$ in $(3.12b)$ and $-0.59$ with a standard error of $0.22$ in $(3.12f)$; thus the net effect of spending unit size on saving is consistently negative. As compared with $(3.12)$, the absolute size of all asset effects is attenuated in $(3.12b)$ and accentuated in $(3.12f)$. These measures are perhaps seriously affected by asset holdings of businesses and currency holdings of farmers.

A comparison of the savings–income relations contained in the three equations from the 1949 data is shown in the accompanying graph. The lines are drawn from the respective equations by assigning constant values to all variables other than $S$ and $Y$. The sample means underlying $(3.12)$ are the particular constants used. The dashed line assigns $H = 1$ in $(3.12)$ (homeowners), while the solid line assigns $H = 0$ in $(3.12)$ (non-home-owners).

Numerical values of the marginal propensity to save determined at various points along these curves are given in Table 13.

TABLE 13

MARGINAL PROPENSITIES TO SAVE, $(3.12)$, $(3.12b)$, AND $(3.12f)$

| Income Level (dollars) | Nonfarm, Nonbusiness Renters | Nonfarm, Nonbusiness Home Owners | Businessmen | Farmers |
|---|---|---|---|---|
| 1,000 | 0.06 | 0.11 | 0.09 | 0.40 |
| 3,000 | 0.18 | 0.23 | 0.28 | 0.73 |
| 4,000 | 0.23 | 0.28 | 0.36 | 0.88 |
| 7,500 | 0.27 | 0.32 | 0.43 | 1.01 |
| 10,000 | 0.30 | 0.35 | 0.48 | 1.09 |

The graph and Table 13 indicate, both as to level and rate of change, a hierarchy of saving behavior, farmers being the highest savers, businessmen being next, and nonfarm nonbusiness being the lowest savers.[18] While there is plausibility in these findings, we must remember that farm income level is understated by the amount of

[18] The values of the marginal propensity to save for farmers are extremely high at income levels greater than $7,500 per year. The excessively large values could be explained by sampling error, but they are also a result of the fact that the savings equation for farmers probably does not extrapolate well to such high levels of *disposable* income. Few farmers receive money-disposable income in excess of $7,500 per year.

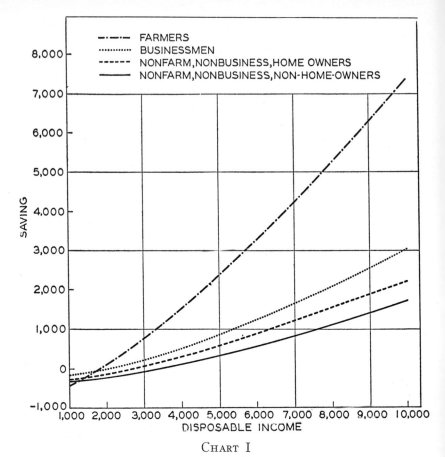

CHART I

Savings–Income Relations for Different Groups, 1949

income in kind and that accounting problems plague the accuracy of many of the business and farm data.

*Estimates from the 1951 Survey of Consumer Finances.* Three equations of the same form as (3.12), (3.12b) and (3.12f) have been estimated from yet another sample for confirmation or rejection of the basic findings. From the 1951 Survey of Consumer Finances we made groupings and estimated equations in essentially the same manner as from the 1950 Survey.

*2,518 home owners and renters*

$$(3.13) \quad S/Y = -0.79 + 0.25 \log Y/N + 0.10 \log N - 0.11L_{-1}/Y$$
$$\qquad\qquad (0.09) \quad (0.02) \qquad\qquad (0.03) \qquad\quad (0.01)$$
$$\qquad\qquad + 0.0000044L_{-1} + 0.00057A + 0.043H$$
$$\qquad\qquad (0.0000018) \qquad (0.00047) \quad (0.014)$$
$$\qquad\qquad\qquad R = 0.36 \qquad S_u = 0.31$$

*326 businessmen*

$$(3.13b) \quad S/Y = -2.81 + 0.73 \log Y/N + 0.59 \log N - 0.13L_{-1}/Y$$
$$\qquad\qquad\quad (0.47) \quad (0.13) \qquad\qquad (0.22) \qquad\quad (0.05)$$
$$\qquad\qquad + 0.0000047L_{-1} + 0.0093A$$
$$\qquad\qquad (0.0000080) \qquad (0.0032)$$
$$\qquad\qquad\qquad R = 0.41 \qquad S_u = 0.66$$

*381 farmers*

$$(3.13f) \quad S/Y = -0.56 + 0.24 \log Y/N + 0.04 \log N - 0.37L_{-1}/Y$$
$$\qquad\qquad\quad (0.38) \quad (0.10) \qquad\qquad (0.18) \qquad\quad (0.04)$$
$$\qquad\qquad + 0.000068L_{-1} + 0.00089A$$
$$\qquad\qquad (0.000014) \qquad (0.00265)$$
$$\qquad\qquad\qquad R = 0.47 \qquad S_u = 0.70$$

These three equations exhibit some differences compared with their counterparts in the 1950 Survey, but the main differences are to be noted in the equations for businessmen and farmers where we have relatively large sampling errors, mainly as a consequence of the smallness of the samples. The equations for nonfarm nonbusiness spending units are similar in nearly all respects except for the fact that liquid-asset effects are comparatively weaker in (3.13) than in (3.12). The inverse relationship between liquid assets and savings is more gently inclined in the lower income groups and changes less with movement up the income scale in (3.13). In general, however, the directions of influence among the major variables are the same in all pairs of equations for the two years.

### DURABLE-GOODS EXPENDITURES

*General structure of equation for expenditure on durables.* A broad classification of consumer decisions on the disposition of income consists of the three categories: expenditures on nondurable goods and services, expenditures on durables, and savings. These three add up to total income. The Surveys of Consumer Finances concentrate on obtaining direct information about income, savings, and durables. Nondurable goods and services, called residual expenditures, are estimated as disposable income minus savings minus expenditures on durables. A natural procedure for us then is to follow up our studies of saving behavior with a separate detailed study of expenditures on durables.

The data on durables are not exhaustive; they cover only certain types of durables, as Lansing has shown in Chapter I. Direct questions are asked about purchases of automobiles, furniture, radios, refrigerators, washing machines, television sets, other household appliances, and a catch-all group consisting of any other major household items. In the study of durables, we encounter the same problem of lack of homogeneity of variances by income classes as we found in the case of savings; therefore we use the expenditure–income ratio as the basic variable. A distinctive feature of the savings equation is the negative values of savings indicated at sufficiently low levels of income. The counterpart for nondurables is a positive expenditure at the same low levels of income. Sound reasons can be advanced for this dual phenomenon; minimum standards for necessities must be met regardless of the level of income. Borrowing, the receipt of gifts, and the use of assets enable low-income households to dissave. Durables covered in the Surveys are not items for which people must spend minimum amounts regardless of their income level. In a relative sense, we may call them luxuries. Thus the first property ascribed to our durable-goods equation is that it be a curve through the origin in the $(E, Y)$-plane; $E =$ expenditures on durables. Published tabulations in the Surveys of Consumer Finances have shown that households have been spending about 10 percent of their income on durables in all income classes.[19] This observation roughly suggests that the durable-goods equation is a straight line through the origin in the $(E, Y)$-plane.

Liquid assets are an enabling factor permitting one to make a down payment or buy durables outright without resort to credit. We expect liquid assets to stimulate the purchase of durables; whereas we expect a negative asset effect in the savings equation. Age of spending unit head is another variable which has different directions of effect in a savings and a durable-goods equation. In the latter case, older people have already accumulated a large part of their durables and have less need for some types; hence, we expect demand to dissipate with age of head. Income change is often suggested as a plausible variable, being perhaps positively correlated with expenditures on durables. We find little statistical evidence of this relation, however, when other variables are simultaneously considered. Simple correlations between durable-goods expenditures and income change alone do appear to be significant. A splitting of the sample into home owners and renters has been considered for the study of durables, but no significant results were found. Household items are, perhaps, more frequently purchased by home owners, but this is not true of automobiles, one of the major items of durable expenditures. We omit the influence of change of residence in our calculations with the reinterview survey because only households who did not move between two survey dates are included in the sample.

*Estimates from the reinterview sample.* Our first estimated equa-

---

[19] See "1950 Survey of Consumer Finances," Part IV, *Federal Reserve Bulletin,* November, 1950, p. 1452, Table 22. In 1949, in contrast to previous years, there is a jump to 16 percent for this statistic in the lowest quintile.

tion for durable-goods expenditures is for 600 cases in the reinterview
survey—all the cases used for estimation of savings equations, with
the exception of 6 whose expenditures were not ascertained.

The result is

(4.1)             $E/Y = 0.17 + 0.027L_{-1}/Y - 0.0023A$
                  (0.03)  (0.006)              (0.0006)

$$R = 0.24 \qquad S_u = 0.17$$

The mean value of $E/Y$ is 0.08, in line with other calculations, but
after liquid assets and age are taken into account the value increases
significantly to 0.17. The marginal propensity to spend depends, however, on the age level and is not more than 0.12 to 0.14 for households in the lowest age brackets. It is interesting that the marginal-
asset effect is small but definitely significant. Equation (4.1) shows
that the marginal-income effect is much larger than the marginal-
asset effect for practically the entire span of ages.

If we retain the form of (4.1) but add $\log Y/N - \log (Y/N)_{-1}$
as a separate variable, we find practically no change in the estimate
of the other coefficients and a small, insignificant negative coefficient
of income change. Explicit tests of an income effect, apart from that
implied in (4.1), by using $\log Y/N$ as a variable similarly show insignificant results. In view of the differences, in terms of necessity
of purchase, between durables and nondurables, we are led to accept
the hypothesis that the equation passes through the origin in the
$(E, Y)$-plane.

The low correlation in (4.1) is actually evidence of a specific type
of dispersion of observations about the equation. In recent surveys it
has been found that only about one-half the sample purchase any
durables during a calendar year. If low-income, low-asset and high-
age values accounted for nearly all the zero purchases, our equation
would probably be quite satisfactory as it stands, but there remains
a large number of zero purchasers at high-income, high-asset, and
low-age levels. Some households have adequate funds for purchase
and are in the age groups that often purchase but do not feel the need

to purchase within some twelve-month period. A variable which may bring out the need for purchase is one indicating the existing capacity of durables already in the possession of each household. The stock of physical consumer wealth is not to our knowledge adequately represented in any survey sample on purchases of durables; therefore we do not feel able to develop an equation that properly explains the large volume of zero purchases. A crude attempt to take account of existing consumer assets was made by using last year's purchases as an additional variable on the assumption that recent past purchases tend to fulfill a need for durables and thus lead to low or zero current expenditures. The variable $(E/Y)_{-1}$ used together with those in (4.1) brings no improvement to our estimated equation. Other coefficients remain unchanged, and the coefficient of the added variable is a small, insignificant positive value.

Another possibility is to assume that households make two types of decisions: (1) they decide on the basis of physical need whether to buy or not to buy; (2) they decide on the basis of income, assets, and age how much to spend on the things they have decided to buy. Among 303 spending units who actually did make a purchase we estimate

$$(4.2) \qquad E/Y = 0.24 + 0.068\,(L_{-1}/Y) - 0.0027A$$
$$\phantom{(4.2) \qquad E/Y =} (0.05) \quad (0.011) \qquad\qquad (0.0011)$$
$$R = 0.34 \qquad S_u = 0.21$$

We have also made a slight modification in the form of the durable-goods equation for this group by adding the variable $L_{-1}$, permitting the marginal propensity to spend to vary by asset level, or the marginal asset effect to vary by income level.

$$(4.3) \quad E/Y = 0.24 + 0.082\,(L_{-1}/Y) - 0.0024A - 0.0000074L_{-1}$$
$$\phantom{(4.3) \quad E/Y =} (0.05) \quad (0.012) \qquad\qquad (0.0011) \qquad (0.0000025)$$
$$R = 0.37 \qquad S_u = 0.21$$

As we should expect, the constant term and the coefficient of $(L_{-1}/Y)$ rise when the zero-purchase cases are omitted. At the same time the multiple correlation increases.

An income change variable of the form $(Y-Y_{-1})/Y_{-1}$ shows practically no relation when added to equation (4.2) or (4.3). The coefficient is negative and small, with practically no effect on the other estimates in the equation.

In the equations of saving behavior we find a negative relation between liquid assets and savings for the sample as a whole. When we permit the asset effect to vary by income level we find the negative effect to be attenuated in the upper income groups. The opposite relations are found in our equations for expenditures on durables. For the sample as a whole or for the entire group of non-zero purchasers we find a positive relation between liquid asset holdings and expenditures. The coefficient of $L_{-1}$ in (4.3) shows, however, that the positive effect of assets on spending falls as income rises. Interestingly enough, the asset effect falls toward zero when the income level is somewhat over \$10,000 in (4.3). In savings equations, however, asset effects reverse sign at much lower income levels.

*Estimates from the 1950 Survey of Consumer Finances.* As in the estimation of savings equations, we have tested our estimates of expenditure equations by computing them with data from an independent sample, in this case nonfarm, nonbusiness spending units in the 1950 Survey of Consumer Finances. For 2,493 such spending units, the estimated equation corresponding to (4.1) is

(4.4)          $$E/Y = 0.18 + 0.0058L_{-1}/Y - 0.0020A$$
                    $$(0.01)\quad(0.0030)\qquad\qquad(0.0002)$$
                    $$R = 0.19\qquad S_u = 0.16$$

These estimates are obtained from unweighted data, whereas weights were used in (4.1)–(4.3). They are also different from (4.1)–(4.3) in that, like all estimates from non-reinterview data, they are based on memory data for beginning-of-year liquid assets.

Equation (4.4) is not unlike (4.1) except for a decrease in the liquid-asset coefficient. The other two are nearly the same as those in (4.1) and the overall correlation is only slightly lower in (4.4).

The data from the 1950 Survey do not show any significant interaction effect between liquid assets and income; thus we gain nothing by adding $L_{-1}$ as a variable to (4.4). We have not experimented with income-change variables explicitly introduced into (4.4), because memory data on these are available only in broad classes. We find, however, some possible evidence of an income-change effect in this sample by calculation of the mean values of $E/Y$ within various classes of income change.

### TABLE 14

#### MEAN RATIOS OF EXPENDITURES ON DURABLE GOODS TO DISPOSABLE INCOME WITHIN INCOME CHANGE GROUPS: NONFARM, NONBUSINESS SPENDING UNITS—1949

| Income Change 1948–1949 | Frequency | Mean Ratio of Expenditure to Income |
|---|---|---|
| +25% or more | 408 | 0.114 |
| +5% to +24% | 657 | 0.110 |
| +4% to −4% | 734 | 0.076 |
| −5% to −24% | 366 | 0.084 |
| −25% or more | 181 | 0.077 |
| Change unknown | 12 | 0.063 |
| Not ascertained | 135 | 0.097 |

The spread in the mean ratio between the groups of positive and negative income change suggests a definite possibility of a positive income change effect on expenditures for durables. The fact that the mean ratio is smaller for the group with unchanged income than for either those with increases or decreases is, however, worth noting and may suggest a somewhat more complicated relationship.

*The liquid-asset effect.* Since our asset concept embraces only liquid assets and not total wealth, we must point out that the relation between assets and expenditures may not be the simple cause–effect pattern we imply by treating lagged assets as a predetermined variable influencing expenditures. Persons holding nonliquid assets may tend to shift to liquid assets just prior to purchase time for expenditures which were decided upon on the basis of entirely different considerations. We do not feel that this behavior accounts in any major way for the observed asset–expenditure relation, but it does arise as a qualification in the interpretation of our equations as causal relationships. The liquid assets held by many people are those accumulated during the war and immediate postwar years in which durable goods were unavailable. They were probably not purposively shifted from nonliquid to liquid form just prior to spending.

### SOME QUALIFICATIONS

*Inadequacies of the data.* We have invested a great deal of research effort in minute and detailed examination of the Survey data because we regard them as revealing and fruitful for economic analysis; yet no sample of information is perfectly suited to our needs, and we must discuss some limitations of our findings.

In order to give a completely well rounded picture of household behavior we need accounting-type data which are not available even in specially designed surveys. From the consumers' balance sheets we need, besides liquid assets, data on other types of wealth such as holdings of private securities, real estate, inventories of durables, and ownership interests in business. Even the Survey concept of liquid assets is not clearly appropriate since it does not include currency holdings. From the consumers' income statements we need information on imputed income, nonmoney income, capital gains, and some transfer payments. As Lansing has shown in Chapter I, there are plausible variants of the savings concept, and among these are some on which data are lacking; therefore we are not able to test certain hypotheses about household behavior.

By selecting a sample referring only to the nonfarm, nonbusiness sector of the population and by separating home owners and renters within that sample we make some progress toward overcoming the lack of information. By sorting out farmers we avoid much of the problem of not having nonmoney income. Farmers together with businessmen account for that section of household balance sheets complicated by business ownership. We also avoid having negative incomes in a nonfarm nonbusiness sample. Renters in our sample have more complete information than home owners because major asset and debt items are occupied dwellings and mortgages. In our renter group we still fail to account for currency holding, ownership of private securities, inventories of consumer durables, ownership of real estate not used for own occupancy, nonmoney income, capital gains, and some transfers. The variables actually included in our equations are so much more important than these excluded items that we feel reasonably confident about our findings.[20] The closeness to, and logical conformity with, the equations estimated for home owners enlarge our confidence in the findings for the nonfarm, nonbusiness sector as a whole.

*Weaknesses of demographic and sociological variables.* Two main demographic variables used in our equations are size of spending unit and age of head, but these undoubtedly leave room for improvement. In some studies the concept of equivalent adults has been used instead of number of persons. Equivalent adults is a weighted sum of number of persons, less weight being given to children than to older persons. A special weight is given to a first child because of the need for initial outlays for equipment. One-person households behave essentially differently from multiple-person households, and all components of saving are not related in the same way to family size, some being positively and others being negatively related. Tabulations show that purchase of durables is strongly related to number of years married, which may be a better variable than age in the equations for expenditures on durables. A comprehensive study of family status and other demographic variables in economic relations is needed. Our equations have picked out only some of the more obvious and simpler effects. In spite of the fact that we feel that research can fruitfully be pushed further in this direction, we attach only limited significance to the absence of more and better demographic variables in our equations, since the economic variables like assets and income are so prominent and dominating.

[20] Our use of the term "renter" is not strictly correct. "Non-home-owners" is more accurate since there are included among our renters some spending units who neither own nor rent. These cases consist of related secondary spending units, domestic servants, and persons in rarer special circumstances. Renters dominate the non-home-owning category by far, and we have not made more than a twofold distinction on home-ownership status. Morgan, however, reports some results separately for the group which does not own or rent.

More subtle types of sociological phenomena than purely demographic variables may be of importance. Studies by Brady and Friedman,[21] later taken up by Duesenberry,[22] attempt to establish from survey data a relation between the savings–income ratio and the position of respondents in the income distribution—in most cases in the income distribution of their own geographical community. The general argument runs to the effect that consumer behavior is patterned after that of neighbors and friends or of other members of the same social class. Unfortunately, our samples are not large enough to permit fine breakdowns by geography, social classes, or small friendship groups.

*Special character of the time period covered.* The entire postwar period, during which the Surveys of Consumer Finances have been conducted, has been one of economic prosperity for the country as a whole. There was a mild downturn in activity from late 1948 to 1949, and there is the inflationary disturbance following the Korean War, yet, on the whole, our experience refers to one type of economic climate. Our equations do not, for this reason, extend without further study or justification to depression conditions. We have not adequately handled the occurrence of negative incomes which would be more important in depression. The asymmetry of income change with the more noticeable effects of income decrease would have to be more carefully assessed in a situation in which most people are experiencing a decline.

[21] Dorothy Brady and Rose Friedman, "Savings and the Income Distribution," *Studies in Income and Wealth,* Vol. X (New York: National Bureau of Economic Research, 1947), pp. 250–66.

[22] J. Duesenberry, *Income, Saving, and the Theory of Consumer Behavior* (Cambridge: Harvard University Press, 1949). Duesenberry actually attempts to construct a particular aggregative savings function on the basis of an elaborate chain of reasoning at the microeconomic level. His analysis of Negro–White savings differentials in support of the relation between the savings–income ratio and percentile income position is open to serious doubt, as is his analysis of the effect of income change. See L. R. Klein and H. W. Mooney, "Negro–White Savings Differentials and the Consumption Function Problem."

# VI: APPLICATIONS OF
# SURVEY METHODS AND DATA
# TO THE ANALYSIS OF
# ECONOMIC FLUCTUATIONS

## by *Lawrence R. Klein*

*Autonomous relations.* Prediction, in a broad sense, is the goal of much of quantitative economic research. Having made quantitative measurement of economic behavior under a particular set of circumstances, we may try to infer some basic properties of behavior that would hold under different future circumstances. In a concrete example, we may study from survey data the relation between the savings–income ratio of respondents and their expectations of income change. These data are gathered in a particular economic framework, but we may believe that the relationship observed is basic enough so that it would still hold if the framework were to undergo only slight changes, with the most essential features remaining the same. As an application of the observed relationship between the saving–income ratio and income expectations, we may determine in a subsequent survey the frequency distribution of income expectations. If this distribution has undergone significant change, we have an advance indicator serving as a prediction of a change in the savings–income ratio.

Relationships derived from observed data should be constructed so as to have "autonomy," i.e., the property of remaining valid under a variety of external conditions. We cannot expect, in our relatively brief experience with economic surveys, to be able to estimate completely autonomous relations. If the general economic framework changes radically from a setting of inflation to one of deflation, the basic patterns of behavior are likely to change. In the postwar Surveys of Consumer Finances the economic setting has remained relatively fixed. The period has been generally one of widespread prosperity, full employment, and inflationary pressure. Relations observed in data from these surveys would not be expected to have autonomy that would render them valid under conditions of a severe depression. But some significant alterations have occurred in the postwar period of which survey relationships have provided useful advance indication; therefore, even though we have not had radical changes invalidating observed relationships, we have had changing situations in which it was urgent to have patterns with the degree of "autonomy" and predictive ability found in the Surveys of Consumer Finances.

*Business cycles in an interrelated economy.* Granted that relationships derived from survey data have a degree of autonomy that render them helpful in prediction, we might usefully consider specific problems that arise in applying them to business-cycle analysis. The main goal of empirical business-cycle analysis, as we see it, is a detailed probing into the nature of forces at work during a current period and the assembly of material for prediction into the future. The material assembled should, if possible, cover all sectors of the economy in order that a well-rounded forecast be made. An obvious danger in studying a single sector is that events in other sectors may cause general economic activity to move counter to predicted activity in the particular sector studied. Moreover, activity in one sector depends upon activity in others; therefore an unconditional forecast cannot be made from the study of one sector alone.

Econometricians consider economic activity as expressible in a system of simultaneous mathematical equations. Some of the equations refer to human behavior patterns in particular sectors of the economy; some refer to the underlying technology; while others refer to institutional or legal practices. By human behavior patterns, we mean relations showing the process by which economic decisions are made. In our network of behavior patterns, we would show, in mathematical form, the relationship of personal savings to income, wealth, income expectations, age, and other variables of the type studied in Chapter V. A closed system of this nature would encompass consumer decisions to save, to spend on durables, to spend on nondurables, to hold wealth; producer decisions to invest in capital goods, to hold inventories, to employ labor, to supply goods to market, to incur debts; banker decisions to grant loans, to vary interest charges, to adjust reserves; and so forth. In addition to these complex behavior patterns we have the technological relations of production showing how outputs are produced from inputs of raw materials, labor, and capital; and institutional relations showing how tax collections depend upon income, how agricultural prices are tied to nonagricultural prices, and how wage rates are tied to the cost of living.

A comprehensive system of interrelationships like these describe the main developments of economic activity and constitute a body of knowledge indispensable in predicting business-cycle movements. Using this theoretical framework for business cycle analysis, we now turn to the question of the use of survey methods and data in implementing the research.

Survey methods may be employed to test a number of existing hypotheses of business-cycle theory, principally hypotheses about patterns of individual behavior that comprise the above-mentioned interrelationships. In addition, surveys may be employed to uncover new types of material, unavailable by other methods, that help us to formulate new hypotheses and new behavior patterns not generally prevalent in existing business-cycle literature.

### THE USE OF SURVEY DATA
### FOR STUDYING CONSUMER BEHAVIOR
### IN BUSINESS-CYCLE THEORY

*Aggregation of microeconomic savings functions and the distribution of income.* Consumer behavior in business-cycle theory is largely discussed in terms of the dependence of aggregate consumer expenditures and savings on aggregate consumer income, income change, and wealth. Other variables such as market interest rates, prices, and income distribution are frequently included. From survey data, as we have already indicated in earlier chapters, microeconomic relations connecting the same types of variables at the individual consumer level can be estimated. An interesting problem for business-cycle theory is to derive aggregative relations or specific properties of them from the microeconomic relations. If survey data show the existence of a linear relation between individual savings and individual income, the corresponding macroeconomic relation would be a linear dependence of aggregate savings on aggregate income. The fact that our empirical studies of survey data show that individual saving behavior cannot be expressed as a simple linear function of income has significant implications for business cycle analysis. As has been pointed out by others previously,[1] we find saving behavior to be nonlinearly related to several variables in addition to income.

From our general equations, the relation between savings and income, other things held constant, shows definite evidence of non-linearity, the marginal propensity to save increasing with income. If the marginal propensity to save were constant for all income levels, we would find that income redistribution would be an ineffective business-cycle control policy for influencing consumer spending or saving. By taking a dollar of income away from a high-income consumer we would observe a decline in savings equal to the increase in savings generated by giving this dollar to a low-income consumer. Changes in savings associated with changes in income measure the marginal propensity to save, and if this parameter is the same at all income levels, we would find saving or consumption unaffected by income redistribution alone. The fact that we find evidence of non-linearity in estimating savings–income patterns from survey data is thus useful knowledge in analyzing business-cycle policy which at-

[1] See, e.g., G. Katona, *Psychological Analysis of Economic Behavior* (New York: McGraw Hill, 1951).

tempts to affect savings through income redistribution. The size of income-redistribution effects depends on the degree of nonlinearity and the amount of income being redistributed. From the estimates in Table 13 of Chapter V, one can see the differences in marginal propensity to save by income levels and thereby judge the size of the effect of various redistribution schemes.

Not only do marginal propensities to save vary by income level because of nonlinearities of the savings–income relation, they also vary between economic and social groups such as farmers, businessmen, and others. The relative sizes of these three population groups partially determine the value of the marginal propensity to save as this concept is used in aggregative business-cycle theory. Looking at the matter from another point of view, we might argue that income-redistribution schemes involving farmers, businessmen, and others affect the level of savings in the economy. Many business-cycle control measures such as farm price supports, agricultural subsidies, loans to new businesses, etc., have an influence on the income and population shares of the three groups and subsequently on the flow of savings.

*Wealth variables in the savings function.* Recent discussions in business-cycle theory have considered at some length the effect of wealth on consumer behavior. Survey data have contributed much to our present understanding of the wealth–savings relationship. These data, by enabling us to estimate properties of such relationships among variables, provide information on various building blocks of business-cycle theory and thereby constitute an important research tool.

In the contributions of Morgan in Chapters III and IV we find significant main effects, in the language of the analysis of variance, of liquid assets on savings and significant interactions between liquid assets and income. These findings, confirmed and extended to parameter estimates in formal equations by this author in Chapter V, cast some light on business-cycle analysis. The accepted interpretation of asset effects among economists, especially those who have not dealt with empirical material on assets and savings, is that the real quantity of savings is negatively correlated with the real value of assets. Some theorists argue that a system of flexible wages and prices will provide a stabilizing influence on economic fluctuations by adjusting the real value of assets to call forth a smaller stream of real savings under deflationary pressure and a larger stream under inflationary pressure. The assumed negative correlation between real savings and real assets leads them to this conclusion. They are also assuming that banking practices are such that the nominal amount of liquid assets in the system is not allowed to fluctuate in the same direction by the same percentage amount as prices. The stock of real wealth may fluctuate for reasons other than those associated with price and wage movements. Decisions of treasury finance and central-bank policy may have direct repercussions on the stock of real wealth, and we shall have to take the wealth–savings relation into account in order to assess the business-cycle implication of such decisions. While many economists would accept the proposition of a negative correlation between real wealth and real savings, there are several who argue that the size of the asset effect on savings is not strong enough to be dependable as a stabilizing force in economic fluctuations. Their arguments point up the need for empirical measurement.

In the samples from the Surveys of Consumer Finances, the net correlation between liquid assets and savings (after taking account of income, income change, and several demographic variables) is negative, in line with the assumptions made in theory. Morgan, as we noted, makes the important finding that there is an interaction effect between liquid assets and income, thus leading to the conclusion that the absolute value of the asset effect diminishes as we move from lower- to higher-income spending units. In fact, the estimated equations show a reversal of direction of the asset effect above income levels of approximately $7,500 per year. If asset effects vary, and even change direction, by income level, business-cycle control mechanisms must discriminate among individuals and give differential treatment to persons at different income positions. This point is seldom recognized in the discussions of business-cycle analysis.

As has been pointed out in the previous chapter, liquid assets do not cover the entire portion of an individual's wealth. We noted that by sorting the samples into different groups, at least one of which holds relatively little in the form of nonliquid assets, we find the same type of relationship between liquid assets and savings; therefore, we do not think that the distinction between liquid assets and total wealth invalidates the application of our findings to the aspect of business-cycle theory considered here. Moreover, tabulations in the Surveys of Consumer Finances show a strong positive correlation between liquid assets and consumer net worth, justifying our use of the former as a proxy variable for the latter.[2]

A more serious problem in applying findings of relationships from survey data to business-cycle analysis is the fact that prices are not variable within a single survey and have not varied appreciably during the postwar years covered by our studies of the successive Surveys of Consumer Finances. If all spending units were to experience the same proportional change in real wealth through movements of prices and wages throughout the whole economy, would the asset effect on savings be the same as that estimated from surveys in which prices are effectively held constant over a short interview period? This is a major question that must be asked of our findings. We need more experience in the collection of survey data in various price situations before we can attempt to answer the question. There have been, however, significant changes in the real value of wealth in the hands of consumers which cannot be traced to price and wage fluctuations alone. The effect of these changes can be judged from survey estimates of behavior patterns. The most striking case is the large amount of liquid-asset accumulation by consumers during World War II. The problem confronting economic analysts in 1946 and

[2] "1950 Survey of Consumer Finances," *Federal Reserve Bulletin* (December 1950), p. 1589.

the period immediately thereafter was to judge the impact of this asset accumulation on consumer spending decisions. The existence of large liquid asset holdings was, on the whole, a stimulus to postwar spending, as would be estimated from the Survey relationships. That the liquid asset holdings were not solely responsible for maintaining the large volume of spending will be argued below in connection with the discussion of other business-cycle variables. The unavailability of survey data on consumer inventories of durable goods prevents us from judging the pure effect of liquid asset holdings—i.e., from making an estimate of what the effect would have been if the assets had been accumulated under conditions other than those of wartime buying restraints and military finance.

### SOME DEMOGRAPHIC VARIABLES IN BUSINESS CYCLES

*Cyclically invariant demographic variables.* In addition to economic variables such as income, assets, income change, and others, numerous demographic factors have been used throughout this volume in studying consumer behavior. Because of the nature of survey samples, we find dispersion, among our statistical observations, of such things as age, number of persons in the spending unit, marital status, race, educational level, etc. These variables must be controlled if we are to estimate the true underlying patterns of behavior in spending and saving. These demographic variables may, however, change little or gradually over time during economic fluctuations and therefore be of little use in business-cycle analysis other than as a means of estimating the relationships we desire from Survey data.[3]

*Internal migration.* Some important demographic variables are cyclically oriented or volatile and do have a significant impact on consumer decisions. In the estimates of equations for durable-goods expenditure from reinterview data it is remarked that the sample consisted entirely of spending units who did not move during the year in which they made expenditures, and no variable on internal

---

[3] In saying that individual demographic variables change little over time, we mean that average values and frequency distributions remain temporally invariant.

migration was used in any of the equations. An indication of the effect of recent moving on durable-goods expenditures is shown in the accompanying table, prepared by Morgan from his basic nonfarm nonbusiness sample in the 1949 Survey (Chapter III).

TABLE 1

MEAN EXPENDITURES ON DURABLE GOODS BY INCOME–CLASSES:
SPENDING UNITS WHO HAVE AND HAVE NOT MOVED RECENTLY

*Dollar amounts*

| | INCOME CLASS (DOLLARS) | | | | | |
|---|---|---|---|---|---|---|
| | 0–999 | 1,000– 1,999 | 2,000– 2,999 | 3,000– 3,999 | 4,000– 4,999 | 5,000 or More |
| Renters | | | | | | |
| Moved 1948–49 | 63 | 93 | 261 | 523 | 979 | 1,007 |
| Not moved since 1945 | 8 | 80 | 97 | 201 | 294 | 335 |
| Home Owners | | | | | | |
| Bought 1948–49 | 398 | 418 | 449 | 603 | 711 | 780 |
| Bought before 1940 | 12 | 71 | 101 | 353 | 368 | 525 |

The figures in this table show striking differences, especially because we have selected extreme groups—those who have moved recently and those who have not moved for several years. The same general results hold, but less consistently, for groups between the extremes. In any event, the point to be made is clear. Erratic demographic variables subject to great changes under the impact of new economic forces must be taken into account in business-cycle analysis. Migration from farm to city is strongly related to business and social conditions, and even among industrial workers the effect of new economic forces such as rearmament induces substantial migration toward specific production centers.

*Racial differentials.* The Negro-White differentials in saving behavior provide another example of strong demographic forces that must be taken into account in assessing the current level of economic activity. It may be thought that as long as the percentage of Negroes in the population remains stable or changes according to a smooth trend, we need not be seriously concerned about a racial variable other than for the indirect purpose of estimating savings patterns from Survey data. In a separate study of data contained in the Surveys of Consumer Finances,[4] it is found that Southern and Northern Negroes exhibit marked differences in saving behavior. The relevant demographic variable for business-cycle studies is not the percentage of Negroes in the entire population but the percentage of Northern and Southern Negroes in the entire population. These variables are much less stable and hence more significant for purposes of studying fluctuations.

### SOME CONSUMER ATTITUDES AND EXPECTATIONS
### IN BUSINESS CYCLES

*Measurement of subjective magnitudes in surveys.* Finally, we must consider the role of consumer attitudes and expectations in business-cycle analysis. In the opening paragraph of this chapter we cited, as an example of the type of relation that could be estimated from survey data and used in economic projections, the relation between the percentage of income saved and the expectation of income change. The derivation of such relationships in a much more complex and detailed analysis provides one of the most important contributions, peculiar to the survey method, for studying business cycles.

Most traditional business-cycle theory is couched in terms of objective measurable variables such as income, prices, production, employment, wages, etc. Subjective anticipations in some models are ignored. In others they are thrown into residual random disturbances or exogenous categories. Sometimes they are used as an excuse for lack of deeper analysis, with economic results being catalogued into various types depending on the "state of expectations." The major new contribution of survey methods is that we can measure expectations, and we can study the quantitative effect of expectations on behavior. Ultimately we may even hope to determine a more funda-

---

[4] H. W. Mooney, "Some Factors Associated with Negro–White Savings Differentials," unpublished Ph.D. thesis, University of Michigan, 1953.

mental set of variables and relations showing how expectations are formed, but this type of study has not yet been made.

Anticipations, expectations, and attitudes determined from survey data can be used in the following way: From successive surveys we can estimate relationships connecting actual behavior with subjective, psychological variables. These relationships may be of two types. Either we can associate individual expectations with individual behavior or we can associate a sequence of frequency distributions of expectations with average behavior. In analyzing the reinterview sample in an earlier chapter we presented the relationship between savings behavior and beginning-of-year income expectations. This type of association is possible only where identical units are interviewed at repeated intervals, for then we can measure expectations held at the beginning of a period (obtained from an earlier interview) and the behavior which subsequently followed (obtained from a later interview). If we have evidence that expectations have not changed during a period, we can, from a single interview, associate past behavior with present expectations and use this as an estimate of the desired relation. We are interested in the relation between prior expectations and subsequent behavior because after the basic relationship has been established we can use it to predict behavior from future surveys on which we ascertain current expectations. Extreme changes in expectations caused by changes in the economic climate make it important to be able to incorporate such subjective variables in our analysis.

*Expectations in successive independent samples.* When reinterviews of identical individuals are not available, we can still use expectations for predictive purposes. From a sequence of past surveys we can determine successive frequency distributions of expectations. We then relate the expectations of each survey to the actual behavior reported on the following survey. This shows us how community expectations are translated into community behavior. In new situations we predict future activity by studying the most recently collected distributions of expectation, among other sources of predictive information. As an example of the application of this technique, let us examine the data in Table 2 on successive frequency distributions of price and income expectations.

TABLE 2

EXPECTED CHANGE IN CONSUMER PRICES AND INCOMES[a]

PERCENTAGE DISTRIBUTION OF SPENDING UNITS

| EXPECTED CHANGE | Early 1951 | Early 1950 | July 1949 | Early 1949 | July 1948 | Early 1948 | July 1947 | Early 1947 |
|---|---|---|---|---|---|---|---|---|
| In Price | | | | | | | | |
| Increase | 67 | 12 | 7 | 8 | 42 | 33 | 32 | 13 |
| None | 16 | 36 | 34 | 20 | 25 | 24 | 29 | 22 |
| Decrease | 2 | 36 | 48 | 55 | 15 | 28 | 29 | 46 |
| Uncertain | 14 | 15 | 10 | 15 | 16 | 12 | 9 | 17 |
| Not ascertained | 1 | 1 | 1 | 2 | 2 | 3 | 1 | 2 |
| | 100 | 100 | 100 | 100 | 100 | 100 | 100 | 100 |
| In Income | | | | | | | | |
| Increase | 39 | 30 | 23 | 27 | 26 | 28 | 23 | 23 |
| None | 35 | 43 | 41 | 46 | 42 | 47 | 49 | 42 |
| Decrease | 13 | 16 | 18 | 17 | 8 | 13 | 8 | 14 |
| Uncertain | 12 | 9 | 17 | 9 | 22 | 9 | 18 | 19 |
| Not ascertained | 1 | 2 | 1 | 1 | 2 | 3 | 2 | 2 |
| | 100 | 100 | 100 | 100 | 100 | 100 | 100 | 100 |

[a] Source: "1951 Survey of Consumer Finances, Part I," *Federal Reserve Bulletin,* XXXVII (June, 1951), 632, Table 5.

In general we would predict that favorable income expectations would stimulate consumer spending. Income expectations appear to have been high in early 1951, but simultaneously consumers expected price increases much more frequently than in other years. Supplementary information gathered in the 1951 Survey showed that consumers did not "feel better off." A slightly larger percentage than in the previous year felt worse off, principally because of price rises. Although consumers frequently expected increases in money income, they did not expect increases in real income. In answer to another question, respondents in the survey expressed much more frequently than in 1950 that 1951 was not a good year in which to purchase durable consumer goods because prices were too high. In assembling various expectations and attitudinal data, authors of the Surveys of Consumer Finances were led to predict a "buying lull" for 1951, and the correctness of this position is well known now from published records.[5]

Income expectations were relatively favorable in early 1950 and not offset by frequent expectations of price increases. Purchases of consumer durables were at an exceedingly high rate in 1950, but, of course, many of these are directly attributable to the Korean War. In the first half of 1950, before the outbreak of war, consumer spending grew, although not as rapidly as in the last half of the year.

In early 1949, when depression forecasts were being made by many business cycle analysts, the combined expectations of prices and incomes pointed to favorable buying conditions which actually did become translated into fact during the year. More consumers than ever before bought durable goods in 1949, and they spent larger amounts than had been previously recorded.

As an alternative approach to the use of indirect measures such as distributions of income expectations, price expectations, or general economic outlook, which are combined with derived relationships of actual behavior, we may use direct questions posed to consumers about their buying intentions. A crude method of prediction would be simply to ask people if they plan to buy a group of commodities and correlate trends in the frequency of buying intentions with actual purchases. High (low) frequencies of buying intentions expressed in a survey at the beginning of a period would lead, with this approach, to bold forecasts of high (low) levels of purchasing during the period.

*Realization of expectations.* A deeper analysis of buying intentions, however, would be to associate them with the determinants of

[5] See Chapter II for a more thorough analysis of consumer attitudes and economic activity in recent years.

## TABLE 3

REALIZATION OF EXPECTATIONS OF NEW AND USED CAR PURCHASES
*Percentage distributions of spending units*

INTENTIONS, EARLY 1948

| PURCHASES, 1948 | DEFINITELY WILL BUY | | PROBABLY WILL BUY | | UNDECIDED | | DO NOT EXPECT TO BUY |
|---|---|---|---|---|---|---|---|
| | *New* | *Used* | *New* | *Used* | *New* | *Used* | |
| Bought new | 57 | | 32 | | 7 | | 4 |
| Bought used | 10 | 54 | 10 | 42 | 11 | 86 | 7 |
| Did not buy | 33 | 46 | 58 | 58 | 82 | 14 | 89 |
| | 100 | 100 | 100 | 100 | 100 | 100 | 100 |

plan fulfillment. From a study of past data we can ascertain major factors determining whether or not buying plans are fulfilled. This can be done either from reinterview surveys or by matching intentions, purchases, and related variables on successive surveys from independent samples.

In a study of fulfillment of intentions to purchase automobiles, S. B. Withey of the Survey Research Center has prepared distributions on which the following tables are based.[6]

## TABLE 4

INCOME CHANGE AND REALIZATION OF CAR PURCHASE INTENTIONS
*Percentage distributions of spending units*

| INCOME CHANGE 1947–48 | EXPECTED TO BUY NEW CAR | | DID NOT EXPECT TO BUY NEW CAR | |
|---|---|---|---|---|
| | *Bought New Car* | *Did Not Buy New Car* | *Bought New Car* | *Did Not Buy New Car* |
| Increased | 63 | 43 | 63 | 55 |
| Approximately no change | 12 | 9 | 20 | 13 |
| Decreased | 23 | 37 | 11 | 29 |
| Not ascertained | 2 | 11 | 6 | 3 |
| | 100 | 100 | 100 | 100 |

[6] Included in J. B. Lansing and S. B. Withey, "Consumer Anticipations: Their Use in Forecasting Consumer Behavior," *Midwest Conference on Research in Income and Wealth*, National Bureau of Economic Research (Ann Arbor, Michigan, 1951).

This sequence of tables shows that we should not rely exclusively on direct statements of intentions to purchase for prediction and that by relating intentions to other variables in a more rounded economic model we can improve the predictive performance of intentions data. There are significant numbers of persons who stated that they definitely or probably would purchase a given type of car but did not do so. Smaller frequencies purchased without having stated that they intended to do so. Tables 4 and 5 indicate that income change and income expectations or their realizations are correlated with the carrying out of intentions to purchase. Having an income

## TABLE 5

### REALIZATION OF INCOME EXPECTATION AND REALIZATION OF CAR PURCHASE INTENTIONS

*Percentage distributions of spending units*

| REALIZATION OF INCOME EXPECTATIONS | EXPECTED TO BUY NEW CAR | | DID NOT EXPECT TO BUY NEW CAR | |
|---|---|---|---|---|
| | *Bought New Car* | *Did Not Buy Car* | *Bought New Car* | *Did Not Buy Car* |
| Received more than expected income | 27 | 17 | 63 | 30 |
| Received expected income | 50 | 40 | 20 | 32 |
| Received less than expected income | 17 | 32 | 4 | 22 |
| Not ascertained | 6 | 11 | 13 | 16 |
| | 100 | 100 | 100 | 100 |

increase or getting at least as much income as expected is significant in leading one to fulfill purchase intentions. These variables are also useful in showing why some people purchase after having said that they did not plan to buy. Other economic variables, demographic variables, and the state of consumer inventories are also potentially useful in studies of plan fulfillment. In order to interpret survey data on purchase expectations we must have some knowledge of the simultaneous course of personal income movements, and these may be affected by events both outside and inside the consumer sector of the economy. The fact that purchase plans have to be inserted into a broader framework leads us again to our earlier point that a comprehensive system of relations covering many sectors of the economy must form the basis for accurate business-cycle analysis.

### SURVEY DATA FOR THE DETECTION OF STRUCTURAL CHANGE

*Problems of structural change and the use of historical records.* Structural change in the network of interrelationships describing the level and movement of economic activity presents one of the most difficult problems in forecasting. We attempt to build up our system of "autonomous" relations by studying historical material and then project into the future those relations which held in the past. With changes in technology, tastes, habits, and individual psychology continuously occurring, we must be very cautious in using our interpretation of history in future situations. Many historical studies are heavily weighted with data from the distant past and therefore are outmoded as far as present behavior patterns are concerned.

*Structural change and relationships estimated from survey data.* A possible way of attempting to keep pace with structural change is opened up by the use of survey data. If survey samples covering data on some particular aspect of behavior we are studying are made available at regular intervals, we can study a succession over time of estimates of the same relationship and measure fluctuations in the basic parameters. In making projections when parameters are changing, the relationship derived from or modified by the latest available survey data will probably give a good statistical estimate of the pattern to be used for the next future period. There is much serial correlation in economic behavior, and there is also much change. An efficient way of taking account of these two facts in estimating autonomous relations for prediction is to use the relations derived from the latest set of survey data.

We shall never be able to make exact corrections for structural change, because we do not know the future data; but it does seem better to try to keep up with structural change through repetitive examination of survey data than to rely blindly and solely on distant historical records.

## PROGRAMMATIC CONCLUSIONS

*More comprehensive and better data.* A program for developments in survey methods and data to be used in business-cycle analysis is in order. In addition to the past applications of survey data and their rapid development since 1946, there are numerous unexplored avenues which appear to have potentialities for our purposes.

Within the framework of consumer surveys alone, we may view our program as the derivation of improved estimates of household behavior patterns. Improvements may be made through the collection of data on new variables and different types of samples. In analyzing our present data for business cycle projections we have often felt the need for comprehensive statistics on consumer inventories, more precise measures of other nonliquid assets, and more detailed accounting pictures of entrepreneurs (business and farm). It is hoped that data on consumer inventories would improve our analysis of expenditures on consumer durables and that data on other nonliquid assets would contribute to the better estimation of many types of relationships. Businessmen and farmers, although comprising much less than one-fourth of all spending units, are volatile, strategic groups in economic fluctuations. They account for a large share of activity, but a more careful study of their behavior cannot be made unless the intertwining of their various production and household accounts is analyzed. The complication involved in adding questions on detailed production accounts to surveys that are already lengthy in pure household items deserves major consideration, yet progress in this area is possible and should be rewarding.

*Experimental study of attitudinal and demographic variables.* The use of attitudinal or psychological variables in quantitative economics is new, and inevitably the first work of this type will not hit upon the most relevant selection of such variables nor the most efficient statistical technique of analyzing their influence. We are now in the position of trying to find out what group of attitudinal variables shows predictive powers for consumer behavior. Those that have been selected have usually made contributions to our understanding of business cycles and some few have been discarded on diverse empirical grounds, but a great deal of practical experimentation must be carried out under changing economic conditions before we can become committed to any particular group of variables. Deeper theoretical analysis, especially that which would serve to explain the genesis of attitudinal variables as *endogenous* magnitudes in a wider behavioral process, is needed as a leg in any future research program.

Similar to the empirical experimentation with alternative attitudinal variables is the "cut-and-try" treatment of demographic variables. These are by no means straightforward magnitudes such as age, number of children, number of adults, etc. The demographic-structure variable used by Morgan in his studies of savings behavior is an example of a more delicate and sensitive demographic variable requiring expert study in its development and application. The same is true of yet undeveloped measures of social class and group membership.

*Specially designed samples.* New types of samples are required to collect data relevant to the study of some interesting demographic variables. Samples of households in given regions or social classes are needed to isolate some sociological phenomena. In the studies of racial differences in savings behavior it has been found that Southern and Northern Negroes do not exhibit similar patterns. If we combine this information with the known fact that Negroes are migrating in large numbers from the South to Northern cities, we are led to look for an answer to the question, "Do migrating Southern Negroes adopt the economic behavior patterns of Northern Negroes, and if so, what is the time lag involved?" This question requires a specially designed sample for the preparation of an adequate answer. Other demographic and sociological variables also require special samples, thus providing a large backlog of research problems in any future program.

Reinterview samples have been extremely productive in a variety of ways. In this volume we have presented uses of reinterview material in estimating behavior patterns to be employed in business-cycle analysis and in studying directly the fullfillment of expectations. In order to gain an insight into many consumer decisions that would affect the course of business cycles, we could attempt to reinterview households on repeated occasions for a period as long as a decade. We would then be in a position to study family-size planning, plans for purchasing durables, the wealth accumulation process, and many other consumer acts that are obviously important for understanding economic fluctuations. The sampling problems, alone, are exceedingly difficult in decade studies, but reinterviews on this scale are possible and represent a direction which future research may very well follow.

*Combining sample survey and aggregative time-series data.* Ideally, we should like to have a systematic basis for pooling survey data with the time-series aggregates now used widely in business-cycle research. At present we can check estimates of some parameters of aggregative relationships from corresponding estimates made in survey data. The aggregation problem—the derivation of a macroeconomic relationship from microeconomic data—has not yet been solved in empirical applications; therefore the pooling of the two types of data is incomplete. Research on the correspondences between estimates of relations from time series aggregates and from survey data is in need of development, particularly because some degree of aggregation is necessary if we are to get a comprehensive view of the economy as a whole, embracing simultaneously the household, business, financial, government, and foreign sectors.

At the microeconomic level, there are numerous possibilities for future research in that surveys of individual businesses and financial institutions have not been carried so far as surveys of individual consumers. The postwar surveys of business intentions to invest in new plant and equipment[7] certainly carry us measurably along the

---

[7] Surveys conducted jointly by the U. S. Department of Commerce and the Securities and Exchange Commission are reported periodically in the *Survey of Current Business.* See, for example, Lawrence Bridge and Vito Natrella, "Investment Programs and Sales Expectations in 1953," *Survey of Current Business,* XXXIII (April 1953), 7–11.

road toward enlarging our body of microeconomic data, but these surveys too must undergo the same types of future research development that we have put forward for consumer surveys if we are to collect more information necessary to an understanding of business cycles.

# SELECTED RESEARCH PUBLICATIONS
## from the ECONOMIC BEHAVIOR PROGRAM
## OF THE SURVEY RESEARCH CENTER

### SURVEY REPORTS

"Surveys of Consumer Finances," *Federal Reserve Bulletin*
  1946 Survey: June, July, and August, 1946
  1947 Survey: June, July, August, and October, 1947
  1948 Survey: June, July, August, September, and November, 1948
  1949 Survey: June, July, August, October, November, 1949, and
    January, 1950
  1950 Survey: April, June, July, August, November, and December,
    1950
  1951 Survey: April, June, July, August, September, and December,
    1951
  1952 Survey: April, July, August, and September, 1952
  1953 Survey: March, June, July, August, and September, 1953
Industrial Mobility in Michigan: A Sample Survey of Michigan Manu-
  facturers. Ann Arbor: Survey Research Center, University of Michigan, December, 1950. 77 pp.
Life Insurance Ownership among American Families, 1952: Special
  Tabulations prepared for the Institute of Life Insurance. Ann Arbor:
  Survey Research Center, University of Michigan, 1953. Similar annual
  reports are available for five previous years.
What People Want when They Buy a House. Washington: Housing
  and Home Finance Agency (in press).

### ARTICLES AND BOOKS BY INDIVIDUAL AUTHORS

Fisher, Janet. "Income, Spending, and Saving Patterns of Consumer
  Units in Different Age Groups," *Studies in Income and Wealth,* XV
  (New York: National Bureau of Economic Research, 1952), 75–102.
——— "Postwar Changes in Income and Savings among Consumers

in Different Age Groups," *Econometrica,* XX (January, 1952), pp. 47–70.

Katona, George. "Analysis of Dissaving," *American Economic Review,* XXXIX (June, 1949), 673–88.

——— "Contribution of Psychological Data to Economic Analysis," *Journal of the American Statistical Association,* XLII (September, 1947), 449–59.

——— "Effect of Income Changes on the Rate of Saving," *The Review of Economics and Statistics,* XXXI (May, 1949), 95–103.

——— "Expectations and Decisions in Economic Behavior," in D. Lerner and H. Lasswell, eds., The Policy Sciences (Stanford: Stanford University Press, 1951), pp. 219-32.

——— "Financial Surveys among Consumers," *Human Relations,* II (January, 1949), 3–11.

——— Psychological Analysis of Economic Behavior. New York: McGraw-Hill, 1951. 347 pp.

Katona, George, and Janet Fisher. "Postwar Income Changes of Identical Consumer Units," *Studies in Income and Wealth,* XIII (New York: National Bureau of Economic Research, 1951), 62–119.

Katona, George, and Lawrence R. Klein. "Psychological Data in Business Cycle Research," *American Journal of Economics and Sociology,* XII (October, 1952), 11–22.

Katona, George, John B. Lansing, and P. de Janosi. "Stock Ownership among American Families," *Michigan Business Review,* V (January, 1953), 12–16.

Katona, George, and James N. Morgan. "The Quantitative Study of Factors Determining Business Decisions," *The Quarterly Journal of Economics,* LXVI (February, 1952), 67–90.

Katona, George, and E. Mueller. Consumer Attitudes and Demand, 1950–1952. Ann Arbor: Survey Research Center, University of Michigan, 1953. 119 pp.

Klein, Lawrence R. "Assets, Debts, and Economic Behavior," *Studies in Income and Wealth,* XIV (New York: National Bureau of Economic Research, 1951), 195–227.

——— "Estimating Patterns of Savings Behavior from Sample Survey Data," *Econometrica,* XIX (October, 1951), 438–54.

——— "Savings Concepts and Data: The Needs of Economic Analysis and Policy," in W. W. Heller, F. M. Boddy, and C. L. Nelson, eds., Savings in the Modern Economy (Minneapolis: University of Minnesota Press, 1953), pp. 104–17.

Klein, Lawrence R., and J. Margolis. "Statistical Studies of Unincorporated Business," *The Review of Economics and Statistics,* XXXVI (February, 1954), 33–46.

Klein, Lawrence R., and H. W. Mooney. "Negro-White Savings Differentials and the Consumption Function Problem," *Econometrica,* XXI (July, 1953), 425–56.

Klein, Lawrence R., and James N. Morgan. "Results of Alternative Statistical Treatments of Sample Survey Data," *Journal of the American Statistical Association,* XLVI (December, 1951), 442–60.

Lansing, John B., and L. Kish. "Response Errors in Estimating the Value of Homes," *Journal of the American Statistical Association* (forthcoming).

Lansing, John B., and E. S. Maynes. "Inflation and Savings by Consumers," *The Journal of Political Economy,* LX (October, 1952), 383–91.

Lansing, John B., and S. B. Withey. "Consumer Anticipations: Their Use in Forecasting Consumer Behavior," *Studies in Income and Wealth,* Vol. XVII (New York: National Bureau of Economic Research, in press).

Morgan, James N. "Individual Savings in 1947 and 1948," *American Economic Review,* XL (1950), 381–88.

———— "The Motivations of Savers," in W. W. Heller, F. M. Boddy, and C. L. Nelson, eds., Savings in the Modern Economy (Minneapolis: University of Minnesota Press, 1953), pp. 213–17.

———— "The Structure of Aggregate Personal Saving," *The Journal of Political Economy,* LIX (December, 1951), 528–34; "Correction and Addendum," LXI (December, 1953), 536.

# INDEX